D1164080

About Island Press

Island Press, a nonprofit organization, publishes and distributes the most advanced thinking on the conservation of our natural resources—books about soil, land, water, forests, wildlife, and hazardous and toxic wastes. These books are practical tools used by public officials, business and industry leaders, natural resource managers, and concerned citizens working to solve both local and global resource problems.

Founded in 1978, Island Press reorganized in 1984 to meet the increasing demand for substantive books on all resource-related issues. Island Press publishes and distributes under its own imprint and offers these services to other nonprofit organizations.

Support for Island Press is provided by Geraldine R. Dodge Foundation, The Energy Foundation, The Charles Engelhard Foundation, The Ford Foundation, Glen Eagles Foundation, The George Gund Foundation, William and Flora Hewlett Foundation, The Joyce Foundation, The John D. and Catherine T. MacArthur Foundation, The Andrew W. Mellon Foundation, The Joyce Mertz-Gilmore Foundation, The New-Land Foundation, The J. N. Pew, Jr. Charitable Trust, Alida Rockefeller, The Rockefeller Brothers Fund, The Rockefeller Foundation, The Florence and John Schumann Foundation, The Tides Foundation, and individual donors.

Taking Out
THE
Trash

Taking Out
THE
Trash

A No-Nonsense Guide to Recycling

JENNIFER CARLESS

ISLAND PRESS

Washington, D.C. □ Covelo, California

Library of Congress Cataloging-in-Publication Data

Carless, Jennifer
    Taking out the trash : a no-nonsense guide to recycling /
Jennifer Carless.
        p.   cm.
    Includes bibliographical references and index.
    ISBN: 1-55963-171-6 (alk. paper). —ISBN 1-55963-170-8
(pbk. : alk. paper)
        1. Recycling (Waste, etc.)—United States. 2. Recycling
(Waste, etc.) 3. Recycling (Waste, etc.)—United States—
Citizen participation. 4. Recycling (Waste, etc.)—Citizen
participation.
I Title.
TD794.5.C37   1992
363.72'82—dc20   91-43855
                                                            CIP

Printed on recycled, acid-free paper

Manufactured in the United States of America

10 9 8 7 6 5 4 3 2 1

To my parents, Chris and Penny,

and to Peter

Contents

Preface

Recycling is an essential step toward solving this country's solid waste problems, but it has much farther-ranging effects. For those who are concerned about clean air and water or worried about our dwindling forests and wildlife habitats and our dependence on fossil fuels, this book will show how recycling helps work toward practical solutions to these problems and more.

The following chapters survey the full spectrum of issues surrounding recycling in the United States today. Why do we need to do it? How is it actually done? What actually happens to all these recyclables? What can everyone do to help? What are communities, industry, and the government doing? And, finally, what hurdles associated with recycling need to be overcome? These questions, and more, are all addressed.

The book is not packed full of statistics. Hard facts have been used to illustrate specific points, but it is not necessary to present volumes of statistics to demonstrate the common sense of recycling. Additionally, every effort has been made to use only statistics that are generally accepted to be true.

While all the data offered here are believed to represent the best current information available, many are estimates because states are just beginning to monitor recycling and other waste management practices. That some of these figures are estimates does not lessen their value, however; they still provide a good overall understanding of this nation's current recycling practices and a basis from which to make comparisons and future projections.

There is one important thing to keep in mind while reading this book: Buy Recycled. If no other point comes through in this book, the concept of developing markets for recycled products must. Manufacturers will be encouraged to use recycled materials in their products only if there is a consumer demand—your demand—for recycled content.

Taking Out
THE
Trash

Introduction

Recycling is getting more and more publicity these days, but what exactly is it? Recycling is returning materials to their raw material components and then using these again to supplement or replace new (virgin) materials in the manufacture of a new product. The process involves several steps: separating materials from the waste stream, collecting them, processing them, and ultimately reusing them either as an entirely new product or as part of a new product. It is important to understand at the outset that a material has not been recycled simply by having been collected from a curbside or taken to a buy-back center: it is only truly recycled once it has been turned into another product.

In a more general sense, recycling also means simply putting something you were going to throw away to good use. We do this daily when we donate clothes to charitable organizations or when we reuse a plastic container to store food in the refrigerator.

Throughout this book you'll encounter examples of recycled products. Some of the more common ones include newsprint, aluminum cans, and glass. To appreciate the value of these commodities, we must stop thinking of recyclables as garbage or waste, which have negative connotations, and start thinking of them as secondary raw materials. Recyclable materials are not trash; they are resources.

TOWARD AN INTEGRATED SOLUTION

Most experts believe that to control our increasing waste disposal problems in this country we need to adopt an integrated waste management approach. Although one can find diverse definitions of this concept, most agree on its general principles. An integrated approach to managing our waste involves source reduction, reuse, recycling, and then (and only then) either landfilling or incineration as a final disposal method. (Landfills and incinerators are discussed in Chapter 1.) In other words, the goal is to eliminate as much as possible of our waste stream by either reducing the amount of waste we generate in the first place or at least reusing or recycling everything possible. While this book focuses on recycling, keep in mind that it's one part of an overall solution.

Source reduction, also called waste reduction, can be accomplished in many ways. Buying in bulk, avoiding disposable products, and buying durable (and repairable) goods are all excellent waste reduction strategies. Industry can help by reducing the size or weight of a product or its packaging. As an example, today's aluminum can is lighter than its counterpart of years ago, as is a two-liter plastic container.

Reusing things is simple once the habit is established. Using glass bottles to hold frozen juice, saving wrapping paper, taking shopping bags to the store—all are examples of reusing materials. Photocopying and writing on both sides of paper and reusing envelopes are others.

WHY RECYCLE?

Recycling benefits everyone, both in obvious ways and in ways many people haven't even considered. The most obvious benefit to recycling is that it saves landfill space, which is certainly very important. Recycling does much more, however. It helps all of us in a multitude of subtle ways. The environment, individuals, local communities, and industry all realize concrete advantages from recycling reusable materials. Recycling is easy and provides immediate results.

Environmental Benefits

First and foremost in most people's eyes are the environmental advantages of recycling. These are numerous. Our land, air, and water are affected by everything we do—and by everything we don't do. Recycling allows us to conserve our precious natural resources and energy, contributes significantly to a reduction in pollution, and eliminates the negative environmental impact of alternative disposal methods such as landfilling and incineration. It helps to preserve treasured wildlife habitats and vital ecosystems.

The conservation of our natural resources is certainly one of the most compelling reasons to recycle. Most of the products we use daily have been manufactured from extracted virgin materials. But by recycling paper products, glass, metals, aluminum, yard wastes, and many other materials, we can significantly reduce the demand for raw materials to produce the goods we consume. As an example, seventeen pulp trees are saved by each ton of paper made from recycled materials. In addition to saving resources, recycling helps preserve the natural landscape by requiring less mining of raw materials.

Recycling results in significant savings in other areas as well: energy, water, raw materials, and capital can all be saved by reusing what we have already produced. Approximately half the water is needed to manufacture recycled paper than is needed to produce paper from virgin pulp. Another example can be found in the aluminum industry. Alcoa, a major aluminum recycling company, states that an industrial facility to melt used aluminum cans may be built in half the time and one-tenth the cost of the facilities required to mine and refine ore to produce aluminum.

Recycling saves enormous amounts of our precious energy and the fuels which go to produce that energy because manufacturing new products from secondary, as opposed to raw, materials is typically more efficient. Our waste stream is a huge source of untapped energy that sadly, when recycling doesn't happen, literally goes to waste.

Let's take just one illustration of the energy efficiency to be gained from recycling: the production of recycled paper requires anywhere between 23 and 74 percent less energy per ton than does that of virgin paper. Another illustration: producing one aluminum can from recycled aluminum rather than from raw materials saves the energy equivalent of one-half of that can filled with gasoline. In fact, just by increasing the levels of steel and paper recycling in this country we could afford to shut down numerous nuclear power plants.

When recycled materials are used in the manufacturing process instead of virgin materials, there is almost always a significant reduction of harmful emissions. Both air and water pollution can be significantly reduced. Manufacturing with scrap paper, for example, results in lower levels of harmful emissions into the environment compared to the pollution that results from virgin wood pulp paper manufacture. Specifically, the EPA has found that a paper mill can reduce its air pollution by 74 percent and its water pollution by 35 percent by using wastepaper instead of virgin pulp. This means that every ton of paper made from recycled pulp keeps nearly 60 pounds of air pollutants out of the atmosphere.

Our water is affected in much the same way. Factories using raw materials pollute streams and rivers into which they dump their waste more than factories using recyclables. A steel mill, for example, can reduce its water pollution by 76 percent and its mining wastes by 97 percent using scrap metal as a feedstock rather than iron ore, according to the Institute of Scrap Recycling Industries (ISRI).

Everything we do not recycle has a chance of either contributing to our general litter problem or being dumped into the ocean. No one needs convincing of our litter problem, and much of what we see strewn on the side of the road or in our parks is paper, aluminum, or plastic—almost all recyclable. The litter in our oceans is perhaps less obvious, but nonetheless constitutes a real disaster. Plastic is a particular problem—more than 45,000 tons of plastic waste are dumped in the world's oceans every year. Six-pack rings, fishing line, and strapping bands entangle and kill seabirds, fish, and mammals in alarming numbers each year. The National Oceanic and Atmospheric Administration (NOAA) believes that approximately 30,000 northern fur seals alone die yearly from entanglement in netting.

Apart from the positive reasons for recycling, other incentives stem from the negative environmental impact of alternative disposal methods. Anything we do not recycle will probably find its way to an incinerator or a landfill. There are significant concerns about air pollution from incinerators that burn municipal solid waste, much of which could have been kept out and reused. Likewise, both ground and water pollution is caused when landfills leak—which older ones tend to do with frightening regularity.

Continued reliance on landfills without the serious development of safe alternatives such as recycling simply exacerbates our nation's significant problem of the shrinking availability of landfill space. For each ton of wastepaper separated from municipal solid waste, for example, ISRI notes that more than 3 cubic yards of landfill space are saved.

Recycling, coupled with source reduction, is the best way to lessen our reliance on landfills and incinerators. Although the EPA has set a goal of 25 percent of our solid waste to be recycled, some experts estimate that up to 80 percent of the household waste stream can be recycled. This shows how far we still have to go from the current 13 percent that we are recycling. Fully comprehensive recycling programs can eliminate the need for expensive and harmful incinerators and greatly reduce our reliance on the ever-shrinking supply of landfill space.

Social and Economic Benefits

Individuals and local communities benefit from recycling programs, and not just from living in a cleaner environment. There are economic advantages, too. From the neighborhood children who may collect bottles and cans to earn extra pocket money to our nation's balance of trade, recycling makes economic sense for everyone.

One of the areas in which recycling saves money is in avoided waste disposal costs, and this is true even for an individual household. A family that puts out two garbage cans for collection each week can easily reduce its waste to one can by recycling basics like newspapers, plastics, glass, and aluminum and by avoiding throwaway products at the store. Depending on local charges, this can save a family about half of its disposal costs each month.

And if individual families are saving, it makes sense that the communities which house them are going to notice significant savings as well. Typically, a community is charged on a per-ton basis to dispose of its waste; less to throw away means less cost to the local government. This could mean lower service charges to residents. The per-ton cost to a community for recycling is usually significantly lower than the per-ton cost to landfill or incinerate. The Steel Can Recycling Institute has said that at current average landfill tipping fees, steel recycling alone saves us more than $2 billion per year in avoided solid waste disposal costs.

Recycling programs, being labor intensive, also provide jobs in the community and can help stimulate local economies. In fact, the recycling industry creates far more jobs than either incineration or landfilling. The paper, glass, and aluminum recycling industries employ hundreds of thousands of people across the country and pay millions of dollars in taxes yearly.

The collection, processing, and marketing of recyclables all require workers. Curbside collection requires drivers and collectors. Much of the quality control in recycling is still done by hand—glass is sorted by color, plastics must be sorted by resin types, and contaminants must be discarded from all types of recyclables. Many drop-off and pay-back centers need to be staffed also, as do the recycling stations at local landfills.

Not only individuals but community groups and charities benefit from participation in recycling schemes. In California, for example, the Boy Scouts, the Lion's Club, and the California Grey Bears are just a few such organizations that have been involved in the collection of recyclables for some time. With recycling funds such groups are able to expand the scope of their activities.

Local government officials across the country have found that the establishment of recycling programs in their communities has helped to develop an increased awareness of litter problems and a heightened concern for the environment in general. Recycling also develops a sense of pride in the community, which is able to see significant economic and environmental payoffs from its efforts.

Benefits to Industry

Business and industry both realize concrete benefits from recycling also. For the manufacturing industries, avoided disposal costs, savings from lower energy bills, and avoided costs for pollution control equipment can add up to big savings, which are directly related to the company's profits.

Not only manufacturing companies see cost savings. Companies that institute a comprehensive office recycling program can save thousands of dollars each year in avoided disposal costs. Selling the collected recyclables also contributes positively to the balance sheet.

Recycling even has an effect on our national economy. Scrap paper exports, for example, contribute significantly to both our national economy and our international trade position. Total paper stock exports in recent years have averaged more than $500 million annually.

Keeping in mind the many benefits of recycling, clearly it deserves serious consideration in relation to our current waste disposal methods. In understanding how we dispose of our garbage now, and the problems associated with these methods, we can further see the necessity of a full-scale recycling effort nationwide.

1 Where We've Come From

People have been creating garbage in some form or another since the dawn of creation. When life was simpler, however, there was less garbage to deal with and much less controversy about how to dispose of it.

To the earliest humans, who frequently moved from place to place, garbage was not a problem because they just left it behind them. Then, as people began to settle down, they are believed to have simply littered their floors until it became awkward, or unbearable, at which time they covered the garbage with a layer of dirt or clay and started again with a clean floor. Eventually their ceilings had to be raised, of course, but this too has been noted in history.

DISPOSAL OVER THE YEARS

Many other disposal methods have been implemented over the years. Household garbage and debris were for years thrown out into the street, where pigs or other animals ate anything edible and scavengers and scrap merchants also took their share. Anything unwanted simply remained where it was dropped. The streets of European and American cities until as recently as the nineteenth century were filthy beyond the most fertile imagination. Health concerns eventually prompted people to do something about haphazard dumping.

The methods that we associate with waste management today began to appear toward the turn of the century. Although people have burned garbage throughout history, incinerators as we know them today began to appear in the late 1890s. At the turn of the century New York City had a mass-burn incinerator with an 800 tons-per-day (TPD) capacity, and by the 1920s incineration had become the main method of garbage disposal across the country. At that time several hundred incinerators were in use.

A technique known as reduction, imported from Europe, also enjoyed a certain popularity around that time. Wet garbage and animal remains were literally stewed to produce a greasy substance that was then sold for use in manufacturing such items as soaps, candles, and, yes, perfume. The problem with the reduction process was that the plants emitted an unbearable odor in addition to leaving an unpleasant residue that polluted nearby waterways.

Beginning in the 1920s, landfilling was used to reclaim wetlands with alternate layers of garbage and dirt. Then for years we swung back and forth in our choice for waste disposal between incineration and landfills. New air control laws that came into effect in the 1960s—as well as public dislike for the fumes and smoke from incinerators—are thought to be the causes for an enormous cutback in the use of incineration facilities in the latter part of that decade. In the 1960s as well as in the following decade, landfills were heralded as the sanitary solution to our waste disposal problems.

The energy crisis in the mid-1970s drove the federal government back toward the use of incineration. It promoted the generation of electricity by burning our municipal solid waste and emphasized the role of such incineration facilities toward our goal of energy self-sufficiency. Incinerators were no longer just incinerators, they were now resource-recovery plants. In addition to disposing of our garbage, they could separate out any valuable materials and even provide energy to nearby homes and businesses.

The two methods, landfilling and incineration, developed in tandem for a short time, but during the 1970s and 1980s landfilling became by far the most common method of disposal in all but a small number of states as the resource-recovery plants ran into problems marketing their recovered materials and slowly waned in popularity. Despite the more recent preference for landfills, creation of new sites is becoming a serious problem. Twenty years ago, more than 300 new landfills were built each year across the country, but in the last decade, according to the National Solid Wastes Management Association (NSWMA), that number has shrunk to between 50 and 200 per year. Even if we only created garbage at a level rate in the future, we would still run short of landfill space eventually.

A new type of incineration, called mass burn, may be more popular, but this method still carries with it serious doubts as to the safety of the emissions that are released from the plants. With landfill capacity dwindling and new sites more and more difficult to procure, the current surge in popularity of recycling has perhaps come at just the right time.

THE SITUATION TODAY

To appreciate the importance of recycling, it is necessary to understand a few things about our current waste management system. How we deal with our garbage, what it consists of, and what problems are associated with our current system are all key factors to consider.

What Is Solid Waste?

What most people just call garbage is termed solid waste by the industry that handles it, and the term municipal solid waste (MSW) refers to the overall garbage created by a community or entity. This means household waste as well as the waste created by the businesses, schools, and institutions in an area.

Estimates vary as to how much garbage each one of us produces, but no one disputes that we dispose of significantly more waste per person in this country than in most other nations. As an average, it has been estimated that we each dispose of 3.5 pounds of garbage each day. (Some studies say this figure is as high as 5 to 8 pounds per day, while some say it is as low as 1.5 pounds per day.) If that figure shocks you, take a minute to think about how fast your garbage cans fill up at home—and then think about how much you as an individual are responsible for throwing away at your office. You will see that it all adds up. The actual number is not important here, but it is important to understand that we do create an enormous amount of waste, and that we all must take responsibility for our share.

As these figures are averages, however, we can be comforted to know

that not all of us are so wasteful. As our waste generation varies significantly from individual to individual, it also varies from one region of
the country to another: rural states tend to have lower per capita generation rates than do states with higher concentrations of people.

What's in Our Waste Stream?

What are we throwing away in such large quantities? Here, in round
terms, is a breakdown of our nation's garbage (municipal waste) by
weight:

40%	paper and paperboard
18%	yard wastes
9%	metals
8%	plastics
7%	glass
7%	food wastes
4%	wood
3%	rubber, leather
2%	textiles
3%	miscellaneous

Source: EPA.
Note: Percentages do not equal 100 because of rounding.

Various organizations have statistics that vary by 1 or 2 percent either
way from these figures, but these are a fair representation of what most
people accept to be true. These percentages have not varied significantly over the past several years.

Even a cursory look at the materials listed above shows that a very
large portion of our waste is recyclable. We will see throughout the
book that recycling programs for many of these materials, such as paper,
glass, and metals, are already in existence across the country. Yard
wastes, too, have been composted and blended with other ingredients
to make compost and other materials for years. Textiles can be recycled,
and studies are being done to learn more and better uses of used rubber,
particularly from automobile tires. Later sections of this book will explain why more of these materials are not currently being recycled and
what can be done to change this situation.

Where Does Our Garbage Go?

As a nation we dispose of our solid waste as follows:
- Landfills: 73 percent
- Incinerated: 14 percent
- Recycled: 13 percent

Again, these figures (based on EPA data) can vary by a few percentage points in different studies. The proportions are expected to change significantly in the next several years, however. An ever-decreasing number of available landfill sites, public concern over their safety, even stronger safety concerns about incineration procedures, a growing awareness of the benefits of recycling—all will contribute to a drastic change in the way we dispose of our garbage into the twenty-first century.

The figures cited above represent national averages, but waste disposal practices vary widely among the fifty states. Although landfilling is by far the most common method of disposal, some states rely much more heavily on incineration. Connecticut and Maine, for example, incinerate 62 and 37 percent of their MSW respectively. Few other states rely so heavily on incineration, however.

Over the last several years, states have begun to keep track (or better track) of the amount of recycling taking place within their borders. Many have estimates, some of which qualify more as guesses. Some of the states with the highest estimated recycling rates are Washington (28 percent), New Jersey (25 percent), Oregon (23–25 percent), Vermont (18 percent), Illinois (17–18 percent), and Maine (17 percent). The District of Columbia recycles just over 20 percent of its solid waste stream.

Curbside recycling is gaining popularity around the country. Although not all states have accurate information about curbside programs yet, BioCycle magazine estimates that there were 2,700 operating throughout the country at the end of 1990. In terms of population served by the curbside programs, he cites some of the leading states (again, at the end of 1990) as New Jersey (7 million), California (6.4 million), Pennsylvania (5.5 million), and Florida (5 million).

Costs and Problems

There are several problems with the way we currently dispose of our garbage. Diminishing landfill space, safety concerns about both landfills and incinerators, and disposal costs are all issues that must be addressed.

While landfills across the country are closing either because they have reached capacity or because of failure to meet environmental safety standards, it is increasingly difficult to find suitable sites for new ones—largely due to concern from local citizens about potential environmental hazards. The EPA estimates that between 1978 and 1988, some 70 percent of the nation's landfills—approximately 14,000 facilities—closed. It also estimates that by 1995 half of the remaining landfills will have reached capacity. This situation can be traced to a number of factors, according to the National Solid Wastes Management Association. First, our population has increased by 34 percent since 1960 and we have increased the amount of garbage we generate as a nation by approximately 1 percent each year during that time. Also, as noted earlier, many fewer landfills are being built today.

It is important to note, however, that while these figures are significant and indicate that we must find alternatives quickly, they do not necessarily signal a need for panic. Almost half of our states still have landfill capacity greater than ten years. We have the capability of extending the life of all landfills tremendously by implementing comprehensive waste reduction and recycling programs.

Incinerators, our other method of waste disposal, have been severely criticized by the public and environmental organizations for emitting toxic chemicals. Although the proponents of these incinerators have declared them safe of toxic emissions and attempt to make them more appealing by citing their ability to produce power, their cries seem to be falling largely on deaf ears.

The costs involved with waste disposal by landfill or incinerator are also key factors in our current problem. Newsweek reported (27 November 1989, p. 67) that Long Island townships, for example, each spent an average of $23 million each year at that time to dispose of their garbage in other states. Such facts cannot be ignored by those trying to balance stretched budgets.

THE ALTERNATIVES

The rhetoric surrounding the two current alternatives to recycling—landfills and incinerators—is filled with contradictions and confusion. Proponents of both of these disposal methods proclaim their safety and efficiency, while citizens, environmental groups, and independent researchers regularly dispute such claims. To add to the confusion, results from various studies are often contradictory. One study may say the emissions from an incinerator are below required levels while another may say they are well above these levels.

Amid all this confusion, what does seem to be clear is that no one knows for certain the answers to some very disturbing questions. How dangerous is it to live near a landfill or incinerator site? What amount of dioxin in our immediate environment is safe? Such questions are of interest to us all. Even with the strictest measures imaginable, we will still create waste requiring disposal. So we must find safe, suitable methods to do this. Recycling is an ideal choice because of its environmental, economic, and social benefits. Currently, however, its development competes with incineration and landfilling.

Incinerators

At modern incineration plants, solid waste is fed into a huge furnace and burned at temperatures up to 2,400 degrees Fahrenheit. If the plant is used to produce energy, then the mass of burning waste is used to heat water, the steam from which drives a turbine to generate electricity. What remains after being burned is a combination of solid residue and gases. By volume, burning garbage eliminates anywhere between 50 and 90 percent of the original volume of waste (depending on whom you ask), so there is less waste to send to the landfill. There are, however, serious questions about the safety of the ash and residue that remain.

Today, according to the EPA, there are some 130 facilities across the country, which dispose of approximately 25 million tons of garbage annually. A variety of terms are used to describe incineration plants:

• *Mass burn:* This term implies that everything which goes into the plant is burned; no preprocessing of the waste is done other than to remove items too large to go through the processor. No recyclable materials are extracted before burning. The EPA indicates that all but a very few mass-burn incinerators operating today produce energy.

• *Refuse-derived fuel (RDF)/resource-recovery/waste-to-energy:* These are all names for a plant that is used to create energy. RDF plants remove noncombustible wastes and process the rest into fuel with a high Btu content. These plants do not necessarily remove recyclables first. In fact, opponents believe they rarely do so because of their need for as much solid waste as possible to produce energy.

It must be explained at the start that incineration and recycling are two fundamentally opposed methods for waste disposal. Incinerators reduce the potential for recycling by diverting materials out of the recycling process to burn them. Moreover, incinerators are very expensive—estimates for their construction range anywhere from $100 million to $500 million per incinerator. To secure a return on such an investment, operators have often required communities to sign what is referred to as a "put or pay" contract. This essentially means that the community guarantees the plant a certain amount of garbage on a regular basis and that it will be charged if it delivers less than the agreed amount.

The implications of such an arrangement for recycling efforts are obvious: if the community is at all concerned about meeting its quota, it is certainly not going to encourage its citizens to recycle. As a result, tons of useful recyclable material are burned, potentially causing harmful emissions, instead of being put to use again as another product.

Proponents of incineration plants cite many benefits to their system. Among these are energy production and significant reduction of required landfill space. They cite the capability of producing energy without significantly harming the environment. An incineration plant, they say, can take our garbage and not only shrink it to a fraction of its original size, but give us relatively inexpensive energy in the bargain. Millions of watts of power can be produced around the clock while disposing of our solid waste. The Council for Solid Waste Solutions (a group of companies from the plastics industry) reports that a 550 ton-per-day capacity plant will produce 11 megawatts of power each day, which is sufficient to provide electric power to 6,500 residential customers for one day. The existing waste-to-energy facilities in the United States are estimated to produce enough electricity to power 1.2 million homes. Proponents claim that by incinerating we are also reducing our reliance on fossil fuels such as oil and coal.

Finally, we are told that these incineration plants are safe—that they do not emit harmful toxics in amounts we need worry about. The pollution control devices in modern incinerators consist of three basic components: scrubbers, electrostatic precipitators, and baghouses. These are designed to capture the toxic emissions before they are released into the environment. Scrubbers are meant to remove acid gases from the flue gas stream. They do this by mixing the gaseous waste stream with a lime solution that neutralizes the acids. Electrostatic precipitators use an electric charge to remove harmful particles from the emissions. Finally, baghouses are just what their name implies: heat-resistant bags. They are the last stage in pollution control and consist of a fabric filter attached to the stacks that catches material before it escapes.

But environmental organizations and members of the public alike are not convinced that the incineration industry's claims are accurate. They cite toxic emissions and ash residue, insufficient safety devices, and unacceptably high construction costs as reasons to eliminate our reliance on incineration in this country.

Critics say incinerators create as many problems as they might solve. People are particularly concerned about toxic air pollutants, including dioxins, which are released from some incinerators. Even with the best possible pollution control devices, incinerators have been accused of loading the environment with acid-rain-causing gases such as hydrogen chloride and sulfur dioxide, toxic heavy metals such as lead, mercury, and cadmium, and classes of chemicals called dioxins and furans that have been associated with various forms of cancer and birth defects. The EPA acknowledges the health-related risks of these emissions. Scientists have identified hundreds of toxic or potentially toxic chemicals in municipal waste incinerator emissions and ash residues.

The risks to our health from these emissions may not be simply those of direct inhalation, either. While the debate persists as to whether or not the dioxin levels emitted from incinerator plants are safe for humans, researchers are becoming concerned that the toxicity of these chemicals may also reach us in a more roundabout manner.

Concern has increased about the possibility that dioxins and other toxic substances are building up not only in our atmosphere but in the tissues of animals, including humans. Scientists are concerned that the presence of dioxins in mothers' tissues may be responsible for birth defects in the offspring of certain bird and mammal species. So we are not only potentially taking a direct hit from these toxics, but an indirect one as well.

Consuming food produced near an incineration facility can also be dangerous. A study by the Danish EPA estimated that, for members of a community located near an incinerator, consuming the local dairy products or local produce posed risks 481 times higher than respiratory exposure.

In addition to the toxic substances released into the atmosphere through the stacks of an incineration facility, there is also a problem with the ash left over after burning waste. Incinerators produce two types of ash. *Fly ash*, as its name implies, flies up the stacks and either escapes into the atmosphere as tiny particles or is trapped by pollution control devices in the stacks. *Bottom ash* (the largest portion of residue ash) is the ash remaining in the burning chambers after combustion.

This brings us to landfills. Incinerators do not eliminate the necessity for landfills because the ash still has to go somewhere, and that in itself is a problem. The National Toxics Campaign believes that, because so many different substances have been burned together in an incinerator, the resultant ash is more toxic than the original garbage. Because of this some facilities have trouble finding landfills to take the ash.

Estimates vary widely as to what percentage of the original volume of garbage burned in an incinerator actually remains as ash and residue. Proponents of such facilities claim a 90 percent reduction rate, meaning that only 10 percent of the original garbage has to be landfilled. Others believe that up to 50 percent of the original garbage still remains after burning it. Incineration opponents argue that the 90 percent figure does not take into account several factors. For example, normal incineration commonly means inefficient and incomplete burning. Also, during shut-

downs for repairs and maintenance, the garbage does not get incinerated but gets bypassed and goes directly to the landfill. Finally, bulky
items such as tires, large appliances, and mattresses are commonly removed before burning.

Incineration is vigorously opposed by environmental organizations
and a large portion of the general public. Critics say that names such as
waste-to-energy and resource recovery for these plants amount to nothing more than a marketing ploy.

The EPA estimates that over 200 new municipal incinerators are currently planned or under construction, at a cost of over $18 billion. More
than sixty plants have recently been blocked, canceled, or delayed,
however, because of cost or environmental concerns. Many of our nation's cities, including Seattle, Austin, Philadelphia, and Los Angeles,
have canceled plans for incinerators in favor of comprehensive recycling
programs.

Sanitary Landfills

Though by no means a trouble-free alternative, landfills are generally
considered to be a favorite over incineration as a waste disposal option.
Currently, about 73 percent of our nation's solid waste is disposed of in
sanitary landfills.

There are three main issues regarding the use of landfills as a disposal
method: the growing lack of available landfill space, related disposal
costs, and environmental and health concerns. The first is probably the
best-known concern. A lot has been written in the press about the crisis
of landfill space, implying that in a year or two America won't have
anywhere to put its waste. No one would disagree that the problem is
serious, but it's one that is rather difficult to quantify, as no one knows
for certain how many new landfills will open in the next few years.

Dwindling landfill space is considered to be a particular problem in
the Northeast where the population is more dense and land more
scarce. The EPA lists 5,499 landfills operating in 1988—with an annual
intake of 187 million tons (including industrial and other wastes)—and
projects that these figures will decrease to 2,157 landfills with an annual
intake of 76 million tons by the year 2000. These statistics support the

idea that our landfill capacity is shrinking rapidly: we are not replacing landfill capacity at the rate with which we are using it up.

Studies have shown that people have several misconceptions about landfills. For example, the general notion that much of our garbage biodegrades in our landfills is largely a myth. Part of the trouble in getting people to compost their food wastes, or separate their paper, is that people believe that these materials will biodegrade, or disintegrate, over a period of years in a landfill and are therefore not a problem.

The Garbage Project, an anthropological study of our waste conducted by a group at the University of Arizona, has unearthed hot dogs, corn cobs, and grapes that were twenty-five years old and still recognizable—as well as newspapers dating back to 1952 that were still easily readable. These findings clearly indicate that a lot of what we throw away doesn't biodegrade in a landfill, even if it is quite capable of biodegrading elsewhere (in a home compost system, for example). This is mainly because of the lack of oxygen and the absence of certain organisms in landfills that are necessary to allow degradation.

What's in these landfills taking up so much space? Interestingly, there is also a great deal of misconception regarding the contents of our sanitary landfills. Whereas many people would cite some of the more visible portions of our waste stream, such as plastics, fast-food packaging, and disposable diapers, as accounting for a high percentage of our landfills' contents, these are actually not the most problematic elements. While these materials do contribute significantly to our disposal problems and we waste them in horrendously large amounts, they are not, surprisingly, the real villains. As shown earlier in this chapter, paper and paperboard make up about 40 percent of the waste in our landfills. When the Garbage Project dug trenches through the landfills they studied, they found layer upon layer of telephone books, with newspapers almost equally prevalent.

The majority of what remains of our waste, the yard wastes, metals, glass, food wastes, and plastics, just like the paper and paperboard, is almost all recyclable or would make good compost material. This goes to show that much of what we throw away doesn't need to end up in landfills. If it were diverted, the problem of declining landfill capacity would be considerably less severe.

Cost of disposal in sanitary landfills is another issue. As available landfill space decreases, tipping fees are escalating, as well as the transportation costs involved in carrying the garbage farther away to find a dumping site. New Jersey's landfill tipping fees, for example, have gone from approximately $5 per ton ten years ago to an average of $60 or $65 per ton today. New Jersey and other eastern states often send their garbage as far away as New Mexico for disposal. Building costs for a new landfill are running as high as $60 million. High disposal costs are significantly influencing many cities, counties, and states to take a hard look at recycling.

Landfills have changed dramatically over the years. Today's facilities are considerably safer, both for the environment and for public health, than those constructed in the past. The open dumps of previous decades, where waste was burned or simply piled up, often were neither lined nor monitored—creating public health hazards due to the rodents and insects attracted by the waste and creating environmental hazards because the contaminated liquids they contained leaked into underground water supplies.

Today's landfills are supposed to adhere to much more stringent safety regulations. Not only is their construction more carefully regulated, but the location is more carefully monitored also. Typically, a sanitary landfill today is a huge depression in the earth that is lined with a protective material. Into it each day's garbage is dumped and covered with a layer of dirt or plastic.

In addition to the lining, typical safeguards in today's landfills include a drainage system and sometimes equipment to deal with the gases created by deteriorating waste. The protective liners can be made of compacted clay or plastic and are designed to prevent filtration. The drainage systems allow rainwater and other liquids to pass through the waste and are then pumped to the surface where they are treated and discharged. In some landfills equipment collects the gases created from the waste and pumps it through pipelines for use as a commercial fuel. In most cases landfills are surrounded by huge mounds of dirt to prevent the waste from being blown away from the area as well as to block them from public view. When landfills are filled to capacity, they are sealed with clay and dirt. (Sealed landfills often serve a second purpose: JFK

Airport in New York sits on an old landfill, as do golf courses across the country.)

This does not mean, however, that landfills are without their problems. The safety measures depicted above represent an ideal. Older landfills do not reach it because they often have no protective devices. And modern landfills do not always achieve the ideal either, often being accused of having substandard safety equipment. Numerous landfills are on the national register of Superfund sites for having created environmental problems.

The two major environmental risks from a landfill are leachate and methane gas. Leachate is the highly contaminated liquid that can leak out from a landfill. It can come either from rain entering the landfill or from the moisture already in the garbage when it is thrown away. The groundwater beneath a landfill is particularly at risk, and contamination of drinking water sources happens unfortunately all too often.

But it is not just the ground that can be affected adversely by landfill sites. They can pollute the surrounding air, as well, creating health hazards for those who breathe the air locally. Methane gas, created by the decomposition of organic matter in the landfill, can also cause explosions if not adequately vented. Methane escaping from landfills is also thought to be a significant contributor to the greenhouse effect.

The trouble with landfills constructed years ago is that they were built at a time when there were many less toxic substances being sent to a landfill. Although industrial waste was certainly potentially hazardous, household waste was generally not so dangerous then. Today we have many more chemicals and toxic materials around the house, and unfortunately these end up in our landfills. Older landfills were not built to deal with these toxic wastes, and even today's landfills, with all their new safety equipment, simply don't achieve 100 percent safety.

Older landfills were also built in inappropriate places, as on wetlands and marshes. It was thought at first that garbage disposal on such sites was making use of otherwise useless land—"reclaiming" it—but eventually we learned that landfills located in moist places experience serious seepage problems.

Even recently built landfills are suspected of not being nearly as safe as they could be. The most basic protective device used in a landfill, the liner, is said by environmental activists to be unsatisfactory. The liners have been described as either a dime-thick sheet of plastic, laid out in 20-foot strips and glued together, or simply clay dirt. The Citizens Clearinghouse for Hazardous Wastes (CCHW), a group mobilized in response to the Love Canal disaster, cites an example of a landfill liner that leaked within forty-eight hours of use, even though it met all state and federal regulations. Many landfills have no method of dealing with methane gases.

What all this means is that a landfill can potentially be as dangerous as an incineration site—if it is not supervised and maintained properly or if hazardous materials, which are not meant to end up in an ordinary landfill, are not detected. Examples of toxic seepage from landfill sites are unfortunately much too common. As an example, during the week of 28 June 1991 residents of a neighborhood near Savannah, Georgia, had to leave their homes suddenly because of the discovery of dangerous methane leaks from an old landfill upon which the neighborhood had been built. CCHW notes that even if you don't live near a site, you could be affected by a variety of side-effects. These include airborne toxics that travel for miles and contaminated food and water supplies.

It is not surprising, then, that one of the major problems with increasing our current landfill capacity is the public outcry against landfills: people simply don't want a landfill near where they live. Even if landfills were the safest solution possible, a massive wall of public disapproval is blocking the way for future sites.

Few people see a future without landfills, however. Waste that cannot be recycled and residue from incinerators will always need to be put somewhere. A goal to strive for, then, is to make landfills safe and to reduce significantly our dependence on them.

Time for a Serious Look at Recycling

It is clear that the information regarding our waste disposal practices is often confusing. Statistics are often hard to come by—and, once armed with them, one undoubtedly runs across a new set that doesn't quite match ours. There are those who support incineration as a method of waste disposal, and there are many more who don't. The case is equally true for landfilling, which also has its proponents and opponents.

All this brings us to recycling as a disposal method. Although we currently recycle only about 13 percent of our waste as a national average, many states and areas have significantly higher rates and even the EPA has targeted a national source reduction and recycling rate of 25 percent by 1992. In the past, municipal authorities have tended to believe that recycling was too difficult to organize and that Americans would not sort their waste. But rapidly rising disposal costs and opposition to landfills and incinerators have forced state and county officials to take a serious look at recycling as an alternative.

Clearly our current waste disposal problems have not occurred overnight. The planet's increasing population and the ensuing space constraints mean that we need to pay more attention to our disposal methods than in the past. It is only as the problem reaches crisis level that federal, state, and local officials are being forced to look at the issue and search out safe, viable alternatives.

2 The Basics of Recycling

In light of our nation's current solid waste disposal crisis, it is obvious that recycling can—and must—play an important role in the future management of waste in this country. Whereas recycling was a fact of life hundreds of years ago, it became no more than an afterthought for years . . . until environmental, economic, and subsequent legal pressures in recent decades have forced individuals and communities alike to recognize the benefits of this waste processing method.

A BRIEF HISTORY OF RECYCLING

Recycling is not a new idea. It, too, like general waste management, has been around for centuries. Scrap merchants and scavengers collected what others no longer wanted and either repaired the item or turned it into something else that could serve a useful purpose. In fact, the scrap recycling industry estimates that people were reusing metal scrap as far back as 3000 B.C. or so, while the reuse of wastepaper and textiles goes back about half that far.

More recently, our nation pulled together during World War II to preserve or reuse vital resources that were in short supply. Rubber, metals, glass, tin cans, scrap iron, cooking grease, string, razor blades, and countless other materials were all saved either to conserve fuel and energy or simply to keep items that were difficult to obtain. After the war, when things once again became easier to obtain, we slipped into habits that persist today and are extremely hard to break: we throw things away without thinking rather than finding another use for them. Industry has aggravated the situation over the years with the introduction of disposable goods in alarming numbers.

The recycling philosophy regaining momentum in today's overpackaged, waste-oriented society can be traced back to the 1960s. At that time, even without the pressures that today are forcing people to look at recycling as a viable solution to our disposal problems, people began to realize that we were throwing away valuable resources and polluting our environment.

What started as a grassroots movement soon developed further when stricter environmental controls on landfills and incineration plants made the costs of waste disposal much higher. Suddenly garbage became a potentially profitable business, and like any good capitalist society, Americans rushed forward to investigate a previously untapped market. Growing public concern about pollution and land waste spurred these efforts. In response to the public outcry, Congress passed the Resource Recovery Act of 1970 and then the Resource Conservation and Recovery Act of 1976. (More about these in Chapter 7.)

The recycling industry has been developing rapidly over the past decade even though the majority of the population has been unaware of its existence. What began as community newspaper collection sites has developed into a multimillion-dollar industry that has spread across the nation in various shapes and sizes. Communities from California to Maine now have the opportunity to separate not only newspaper but plastics, paper products, glass, aluminum, and various other materials from their garbage and thus significantly affect our overall waste generation. Some of us are lucky enough to be served by a curbside collection system that picks up our recyclables literally from our curbs, and many more have access to buy-back or drop-off centers. And those who don't can expect to have the opportunity shortly—for recycling is proving itself to be a far superior method of dealing with our waste disposal problem than either of its alternative methods, landfills and incinerators.

CURRENT COLLECTION METHODS

Many communities across the United States now have some sort of residential recycling program in place. A community must develop a system that suits its particular situation, taking into account such variables as demographics and local markets for recyclables. Clearly, rural communities are not suited to the same sort of collection methods that would best serve Manhattan. Likewise, if a city consists mainly of multifamily buildings, it may need a different system than a community in which single-family dwellings are the norm. In any case, the program must be convenient for the residents and economically feasible for the community. Separating trash and recyclables is not difficult once the pattern is established: the Glass Packaging Institute estimates that it takes only fifteen minutes per week.

Curbside Programs

Curbside collection of recyclable materials is the most effective method of residential recycling because it is the most convenient for consumers. In fact the very idea behind curbside collection is just that: to make it as easy for residents to recycle as it is to throw the materials away. At the end of 1990 there were thought to be 2,700 active curbside programs in forty-eight states according to *BioCycle* magazine.

In a typical curbside program, recyclables are picked up just like the regular household garbage: in their own containers at the curb. Both one-bin and multibin systems are used. In the former case, residents do not separate the recyclables themselves but put them all in one bin at the curb; in the latter, residents typically separate their waste into aluminum, glass, plastic, and paper (or some combination of these, depending on the program) and have a container for each at the curb. Most communities provide containers for their residents. This policy ensures higher participation, as residents don't have to hunt down their own containers, and also allows the containers to be color-coded for the different materials, speeding up the collection process. Typically, the containers are sturdy plastic bins (usually made of recycled plastic) or reusable bags.

There are benefits to each of these systems, and it is up to each community to decide which approach works best. The one-bin system requires less work for consumers but demands more staff or equipment somewhere along the line to separate the materials. This method also allows the flexibility of adding new recyclable materials to your com-

munity program without issuing every household with a new container.
The multibin system requires the consumers to separate the recyclables
but then saves on the extra labor required to do this at a later stage.
Multibin systems must also have collection vehicles with separate com-
partments.

A curbside program is more likely to succeed if collection is scheduled for the same day as regular garbage pickup. This practice eliminates any confusion and allows recycling to become part of an established routine. Another key to success is proper community education
before the program begins. Since people will not go out of their way to
learn about a new program, participation must be encouraged by first
explaining how the program will work and then clearly detailing what
materials will be accepted.

A variety of materials are collected in curbside programs across the
country. Newspaper is by far the most commonly collected item: it is
estimated to account for well over half of all materials collected by
volume. Newsprint is followed by glass. Aluminum cans, steel cans, and
plastic are often collected too.

Curbside collection is also the most expensive method of collecting
recyclables from residential areas. In fact, in its July 1990 issue, *BioCycle*
magazine cited estimates that the cost is running at almost $2 per
household per month for new programs. Not only are new collection
vehicles expensive, but just providing households with bins or plastic
bags for their recyclables can be an enormous expense. Even so, the
high success rate of curbside collection in comparison to the other options still appears to make it well worth the initial expense. Regular
collection of high-quality recyclables not only can earn a community
money from the sale of these materials but it saves considerable money
in avoided disposal costs.

Approximately half of the curbside programs currently in use across
the country are mandatory. To ensure participation, some cities conduct
random checks of a household's garbage and can levy fines if recyclables
are found among the "regular" garbage. New York, for example, fines
residents up to $500 for failure to separate recyclables. The state of
New Jersey is thought to have one of the most comprehensive curbside
recycling programs in the country. In that state's mandatory program,

established in 1987, local communities are required to enforce separation of leaves and at least three other recyclable materials. (They can choose from a list.) The program has proved very successful. It was New Jersey's lack of landfill space that spurred the state into developing this wide-ranging program.

In the twenty-seven states that were able to provide numbers in a recent *BioCycle* magazine study, it is estimated that 37 million people are served by curbside recycling programs. Clearly, many more than this number are served, but the infrastructure is not yet in place to get accurate totals. Almost all existing systems are multimaterial programs. This is in stark contrast to the early curbside programs of the 1970s and early 1980s, when only one material, usually newspaper, was picked up through curbside collection. If pending legislation across the nation is any indication, the number of people and communities served by curbside programs will increase substantially over the next few years. Many states are currently considering implementing either voluntary or mandatory curbside programs for their residential areas while others have already made the decision and are just beginning to implement their programs.

Drop-Off Sites

Drop-off centers are the most common method of recycling in the United States. They are the traditional method employed by rural communities, where the housing situation makes curbside collection less practical. It is also the ideal collection method to use in a pilot recycling project, where a community has never engaged in recycling collection before.

Recycling drop-off sites are situated at specific locations around a community and supplied with large containers, usually "igloos," trailers, or large waste bins, clearly marked for the kind of materials they accept. They may be located anywhere with enough space to take the large collection containers, such as the corner of a parking lot, an abandoned lot, or the city landfill. Such sites can be run by a public body, privately, or by some combination of the two. It is very common now for charitable organizations to have drop-off centers from which they sell the donated recyclables to help support their work.

The location for a drop-off center must be convenient for the public. The less people have to go out of their way to recycle, the more successful the program will be. In California, for example, most shopping centers now have recycling igloos in the corner of their parking lots. The materials accepted at a drop-off site are determined by the local markets, but the most common drop-off materials are aluminum, glass, and newspaper. Residents are expected to separate their materials and put each type of recyclable in the appropriate container.

Communities using the drop-off system save the expenses associated with curbside collection. Collection costs are nil because the residents bring their own recyclables to the central site, and virtually no personnel are required as the sites can often be left unstaffed. The only costs involved are for the containers to hold the recyclables and for the transport of materials from the drop-off sites to the processor, but even these costs may be paid by the recycler or broker who eventually takes the materials for processing.

There are three basic drawbacks of a drop-off recycling system: it relies solely on the voluntary participation of the community; it requires residents to save up their recyclables and then transport them to the drop-off center; and, with the prices paid for some recyclable materials today, drop-off centers must be secured to avoid theft. To be successful, a drop-off collection facility must keep the public aware of its location, its hours of operation, and the materials it will accept.

Buy-Back Centers

A buy-back center is just what its name implies: a place where the public can take recyclables and be paid for them. Buy-back centers, unlike drop-off sites, are not so often limited to rural locations. They may be found in both rural and urban areas. Even if a community has a curbside pickup program, there are probably one or more buy-back centers somewhere nearby also.

There are several differences between a drop-off center and a buy-back center other than just the matter of payment. The two approaches to recycling may differ in the types of recyclable materials they will accept, their location, the level of contamination they will accept, and their hours of operation.

Prices will vary according to the current markets for the recyclable materials turned in. Aluminum, for example, usually maintains a relatively stable price, but other materials like glass and particularly newspaper have fluctuated greatly in price over the past few years. In some states with "bottle bills," there may be a statewide price set for bottles and other beverage containers. Most prices are set on a per-pound basis.

The location of a buy-back center will probably not be quite as convenient as that of a drop-off center. This is true for a couple of reasons. First, people will generally go farther out of their way to return materials if they are earning money for them. Second, buy-back centers often need their own lot or yard because they take up more space with storage, equipment, and machinery and because a shopping center is less likely to allow them to locate on their premises if they are making a profit from their collection.

Moreover, a buy-back center is usually more careful about contaminants. It will probably require all recyclables to be separated and insist that all contaminants be removed. Because the buy-back center is paying you for the materials, it will not want to pay for materials it cannot ultimately sell to its end-users.

Because buy-back centers must be staffed, they usually have limited hours in comparison to a drop-off location. Check ahead to find out what hours your local buy-back center keeps.

Charity Drives

From time to time a community group will have a drive to collect certain recyclables that it will then sell to a buy-back center or broker to earn money for a specific project. The Girl Scouts, a church group, or a local elementary school, for example, may pick up your recyclables from your house or ask that you take them to a specific location. Such groups always appreciate the extra effort local residents make to help them out, and donating your recyclables to an organization represents a way for you to help them financially at no loss to yourself.

Landfills

Many communities now include a recycling center at their landfill. There are benefits to combining these two functions—namely, convenience to the patrons of the landfill and the ability to combine several functions in one location.

Typically, the recycling center will be the first stop on the way into the landfill. This location allows people coming to dispose of waste to separate recyclable materials before proceeding to the dumping area. As landfills charge by the load for dumping, the customer can save money by eliminating as much as possible at the recycling center first. This gives a financial incentive—to individuals and commercial users of the landfill alike—to dispose of recyclables separately.

Because of the location of a typical landfill—a large plot of land usually owned or managed by the local community—it allows the community to combine various functions at the same site, saving money both in transport and in the cost of renting or leasing other locations. Often these sites will also take hazardous wastes.

Clearly the collection or disposal methods for recyclable materials vary widely. With the emergence of recycling programs across the country, most communities should by now have at least one of these systems available to them or in some stage of development.

PROCESSING AND TRANSPORTING MATERIALS

Once recyclable materials have been collected, they must be transported and processed before they can be made into new products. A look at the various methods of shipping and processing recyclables will show clearly how the recycling industry is still in a growth stage: if one thing can be said for the processing of recyclables it is that no two programs seem to do it exactly the same way.

Materials Recovery Facilities (MRFs)

Once recyclable materials have been collected, either from a curbside program or from any of the other systems described above, they are typically taken to a sorting and processing facility. These are most commonly known as materials recovery facilities, or MRFs (pronounced "murfs"), but are sometimes also referred to as intermediate processing centers (IPCs) or intermediate processing facilities (IPFs). These deserve special discussion because they often represent state-of-the-art processing methods in this developing field.

A community or region needs to have a reasonably large and continuous supply of recyclables to justify the construction of a MRF. For example, it is estimated that it takes a population of 250,000 to 400,000 to supply recyclables to a MRF with a processing capacity of 100 to 200 tons per day.

The capital costs needed to build a MRF are steep: existing MRFs have cost anywhere from $10,000 to $50,000 per daily ton of waste processed. This means that a present-day facility which can process 200 tons per day probably costs several million dollars to build. Estimated costs for planned MRFs are even higher.

Recyclable materials that have been commingled—gathered in one container without separation—must be separated by type of material and sometimes also by color (glass and plastics, for example). This is what takes place at a MRF, in addition to shredding, crushing, and baling. All this is done by a combination of muscle and machinery.

The machinery used in today's MRFs is varied: large magnet systems can separate ferrous materials from other waste; air separators can be used for lighter materials like paper and plastics; and optical systems to separate glass colors are being developed. Many MRFs also use huge balers to compact and tie together the recyclable materials for transport to end-users. Even so, a large part of the separating is still done by hand as the materials go along a conveyor belt.

There are several benefits to using a MRF. Commingled collection is much easier for participating communities and it tends to increase public participation by allowing residents to put out only one collection bin. Curbside collection of commingled recyclables also takes less time because the truck personnel don't have separate bins to empty. Finally, the MRF centralizes the sorting process and eliminates repetition of the same tasks by all areas or communities who bring their materials to the MRF.

The sticky problem of permits is usually much less pronounced for a community that opens a MRF rather than a landfill or an incinerator. This can mean significant cost and time savings when trying to establish a waste reduction program. In many states there are no permits required at all, while in others the procedure, in comparison to that for landfills or incinerators, is significantly easier.

The first MRFs were started in the early 1980s in Groton, Connecticut, and Islip, New York. Since that time at least 150 more facilities have been opened, most of them on the East Coast. Over fifty more are in various stages of development. With MRFs gaining in popularity, many more can be expected in the years to come. Most MRFs operating today (approximately 80 percent) are privately run. The remaining 20 percent are either publicly run or joint ventures between public and private entities.

Like any new enterprise, MRFs are not without their troubles. Both aluminum can and glass manufacturers have noted concerns about the quality of materials coming to them after having been sorted at commingled materials facilities. Aluminum can manufacturers, for example, are concerned that the quality of the aluminum coming from a MRF is not as good as that from states which have deposit or redemption laws. In these states, there is a closed-loop system in which the aluminum cans go back to the retailer and then straight back to the aluminum can manufacturers, without being commingled with other recyclable materials. When aluminum has been through a MRF, it sometimes becomes mildly contaminated by chips of glass, parts of bimetal cans, or traces of dirt that attach to the aluminum and lower the overall quality of the finished product.

Likewise, glass manufacturers have some concerns about the glass that comes from a MRF. Ceramics—pieces of plates and cups, for example—can get mixed in with the glass cullet and then cause blistering on the newly produced glass bottles. Another problem is the high percentage of glass that comes to a MRF broken and thus has to go through as a mixed-glass classification. Color-separated glass is valued more highly than mixed glass.

These problems are by no means insurmountable, however. Teething problems are a fact in any new venture. Some problems have relatively simple solutions, while others will need to be approached by all the players involved in a joint effort to solve these inconveniences. Contamination of aluminum by dirt can be avoided simply by storing the aluminum indoors or in properly protected areas, for example. Only about half of the existing facilities store their aluminum in this manner, but the new facilities are being built with this in mind. MRF operators are solving the problem of mixed glass by finding new markets for the product: one such use is by asphalt producers to make glasphalt.

Already, during their short lifetime, MRFs have developed significantly from what they once were. Many began as simple covered cement slabs where materials were dumped and sorted by hand, whereas most MRFs constructed today are sophisticated facilities that may employ sorters, magnets, balers, and conveyor belts to deal with the recyclables. They are capable of handling more volume and a wider variety of materials, too. Most started out accepting newsprint, glass, and aluminum and now it is common for a MRF to handle mixed paper and plastics also. The capacity of a MRF varies widely from facility to facility. Some handle 100 or 200 tons per day of recyclables, while others have a capacity of up to 1,600 tons per day.

Experts believe that MRFs are here to stay—in fact, they are expected to develop and do even more than they do currently. Future MRFs are expected to handle commercial waste as well as domestic, for example. They are also expected to further process the materials. It has been suggested, for instance, that MRFs of the future may also pulp paper, rather than just shred and bale it, taking responsibility for one more step in the recycling process. Whatever their future developments, these facilities already represent an important step in the processing chain.

Brokers and Other Intermediary Players

Once recyclables have been collected, there are generally three channels through which they may be sent: end-users, brokers, and internal markets. A MRF may be run by any one of these intermediary players.

End-users are the facilities that actually process or remanufacture the recyclable materials. A paper mill or aluminum plant that takes receipt of recyclable materials directly is an end-user, for example. Some end-users will accept material from the public and prepare it for reuse themselves; others may take it only from brokers. By selling directly to an end-user, a community can probably earn more money because it is leaving out the middleman. But end-users may have more stringent standards as to how recyclables must be prepared.

Brokers are the middlemen. They purchase recyclables from the public, charities, and businesses and then sell them to the end-users. Brokers are popular with end-users because they will guarantee the quality of the materials they are selling. They sort through the materials manually or mechanically and remove as much of the contaminants as possible before delivering the recyclables to the plant where they will be reprocessed. They also have the equipment necessary to bale and otherwise prepare recyclables in the way the end-users prefer.

Internal markets are sources within a community that can use its recyclable materials. This is usually a small market, but one example is collecting newspapers and shredding them to use as bedding for local farmers' livestock.

Transfer stations are often used by the buyers mentioned above or by a MRF. A transfer station is a site where collection trucks take recyclables that are then eventually taken to a MRF, an end-user, or some other step in the processing chain. Transfer stations are useful to help centralize recyclables that have been gathered from various sites.

Although the players and processes mentioned here represent the major links in the processing chain, there is still no standard formula for processing recyclables. Some MRFs take commingled materials and others don't; some collection systems use transfer stations and others don't; sometimes the recyclables will go through many stages before being reprocessed and other times they will go almost directly to the reprocessor.

Most communities work with some combination of the players mentioned above when collecting and selling their recyclables. As the industry develops, the process may become more standardized but for now it is a sometimes confusing combination of all these factors. A community must establish the best way to deal with its particular situation.

WHY SOME THINGS CAN'T BE RECYCLED

Chapter 1 showed that only 13 percent of our municipal solid waste is being recycled nationwide (higher in some individual states). The rest is being buried or burned. So why isn't more being recycled? Many involved in studying our waste habits, including the Citizen's Clearinghouse for Hazardous Wastes, believe that over 80 percent of our solid waste stream is recyclable—that is, technically recyclable.

But what do we mean by "recyclable"? There are two tests for genuine recyclability. First, can a product or material *technically* be recycled? In other words, do we have the technical capability to turn it back into another useful product? Second, is it *practically* recyclable? To be considered practically recyclable it must be recyclable in most communities, meaning that someone will take the material and reprocess it (or ship it to where it can be reprocessed). Its recycling must also be economically feasible.

It is difficult to think of many materials that cannot technically be recycled—either by being reprocessed into another product, reused again for some other purpose, or passed along to someone else for the same purpose. Even the number of products and materials mentioned in these pages covers a wide range of recyclables. The technical aspect of recycling does not appear to be the main deterrent to the development of this field. Even if not everything can be recycled currently, the estimate of over 80 percent of our solid waste is certainly a healthy goal.

Throughout this book reference is made to a number of materials that are indeed recyclable—but not in your area. This is the essence of the problem of what is technically recyclable but not practically so. Making all our waste practically recyclable is a complex issue. A general lack of recycling programs, economic inequities, and poor markets are all separate—but interrelated—problems that stand in the way of practical recycling.

Motor oil is a good example. While many communities now do recycle oil, many others do not because local industry or government have not organized the infrastructure necessary to collect, transport, and process the oil. Finding uses for the collected oil is not the problem.

This dilemma is also applicable to the resident of a small town who wants to know why no one will recycle the plastic containers she has even though they have a recycling symbol on the bottom. While the plastics industry spends huge sums of money telling consumers that plastics are recyclable, only 1 percent or so of all plastics are actually being recycled currently. The facilities are simply not in place to recycle more.

Whether it is *economically* feasible to recycle a product is another issue. Often, virgin raw materials are cheaper than recycled products so there is no incentive for processors to use the recycled materials. Sometimes these economic imbalances are reinforced (or even caused) by government policies—such as depletion allowances for the mining and oil industries—that falsely lower the price of virgin materials as compared to their recycled counterparts. Transportation can also play a role. Often the shipping costs of moving collected recyclables to a processing plant (because processing plants for recyclables are still few and far between) can prove too costly to allow the materials to compete in the marketplace.

Newsprint, as everyone knows, is technically recyclable. It is not always practically recyclable, however, for another reason. Even though newsprint is the most commonly collected material, huge stores of newspapers have many times been taken to an incinerator or landfill because a market glut meant that no paper mills would take all the stored paper. If a product isn't used again, it isn't recycled: simply collecting it means nothing. Reliable markets for recycled materials are essential.

Each of these problems has a separate solution. Government subsidies and economic policies that favor the use of raw materials must be stopped or severely modified if recycling is to develop successfully. The creation of more reprocessing plants for recycled materials across the country is the only way to solve the transport problem. Finally, the biggest impact on recycling will come from the development of markets for products made out of recycled materials. The public must buy recycled products whenever possible if recycling is to develop to its full potential.

These issues must all be dealt with. Simply relying on our past methods will not work. We have seen that the alternatives to recycling are environmentally ugly and economically unattractive. Efforts must be made, then, to take positive steps toward helping recycling play its essential role in the practical solution to our solid waste crisis.

3 Common Recyclables

This chapter introduces the better-known recyclable materials—those which many people are already recycling and for which there are well-established markets. These materials are paper, glass, metals, and plastics.

The potential uses for most recyclables are almost endless. Many materials can be recycled on a closed-loop basis, which means that they go back to make the same product over and over again. Glass and aluminum are closed-loop recyclables. Others, like paper, can be recycled into a variety of different grades and products.

But recycling isn't just collecting newspaper or glass bottles and turning them in to a recycling center. Recycling hasn't occurred until the newspaper or glass is made into another product. We can collect all the aluminum cans in the world, but if they're not used to make new products, they are not being recycled.

The opening sections in this chapter discuss how these materials are recycled, how much we are currently recycling, and what becomes of each material at the end of the recycling process. Then we'll consider paper, glass, metals, and plastic as environmentally sound packaging. The final section discusses composting organic wastes.

PAPER

Using recycled paper instead of virgin materials reduces:
- Energy use by 23 to 74 percent
- Air pollution by 74 percent
- Water pollution by 35 percent
- Water use by 58 percent

The paper industry also benefits: building a mill designed to use wastepaper instead of virgin pulp can cost 50 to 80 percent less.

Everybody knows that paper is made from trees. But not everybody knows that paper used to be made from cloth and plant fibers. In earlier centuries paper was made from cotton and linen scraps and from various shrubs and grasses, particularly hemp. This remained the case until, in the 1860s, the demand for paper forced innovation and people discovered how to use wood pulp in the papermaking process. We are still using trees, although some people are trying to encourage the use of hemp and other plants again.

Currently 40 percent of our nation's municipal solid waste consists of paper and paperboard products. As a nation we use over 75 million tons of paper and paperboard annually—that's approximately 600 pounds per person according to the Institute of Scrap Recycling Industries (ISRI). The White House alone is estimated to throw out nearly a ton of wastepaper daily. The American Paper Institute estimates that, of the paper produced each year, we discard 54 percent of it in municipal waste systems, recycle 28 percent, and use 11 percent for books and other permanent uses, leaving just 7 percent that is unrecoverable.

A study conducted for the National Solid Wastes Management Association concluded that nearly 25 million tons of recyclable paper was recovered in 1988. Of that, nearly 12 million tons was corrugated materials, approximately 8.5 million was printing and writing-quality paper, and 4.5 million was newsprint. While it is encouraging to know that we are recycling paper in such large amounts, the bad news is that over twice as much as we reclaimed—53 million tons—was disposed of in landfills. Miscellaneous disposable paper and paperboard constituted 11.9 million tons, old corrugated materials counted for 11.1 million tons, and newsprint represented 9.2 million tons. Other packaging (7.4 million tons), printing and writing paper (7 million tons), and magazines and inserts (6.4 millions tons) made up the remaining amount disposed of.

The list of paper products recycled in some amount or another is quite long. Telephone books, newspapers, magazines, computer printouts, junk mail, envelopes, office memos, photocopy paper, detergent boxes, tissue boxes, shoe boxes, toilet paper rolls, cereal boxes, cardboard egg cartons, diaper boxes, grocery bags, and cardboard all get recycled to some extent, although your local program may not take all of these products. The most commonly recycled ones are discussed in the following sections.

These products can come back in many shapes and forms. Cereal boxes, toilet tissue, newsprint, and paper towels are some of the more common products with a certain amount of recycled fiber in them. Wastepaper is also used to make insulation, molded packaging, grocery bags, paper for magazines and books, diapers, certain sanitary products, and cushioning materials for packing and shipping. Additionally, it is more and more common today to find stationery, office supplies, and computer paper made with a certain amount of recycled content. Some of the less known uses for recycled paper fibers are wallboard, the insides of automobiles, and animal bedding. Finally, we export our wastepaper to many Asian countries with limited timber supplies.

To get the highest-quality results from recycling paper, a system of grading has been developed over the years from the Paper Stock Institute. Over fifty different grades of scrap paper have been classified this way. Of these many different grades, the types most commonly recycled include newspaper, corrugated materials, mixed papers, and high-grade office paper.

Newsprint

Discussions about recycling paper usually concern newsprint, as it is the most visible type of paper to enter the waste stream. In fact, newspapers constitute the largest single component of landfills. Congressman Esteban Torres, sponsor of the Newspaper Recycling Incentives Act (H.R. 873), has stated that the amount of newsprint we dump in our dwindling landfills each year takes up over 28 million cubic yards of space at a disposal cost of over $255 million annually.

Newsprint is also one of the most commonly recycled materials. But we still have a long way to go: the National Solid Wastes Management Association reports that only about 37 percent of the newspapers consumed in this country was recycled in 1989. The newsprint doesn't necessarily come back to make more newspapers, either: the same organization points out that the recycled-fiber content of North American (United States and Canada) newsprint in 1988 was approximately 9 percent and the virgin fiber was 91 percent.

ISRI reports that in 1988 Americans used 13.2 million tons of newspapers and recycled 4.5 million tons. It is estimated that we throw away the equivalent of 500,000 trees each week. To translate this to a smaller scale, one ton of paper uses seventeen trees. These trees, apart from looking nice, would absorb 250 pounds of carbon dioxide annually. Another commonly cited figure is that a single Sunday edition of the *New York Times* uses 75,000 trees.

Newsprint doesn't only refer to newspapers, however. The pages of your telephone book (although they are usually a slightly lower grade) and many mail inserts are also made of newsprint. In fact, telephone books are an excellent place to start recycling. Think how many telephone books are thrown out each year. Fortunately, some telephone companies are beginning campaigns to collect and recycle their books each year when the new directories come out. If your local telephone company doesn't, suggest that they do.

One new use for old newspapers deserves mention for its unique nature. That application is shredded newsprint as bedding material for livestock. This market developed when farmers in the Midwest began using newsprint in the late 1980s because poor weather conditions sent straw prices soaring. Since then the practice has been catching on, bad weather or not, and it is estimated that over 100,000 tons per year of bedding is being produced.

Farmers cite many advantages to shredded newspaper over traditional straw. Newsprint has proved to be more absorbent, cleaner, and less expensive than other bedding materials. It produces fewer odors and decomposes more quickly in the field. (Like straw, the newsprint is spread in the fields after use as bedding.)

Several initial concerns about the use of newsprint seem to have been answered. Among the major concerns was the toxicity of the heavy metals and dyes in the newspaper inks. This was certainly a problem in the past, but since the early 1980s, when many toxic elements were removed from printing inks, studies have in fact shown that there are fewer heavy metals in newspaper than in straw.

Another concern was the danger to animals posed by staples in inserts or by glass or metal contaminants that might find their way into the newspaper. So far this has not proved to be a problem. Problems of littering the countryside during transport were also expected. As long as the paper is covered during shipping and not left out in the open for a long time once delivered, however, litter problems have been negligible.

Many states and even the EPA are looking at the possible use of newsprint as animal bedding on a more widespread level. Initial use certainly shows that this is an excellent market for old newspapers.

Finding new markets for old newsprint is essential if we are to establish successful recycling for this material. Canada is expected to take more of our old newsprint in the next few years as it develops more de-inking facilities. American consumption is also expected to rise as we build more such facilities, but their construction appears to be progressing slowly. The growth of de-inking facilities, which will in turn increase the demand for old newsprint, is particularly important as it is generally thought that the traditional markets for this material, such as insulation and recycled paperboard, are mostly saturated.

Corrugated Materials

What we all call cardboard, but which the recycling industry refers to as "corrugated materials," often makes up about half the waste of a retail business. It also has the highest recycling rate of any paper grade. In 1988, according to ISRI, almost 10 million tons of corrugated boxes were recycled in the United States, representing approximately 50 percent of the corrugated boxes manufactured here. The center part of these boxes, the corrugated flute, is often made up of 100 percent recycled materials, too.

It may seem surprising that corrugated materials are the most recycled of paper products because households don't use cardboard boxes on a regular basis. But grocery stores, department stores, and other businesses that commonly use these cardboard containers have been recycling them for years and this has created the high recovery rate. In fact, corrugated materials provide the perfect example of the difference business and industry can make by participating in recycling.

Most recycling programs accept corrugated materials. If for some reason your curbside program or local drop-off center doesn't, try asking your supermarket or department store if their storage area is accessible to the public and if they would allow you to add your cardboard to theirs.

If you can find someone to recycle corrugated paper, ask if you can include kraft paper (like brown shopping bags) as well. Most recyclers will take the two together.

High-Grade Paper

Over 4 million tons of office paper are thrown away each year. Businesses, schools, and organizations are beginning to realize the value of some of the paper they discard, however. High-grade office paper includes computer printouts (both green/white and plain white), tabulating cards, copy paper, white stationery, and the cuttings from printing plants.

High-grade paper is usually more valuable in the marketplace than most other types because it can be used as a direct substitute for wood pulp in the papermaking process. It is made with very strong fibers that can be recycled easily into good-quality paper. The green and white computer paper is the most valuable of all. Traditionally, the market for high-grade paper has been steady and many recycling centers accept it.

Many places that take white office paper will also take colored paper as long as it is kept separate from the white. Check with your recycler, though. Because colored paper fetches a lower price than white, some places don't bother collecting it.

Resource Recycling states that printing and writing paper constituted 28 percent (21.8 million tons) of the 76.8 million tons of paper and paperboard produced in the United States in 1988, but wastepaper made up only 6.5 percent of the feedstock for this paper. What this means is that, although printing and writing papers represent the second largest category of paper produced, they have the lowest amount of recycled content, by far, of any sector. This shows that we need to encourage the practice of recycling this high-grade paper and insist on a much greater recycled content in the office paper we buy. (See Steve Apotheker, "Fine

Printing and Writing Paper—It's Recycled, Too," *Resource Recycling* [Portland, Oregon], May 1990.)

Glossy Paper

The glossy paper that most magazines are made out of is not as widely recycled as many other grades. This is for two simple reasons, both having to do with the fact that the paper is heavily coated in clay (which gives it the shine). At first the clay made the paper very difficult to recycle. This is changing, however, and a recent paper-bleaching process actually benefits from the presence of the clay. The other reason is that once the clay was removed, there was very little paper (about half the original volume) to recycle, so it just wasn't economically worthwhile.

It is still relatively difficult to find outlets to accept glossy paper, but call around. If you live near a big city, where substantial amounts can be gathered easily, or if you live near a paper mill that will use the glossy paper, you are more likely to be able to recycle this grade of paper.

Because we are currently throwing away over 6 million tons of magazines annually, we have nowhere to go but up with respect to recycling glossy paper stock. The paper can be used in the bleaching process mentioned above (to make other paper grades brighter) and in lower-grade papers such as paperboard.

End Products from Recycled Paper

You may be surprised to learn that you probably buy and use products made from recycled paper every day. Some of its many uses (cited in ISRI's *Recycling Paper*, 1990) are listed here:

Corrugated Goods. The cardboard box that we all know so well—our stereos, microwaves, radios, and many other things come packed in them—comes back again and again as the same kind of box or is recycled into a variety of other paper products.

Newspapers. Old newspapers can be recycled into newsprint again.

Other uses for old newsprint include insulation, stuffing, and molded paper products.

Printing and Writing Papers. Many printing and writing supplies come with varying amounts of recycled materials in them. Fine stationery; copying, ledger, and other office paper; magazines, books, and brochures; decorative and wrapping papers—all can contain recycled fibers in varying amounts. It is becoming much more common to find a selection of high-quality printing and letterhead papers with some recycled content. Even coated paper stocks suitable for four-color graphics are now available with recycled-fiber content for magazine production.

Tissues and Towels. Approximately 5 million tons of tissue-grade paper, consisting of toilet and facial tissue, paper napkins, towels, diapers, and various other sanitary products, are produced in the United States annually. About 2.5 million tons of wastepaper are used to manufacture these products. According to the American Paper Institute, paper mills rely heavily on high-grade scrap paper generated in manufacturing and converting operations to make these products. Lower grades, such as old newspapers and corrugated boxes, are being used to make paper hand towels and industrial wipes.

Combination Boxboard. Cereal and soap boxes, shoe boxes, tissue boxes, and beer and soft drink carriers are all familiar consumer products made with a high recycled-fiber content, sometimes as high as 100 percent. If your cereal or soap box has gray-colored board on the inside, it is made with recycled scrap paper.

Construction Products. Most consumers are unaware of the role that recycled paper products play in the construction industry. Insulation, gypsum wallboard, roofing paper, flooring, padding, and sound-absorbing materials all use recycled scrap paper. In fact, almost a million tons of scrap paper are used annually as raw material for these products.

Kraft Paper. The brown paper bags we see every day at the supermarket are made from kraft paper. It is also used significantly in shipping sacks for bulk products such as agricultural seeds, animal feeds, fertilizers, and cement, as well as in mail wrappings for magazines and catalogs. Kraft paper is made from recycled scrap paper.

Molded Products. Paper egg cartons, fruit trays, flowerpots, and certain industrial and construction products are made from scrap paper also. The paper scraps are repulped and molded into this special-use packaging.

Developmental Applications. New uses for recycled paper are being researched constantly. For example, research is being conducted to transform old newspapers into pellets to be burned as a new energy source.

Pre-Consumer and Post-Consumer Wastes

In response to consumer demands for recycled paper products, more and more paper manufacturers are advertising recycled content in their products. But before purchasing a product that claims to be made with recycled paper, it is important to ascertain its content of pre-consumer or post-consumer waste. This shows whether or not the product is really using recycled materials.

Post-consumer waste, as the name implies, consists of paper products that have already been used by the consumer. Newspapers, corrugated containers, computer printouts, office paper, telephone books, and magazines that are returned to paper mills and used again are examples of post-consumer waste. Pre-consumer waste, on the other hand, has never made it to the consumer. Wastes from the manufacturing process—like paper and paperboard waste, box waste, printed paper that never reaches the consumer, printing overruns, and obsolete inventories of paper—are examples of pre-consumer waste.

Because pre-consumer waste has always been reused by the paper industry, its use in the manufacturing process shows no special effort to recycle paper. The percentage of post-consumer waste is the important figure. This shows how much effort has gone into recycling paper that otherwise would end up in a landfill or incinerator, which is the vital issue. Pre-consumer waste content is largely irrelevant.

The EPA has established guidelines for state and local government agencies that spend more than $10,000 using federal funds. These agencies are required to have preference programs for paper products made from certain percentages of post-consumer waste. The following percentages are the EPA guidelines for minimum post-consumer waste: toilet tissue—20 percent; paper towels—40 percent; paper napkins—40 percent; facial tissue—5 percent. While these guidelines represent a beginning, most environmental groups criticize them as being too lenient. These groups prefer to encourage consumers to search for products with a post-consumer waste content of at least 50 percent.

Obstacles

If the widespread acceptance of recycled paper is slow in coming, the reasons can be traced to several issues that still plague the industry. The slow development of reliable markets for recycled paper, doubts about its quality, concerns over bleaching processes—all have hampered the full development of the paper recycling industry. These issues must be faced before satisfactory development can be expected.

MARKET DEVELOPMENT

Recently there have been numerous items in the news about gluts of recycled materials, particularly newsprint. One such market glut occurred on the East Coast in 1989 after legislation required curbside collection of recyclables, among them newspapers. This measure sent the price of newsprint on the market plummeting from anywhere around $40 a ton to near − $25 a ton. In other words, you had to pay someone to take away your newspaper; you could not sell it. (It is worth noting here that even − $25 a ton was still cheaper than disposal.)

The mistake in this case was to require collection of the newspaper without making a parallel requirement to *use* recycled newspaper. Any attempt to regulate the development of recycling must look at both sides of the equation: supply and demand. This is a demand-based industry. Recycling will not happen simply by supplying paper producers with recycled materials. We must see that a *market* develops for paper with recycled content.

It is still quite difficult to obtain writing and printing paper with a significant degree of recycled post-consumer waste, and this is because the paper companies have no incentive to produce this type of paper in mass quantities. A small number of individual consumers with good intentions cannot develop the markets alone. Not only must companies, government offices, and schools buy recycled paper, but any legislation requiring collection of newspapers (or other materials) must also help create a demand for that product. Paper manufacturers must be urged to increase their production capacity of recycled paper also.

The paper industry insists it is doing its best. It says that the public keeps changing its mind about what is important and expects the paper industry to adjust immediately. In the 1970s, when the public protested air and water quality, the paper industry did make improvements to appease consumer complaints. Out of these improvements also came better methods of production. Then, as the industry spent money to improve its production of this cleaner (virgin) fiber, suddenly the public wanted recycled content.

When asked why it cannot expand its recycling capacity faster, industry cites both the expense of reequipping for the de-inking of recycled newsprint and the fact that they must honor long-term contracts specifying paper from virgin fiber. These arguments are debatable, however. Industry experts who don't appear enthusiastic quote prices of $50 to $100 million to build de-inking facilities, for example, while those who appear to favor adjustment quote $25 to $50 million. Either way, pressure must be put on the industry to produce more paper with recycled content and on government, businesses, and individuals to buy it.

The American Paper Institute, with the intention of helping to match state and local recycling officials with potential markets for their recycled paper, has produced a directory called *Paper Match*. The directory contains the names, addresses, and phone numbers of domestic paper mills, wastepaper dealers, and recycling centers, listed by state, and is distributed to state and local recycling officials. It can be ordered by calling the institute's Solid Waste Resource Center. (See Appendix A.) This effort is part of the institute's strategy to reach a paper recycling rate of 40 percent by 1995.

DEGRADATION OF QUALITY

The question of degradation in the quality of recycled fibers is another hurdle to overcome. While newsprint, for example, can reportedly be reused up to six or seven times with an acceptable quality level, recycled paper in general is still fighting an image problem. Some consumers shy away from recycled paper, thinking that problems attending the early days of recycling—like variations in quality and a tendency to tear—still exist.

Even if all paper used in the United States were made of 100 percent post-consumer fiber, this would not mean a tree would never have to fall again. Paper fibers do deteriorate after multiple processing. Eventually, after a certain number of times around the block, recycled fiber becomes a disposable product, such as facial or toilet tissue, or the significantly shortened fibers (which deteriorate with each reuse) become unusable. Imported cardboard, for example, sometimes lacks the strength of its domestic counterpart because the fibers have been recycled too many times. The answer here, however, is simply not to recycle the fibers too many times.

ENVIRONMENTAL CONCERNS

Recently there has been some discussion on another aspect of paper recycling: harmful toxic emissions in the various stages of recycling. There are two distinct stages that are cause for concern, the de-inking process and the bleaching process. It is worth noting that both processes are used almost solely because of the consumer's demand for "pure" white paper.

De-inking is mainly associated with newspapers. It is the process of removing the ink from the used newsprint before recycling it into new paper products.

There are currently two basic ways of de-inking old newsprint. The first process, washing, uses toxic chemicals and cannot function correctly if glossy (magazine-type) paper is included. This is the most common process used. The other method, preferred by environmentalists, is the flotation method, which uses fewer chemicals and in fact needs the clay from glossy paper (hence providing an outlet for that less-often recycled paper in addition to providing a cleaner method of de-inking). Moreover, the quality of fiber is usually higher from this method. Inserts and supplements to newspapers can go in either system.

Bleaching occurs in the creation of almost all types of paper, even from virgin fiber, and is another process that causes serious concern. This is the process that converts brown pulp into white.

Most processes use chlorine to bleach the wood or paper fiber. This chlorine bleaching process forms chlorinated compounds known as organochlorines. These organochlorines, including dioxin and furans, are extremely harmful to humans and to wildlife when released either into the air or waterways. Dangerously high levels of dioxin are being found in trout, in human fatty tissues, and in breast milk. Not only is this dioxin getting to the consumer through industry waste, but it is also present in everyday products such as diapers, paper plates, sanitary napkins, toilet paper, coffee filters, paper milk containers, and writing paper because the paper in these products has been bleached with harsh chemicals. Chlorine is not necessary in the bleaching process, however. Bleaching paper fiber with an environmentally benign oxygen-based process—using hydrogen peroxide, for example—would be an effective, and more appropriate, method.

Toward making the paper industry more environmentally sound, environmentalists are calling for several other actions. The use of nontoxic inks in newsprint is one example. The use of benign bleaching is another, but the total elimination of the bleaching process whenever possible would be even more welcome. The goal to strive for is widespread use of unbleached, recycled paper with the highest possible percentage content of post-consumer waste.

How to Prepare Paper for Recycling

Different grades of paper require different preparation. The following guidelines may be helpful, but it's always best to check with your local recycler to be sure of local requirements.

NEWSPRINT

- Include newspapers, comics, and advertising inserts.
- Tie with recyclable twine or place in brown paper bags.

• Use small bundles for easy handling.

• Do not include advertising mail, cardboard, or any other paper or nonpaper product.

• Do not use plastic for bundling or bagging.

• Telephone books: some sources say they are OK if the covers are removed, while others say not to include them. Check locally.

HIGH-GRADE PAPER

• Do not include plastic windows (from envelopes), adhesive (self-sticking) labels, or colored paper (unless your local recycler allows it).

• Do not include nonpaper items such as plastics or large metal objects.

• Do not include fax paper, blueprints, and self-stick notes.

• Small metal items such as paperclips and staples need not be removed.

• Some programs will not accept paper that has been printed with a laser printer. Check locally.

CORRUGATED PAPER

• Flatten the boxes. Most recyclers prefer this, and it's much more convenient to store them flat.

• Tie with twine in small packages about 3 by 3 feet or store in one box.

• Remove nonpaper items like wire, plastic, wood, tape, or food residue.

• Brown paper bags can be included.

GLOSSY PAPER

• Keep separate from all other grades of paper.

• Staples and small paperclips need not be removed.

• Magazines with glued bindings are usually not acceptable.

- Because recyclers may accept different types as "mixed paper," it's necessary to check locally.
- If boxes (shoe, cereal) are accepted, flatten them.

The Mechanics of Recycling Paper

Wastepaper is generally recycled in a pulper—a device that uses water and chemicals to remove inks and other contaminants and turn the paper into a soft, wet material called pulp. The pulp is then sifted through screens (to remove staples, paperclips, and the like) and washed. Then it is usually bleached, although much less bleaching is required than in making paper from virgin pulp.

Clean pulp is mixed with clean water until it becomes a thick, white substance. This is spread into thin layers, heated, dried, and smoothed on a series of rollers, forming sheets of clean finished paper as it dries.

With a few variations for different grades, the process is basically the same for all paper. Most paper can be recycled up to seven or eight times.

GLASS

Recycling glass reduces:
- Energy use by up to 32 percent
- Air pollution by 20 percent
- Mining wastes by 80 percent
- Water use by 50 percent

Bottles and Jars

The National Soft Drink Association estimates that over 5 billion glass bottles and jars are recycled each year. This represents about 2.5 billion pounds of glass.

The beauty of the glass we recycle today is that it is 100 percent recyclable. Bottles and jars can be melted down and turned into new containers in a true example of closed-loop recycling. No other ingredients are needed: for each ton of glass returned to a recycling plant, one ton of glass can be produced. Glass never deteriorates, either: it can be recycled endlessly.

Glass is very popular for food and beverage packaging because of its many useful qualities. It is impermeable, transparent, and sanitary. A glass container also generally costs less than containers made from plastic, paper, or metal. For these reasons, the market for post-consumer glass has traditionally been quite steady, and glass has developed into one of our most commonly recycled materials.

Clear glass is made by taking almost pure silica sand and melting it in huge furnaces with some burnt lime or limestone and soda ash. Crushed glass, called "cullet," is usually added to some extent. In addition to clear glass (what the industry calls flint glass), glass commonly comes in brown and green. Colored glass is made by adding small amounts of metals or salts.

Other Types of Glass

Apart from the bottles and jars used for beverage and food packaging, there are many other types of glass products. Because of their various makeups, however, most are not easily recyclable. Mirrors, drinking glasses, windows, Pyrex, and light bulbs should not be included in your recycling because they are made of different kinds of glass and cannot be treated the same way. These other types make up about 4 percent of our solid waste stream according to *The Recycler's Handbook* (EarthWorks Group, 1990).

To date, no widespread recycling programs have been established for these other types of glass. In general, glass food and beverage containers are the only kinds of glass that are practical for the individual to recycle. A handful of glass reclaimers will accept windowpanes, for example, but these are few and far between. The problem with windowpanes is that you can't determine their composition simply by looking at the glass; costly analysis is required. Some plate and auto window glass is reportedly being used in the fabrication of fiberglass, but fiberglass manufacturers must buy the glass directly from the makers who can tell them its chemical composition.

Recycling glass serves us all. As less glass goes to the landfill, we are helping to deal with the solid waste disposal crisis. Recycling also uses fewer natural resources, because silica, soda ash, and limestone, the main raw ingredients in glass, do not have to be added again when recycled glass is used. Using a ton of crushed glass in the manufacturing process can save 1.2 tons of raw materials.

Moreover, recycling uses less energy. A furnace containing pure raw materials burns at approximately 2,800 degrees. One using pure cullet can run at 2,600. That 200-degree difference translates to a significant energy savings and also prolongs the life of the furnace, which has to work less hard using recycled cullet. The furnace working less hard also means less air pollution during production.

End Products from Recycled Glass

Approximately 25 to 30 percent of manufactured glass is made from recycled glass, which means that the average glass container you buy at the store has about that much recycled content. When glass isn't made into new glass through closed-loop recycling, it can be used in other ways. This is often the case with glass that is for one reason or another unacceptable to glass manufacturers. Broken glass of mixed colors is an example. This glass can be used in the production of fiberglass and reflective beading and as a substitute for stone in glasphalt. Mixed-color cullet can also be used to make green glass.

Obstacles

Contamination is one of the biggest problems of the glass recycling industry. A related problem is obtaining a constant supply of high-quality cullet. Manufacturers can always obtain a certain amount, but because of color mixes and contamination they can never be sure of their supply of high-quality cullet.

The furnaces used to melt the glass have to be set at different levels according to the percentage of recycled cullet used. To avoid adjusting the furnaces daily, many manufacturers settle on a slightly lower percentage of recycled cullet than they have available to ensure that they can always get the same percentage. So although manufacturers sometimes have up to 70 or 80 percent good cullet to work with, the average is still down at 25 or 30 percent because that is the amount they can count on.

Increasing the supply of good-quality cullet is a matter of education and improved quality control. From individuals who put out their recyclables for curbside pickup to the managers of collection centers, everyone must learn to handle and prepare the glass containers properly, thus ensuring a constant supply of high-quality cullet. Moreover, current research on automated color sorting and contaminant-detecting equipment should improve the situation. At present, all quality control is done by hand.

Better quality control and more consistent levels of good-quality cullet will allow the percentage of recycled glass on the market to increase. The glass industry is very much in favor of using recycled cullet instead of virgin materials to produce its glass. It is in its economic interest: cullet costs roughly the same as the equivalent in raw materials, but the cullet saves them energy and wear and tear on the furnaces. It is simply a matter of supplying the glass industry with a constant supply of high-quality materials.

How to Prepare Glass for Recycling

There are certain steps you should follow before recycling glass. These are simple things to do, but they play an important role in ensuring the quality of the recycled product.

- Only glass containers can be recycled: soda, beer, wine, and liquor bottles, as well as juice and food containers, are acceptable.
- Rinse the containers lightly.
- Separate glass by color.
- Keep free from contaminating materials (plastics, paper, corks, lids).
- Do not include broken glass.
- Labels and neck rings need not be removed.

Color separation ensures that the manufacturers can match the color of newly manufactured glass with previous batches. This guarantees their customers a standard color for their products. Color separation can be done in the household, at a drop-off center, or at an intermediate processing center or recycling facility.

Other materials that can contaminate the cullet are ceramics (from coffee cups and china, for example), metals, and dirt. These materials do not melt at the same temperature as the glass does, so they remain in the glass and can damage the furnaces in addition to appearing in the finished product.

Of course, the ultimate recycling is to wash glass bottles and use them again. One company in northern California, Encore!, is doing just that. It grosses $4.25 million a year collecting and sterilizing approximately 40,000 cases of empties each month and selling them back to West Coast wineries, among other businesses. Glass to be used in refillable containers is made about 50 percent heavier than nonrefillable glass and can be reused up to thirty times.

The Mechanics of Recycling Glass

When collection agents deliver the glass to a recycling plant, it is color-separated (if it did not arrive this way) and crushed into cullet: small, uniform pieces about the size of a pea. In some cases, the collection agent will crush the glass into cullet first and deliver the glass already broken to the plant.

The cullet is run through different machines to remove metals and plastic or paper labels. Then it is melted down in huge furnaces and poured into molds to produce clean glass for new bottles and jars.

Two methods are currently being tested for mechanically separating glass by color. Optical sorting tries to compare light reflected from each piece of glass with light reflected from standard pieces of each target color. Magnetic sorting tries to sort clear from colored glass by the iron compounds found in colored glass. These methods have not been developed well enough yet to use on a commercial basis, but their eventual inclusion in the recycling process should make glass recycling even more profitable.

METALS

Of all the various metals that can be recycled, by far the most easily and widely recycled by the public are aluminum cans (beer and other beverage containers) and steel cans (soup, beans, fruit containers). Because they are the metals most commonly recycled by consumers, these two metals will be the focus of this section.

Aluminum

Using recycled aluminum instead of virgin ore:

• Uses 95 percent less energy
• Eliminates 95 percent of air pollution
• Eliminates 97 percent of water pollution
• Saves 4 tons of bauxite and 1,500 pounds of petroleum coke and pitch for every ton of remelted aluminum

The use of aluminum on a large scale is relatively new: it has been produced in commercial quantities for less than 100 years. Considering this, its rapid rise in popularity is quite astounding. Today aluminum is used for the containers of more than 95 percent of all canned beverages.

Aluminum has also become a very popular material to recycle. Americans earn several hundred million dollars every year by saving aluminum cans and turning them in to buy-back centers. (Each can collected earns between one and two cents.) Consumers can earn so much money from recycling aluminum because it is favored by the recycling industry. This is for two reasons. First, aluminum cans are 100 percent recyclable: there are no labels, caps, or tops that must be removed before recycling. Second, the market for used aluminum is excellent because of the energy and raw material savings associated with the use of remelted, as opposed to virgin, aluminum in production. If you are not sure whether a can is aluminum or metal, stick a magnet up to it: magnets do not stick to aluminum. (Scrap metal dealers, however, can use special aluminum "reverse magnets" that help them separate aluminum from waste, making it easier to recycle.)

In addition to cans, many other aluminum products are recyclable. These include pie plates, foil, frozen food and dinner trays, some take-out containers, and containers for puddings and certain prepared meats. There are also a number of heavier aluminum items to keep in mind such as lawn furniture tubing, house siding, downspouts and gutters, storm door and window frames, and even pots and pans. Many aluminum collection centers will not be willing or able to take anything other than beverage cans, however, because of the different grades of alumi- num used in different products, so it's best to check ahead. If your local recycling center can't help you, try a nearby junk yard.

The Aluminum Association states that in 1989 we reached a national recycling rate for aluminum cans of 61 percent. Rates are even higher in states such as California and Texas, which have achieved recycling rates of between 60 and 70 percent. Overall, nationwide we've been recycling over 50 percent of all aluminum cans used since the early 1980s. As aluminum is a closed-loop recyclable, cans that we return for recycling can be remelted and back on supermarket shelves within as little as six weeks. Even though aluminum enjoys a relatively high re- cycling rate in comparison with other materials, we still throw out a shocking amount of the metal. It has been estimated that we throw away enough aluminum annually to rebuild the country's entire commercial air fleet three to four times.

Aluminum is reckoned to be the most energy-intensive material in common use, which makes recycling aluminum all the more important. According to the Aluminum Association, aluminum recycling saves ap- proximately 11 billion kilowatt-hours annually—the energy equivalent of almost 19 million barrels of oil. According to Alcoa, recycling alu- minum has also created approximately 30,000 new jobs in recycling centers, aluminum companies, and related transport and processing in- dustries.

MAKING ALUMINUM

Bauxite, an ore rich in aluminum compounds, is surface-mined. Virtu- ally all the bauxite used by American aluminum companies is mined in Australia, South America, Africa, and the Caribbean. The bauxite is then refined to remove impurities such as iron oxide. This multistage refining process produces a fine, white powder called alumina, a com- pound composed of aluminum and oxygen.

The alumina is shipped to a reduction plant, or smelter, where it is deposited into cells called pots that are generally about 20 feet long, 6 feet wide, and 3 feet deep. A typical reduction plant operates several hundred pots. Once the alumina is in the pots, a powerful and continuous electrical current is used to separate the aluminum and oxygen. As this current is applied, the now-molten aluminum settles to the bottom of each pot.

The process used to separate the aluminum and oxygen is highly energy-intensive. This step is not necessary for recycled aluminum, however, as it has already been done. Recycled aluminum comes into the chain at this point and is then processed just like virgin ore.

The molten aluminum is then taken from the pot to a furnace, where small amounts of other metals are added to the aluminum to produce desired characteristics in the final product. Copper adds strength, for example, and magnesium adds corrosion resistance. The molten metal is then cast into various solid shapes, their sizes and configurations determined by final fabrication requirements. The final product may be any number of things—aluminum cans are just one possibility.

NEW CANS FROM OLD

Aluminum cans are taken from the collection points around your community (or from your curbside collectors) and smashed and baled into large bundles for shipping. They are then taken to a processing plant where the aluminum is shredded, remelted, and cast into a new ingot—a huge slab of aluminum weighing anywhere up to 30,000 tons that can make 1.6 million cans.

After the aluminum has been cast into ingots, these slabs are passed between huge rollers and other equipment to produce a sheet of aluminum with an eventual wall thickness of just 0.0047 of an inch. (Today's aluminum cans are much thinner, hence lighter, than those of earlier years: a can today uses approximately one-third less metal than a can did in 1972.) A new batch of cans is cut from these thin aluminum sheets and then transported to the makers of the beverage, or other product, that will be packaged in the can. When the aluminum cans are filled they find their way back to our store shelves.

Steel

Using recycled iron and steel instead of virgin ore to make new steel results in:

• 74 percent savings in energy
• 90 percent savings in virgin materials used
• 86 percent reduction in air pollution
• 40 percent reduction in water use
• 76 percent reduction in water pollution
• 97 percent reduction in mining wastes
• 105 percent reduction in consumer waste

According to the Steel Can Recycling Institute, steel is America's most recycled material: more than 100 billion pounds of steel products is recycled every year by North American steel mills. The overall recycling rate of steel products in the United States is 66 percent. The American Iron and Steel Institute has stated that over 3.5 billion steel cans were recycled in 1989. More steel is recycled each year than all other materials—paper, glass, aluminum, plastics, and other metals—combined and doubled.

The average consumer is most likely to run across recyclable steel in the form of the cans in which we buy our soup, beans, fruit, coffee, olive oil, or pet food. The tin-plated steel can has been with us since its invention in the 1820s and is widely used for storing, shipping, and preserving many foods and beverages. Security (they are difficult to tamper with) and shelf life are two features that draw manufacturers to steel cans for packaging. Most cans are tin-plated, with approximately 99 percent steel and a 1 percent coating of tin. Sometimes, however, you can have tin-free steel, in which case the coating is chromium oxide, rather than tin.

Steel cans are 100 percent recyclable and are collected as part of many communities' collection programs, although collection sites are perhaps more likely to accept aluminum than steel. Steel makers can also recycle bimetal (steel and aluminum) cans without removing the aluminum tops. If your community does not recycle steel containers, suggest that they contact local scrap yards that already ship steel materials to steel mills. The materials collected through the community recycling efforts could then be provided to the scrap yard to be sent to the mills with their other shipments. Likewise, you might be able to take your own recyclables to a steel scrap yard.

Two primary markets exist for used steel food and beverage cans.

First, detinning companies are increasing capacity as new recycling programs come on line and generate steel cans for recycling. Second, steel mills are using baled steel cans as part of the scrap mix for their furnaces. Steel is recycled from many more sources than just cans. In fact, cans account for only about one-quarter of all steel recycled: most steel gets recycled through the scrap metal business. This business, of which steel recycling is a large part, is a thriving industry in the United States.

Automobiles, household appliances such as refrigerators and ovens, ships, railroad cars, and industrial equipment are just a few other sources of scrap steel, which is reprocessed and comes back to life as a new steel product. According to the Institute of Scrap Recycling Industries, its members prepare approximately 9 million old automobiles each year for recycling. Iron and steel can be remelted repeatedly for the manufacture of all kinds of consumer goods, some of which have been mentioned above. Paint cans are made from steel and are recyclable as well, so long as they are properly cleaned. (Check with your collector before taking them.)

Because they are magnetic, steel cans are one of the easiest materials to include in recycling programs. They can be magnetically separated easily at resource recovery facilities that collect all types of recyclable materials. Moreover, current market capacity exceeds the supply of used steel cans, which means the industry can use all the steel containers we can recycle.

Despite the relative ease of separating steel cans for recycling, however, they are not recycled nearly as often as aluminum cans. Because steel is not as valuable per pound as aluminum and because the cans come in more varieties, deposit laws (which the industry suspects would increase steel can recycling considerably) are basically unworkable.

The Mechanics of Recycling Steel

Steel goes through several steps on its way from the scrap yard or recycling center to becoming a new steel product. First, a steel dealer/processor buys the scrap from a number of sources such as industrial plants, shipyards, demolition yards, or municipalities. The dealer/processor separates the scrap into specific grades of steel to meet the steel industry's specifications. A variety of techniques are used to prepare the specific grades, including torching and shredding the scrap. Shredders can turn a used automobile into fist-sized pieces of scrap in less than one minute.

Brokers help arrange sales between the processor and the plants that will rework the steel. Once at the mill or foundry, the graded scrap can then be remelted into new steel products.

BIMETAL CONTAINERS

Cans made out of two metals are called bimetal containers. The body is usually steel and the lid, aluminum. Since only a small percentage of beverage cans used in this country are made from this combination of materials, you'll need to check with your recycling center to see if they will accept them. In general, bimetal containers can be recycled with steel.

Other Metals

There are many types of metals, however, that are perhaps less well known as recyclables but are being recycled in large quantities none-theless—copper, iron, lead, zinc, and stainless steel, for example. There is a thriving market in scrap materials of all types, and you just need to take a trip to a junkyard or abandoned car lot to see what gets recycled. Old automobiles, refrigerators, ovens and stoves, and many other metal products are recycled by scrap dealers daily.

Metals are often labeled as being either ferrous or nonferrous. This simply refers to their iron content: nonferrous metals such as brass, bronze, aluminum, and copper contain no iron whereas iron and steel are ferrous metals. Iron is the basic metal from which steel is formed: when you add carbon to iron, you get steel. Adding various other elements to the iron and carbon mixture produces a variety of steel grades.

Copper is used for its thermal and electrical conductivity and its chemical stability. Brasses are copper alloys containing zinc, for example. Major sources of recyclable copper are automobile radiators, telephone and utility wire and cable, tubing, electrical motors, generators, ammunition shell cases, plumbing fixtures, and railroad equipment.

Zinc is used as a protective coating on steel, as well as to make die castings for automobile and construction applications. Although the amount of zinc used by the automotive industry has been declining steadily over the past years, the percentage of zinc die-cast scrap recovered from shredded automobiles has increased to virtually 100 percent.

Lead is the subject of much conversation recently because of concerns about its toxicity. The major use of lead is batteries for energy storage, but it is also used in ammunition and electrical cable sheathing. Scrapped batteries account for the majority of recovered lead.

Tin is recyclable, too. It is a silvery metallic material that comes from cassiterite, a very hard and heavy ore. Today most tin is used as a protective coating for steel containers (to prevent corrosion) and in solders and other alloys. Tin is recycled from tin plate and from used container scrap. When someone refers to a tin can, they probably mean a steel can with a very thin layer of tin coating. Although the tin coating can comprise less than 1 percent of a can's weight, it represents as much as one-third of the recycled value of the can.

One of the reasons why these materials are not being recycled more extensively is the difficulty in pulling them out of the products in which they have been used. Recycling copper and brass, for example, involves shredding, cleaning, and remelting the metals. Even then the quality of the end product is often low due to an inability to separate the target metal from other metals and debris.

The use of cryogenics—freezing a metal with liquid nitrogen until it becomes brittle—has been tested but is still prohibitively expensive for widespread use. (Once a piece of metal has been shattered, reclamation of the various metallic ingredients is much easier.)

So although steel and aluminum may be the easiest metals for consumers to recycle, keep in mind that when you throw anything away which has some metal content a scrap yard dealer might be interested in buying the metal from you. It keeps that much more waste from our landfills.

How to Prepare Metals for Recycling

Aluminum and steel cans, like other recyclables, should be prepared for recycling. Different recyclers have specific preferences as to how you must deliver the cans, but the following are good general rules.

ALUMINUM

• Rinse cans lightly.
• Check with your recycler to see if smashed cans are acceptable.
• Remove food residue from aluminum foil and pie plates.

STEEL

• Rinse cans lightly.
• Remove labels.
• Check with your recycler to see if smashed cans are acceptable.
• Remove all attached materials from large steel items like lawn chairs or siding.
• Steel is magnetic, so test it if you are unsure.

PLASTICS

Plastics are synthetic materials. They consist mainly of polymers (molecule clusters) of carbon, oxygen, and hydrogen. To make plastics with different properties, a variety of ingredients such as stabilizers, colorants, or fillers are added.

Because there are so many different plastics available and because they are not easily identifiable simply by looking at them, the plastics industry has come up with a system to help identify and sort plastics, specifically with the idea of recycling in mind.

Plastics Coding

The Plastic Bottle Institute, with its member companies, established the following identification system for plastic container manufacturers to put on their containers as an aid to recyclers and collectors of recycled materials. It is currently a voluntary system, but one that is widely supported by industry members. You will notice these codes within a triangle shape on the bottom of many of the plastic containers you purchase. The following codes represent seven distinct categories of plastic:

1. PETE: polyethylene terephthalate (PET)—a lightweight, transparent plastic that is resistant to chemicals and moisture

2. HDPE: high-density polyethylene—used in milk jugs, two-liter soda bottle bases, and plastic grocery bags

3. V: vinyl/polyvinyl chloride (PVC)—used in flooring, records, vinyl siding, shower curtains, and garden hoses

4. LDPE: low-density polyethylene—used in cellophane wrap, diaper liners, and some squeeze bottles

5. PP: polypropylene—a light, highly resistant, thermoplastic resin used in packaging, coating, pipes, and tubes

6. PS: polystyrene—(generally referred to as "styrofoam")—used in coffee cups, egg cartons, and almost all packing pellets

7. Other: all other resins and multilayered material

Within each of these categories there are many individual types of plastic. In fact, there are hundreds of varieties of plastics. This section will focus on PET and HDPE, the two most commonly recycled plastics. Recycling of any other plastics is negligible.

PET (POLYETHYLENE TEREPHTHALATE)

PET is the most commonly recycled plastic. Approximately 170 million pounds of PET were recycled in 1988, according to the National Solid Wastes Management Association. This figure represents about 16 percent of all packaging made from PET. As of January 1990, some 292 communities in nineteen states were including PET plastic containers in their curbside recycling programs.

PET containers are the plastic bottles with which consumers are most familiar—the popular two-liter soda bottles and plastic liquor bottles, for example. PET containers are transparent (whether they are clear, green, or brown in color) and have a small raised dot, which the industry calls the "gate," in the center of the base. This indicates that the container was injection molded, rather than extruded.

To be absolutely sure you have a PET container, check the industry code imprinted on the container. (See the complete list above). The PET number is 1. Other grades of plastic can be transparent, too, and it is important to keep the different resins separate. For example, a small amount of PVC plastic mixed in with PET can ruin the whole lot when they are recycled.

If you are unclear about any item, call your recycler and ask about it. Often by telling the recycler the product name, they can tell you whether or not they accept that product's container.

Recycled PET ends up in many products:
- Fibers (for carpet yarns, paint brush bristles, twine, rope, scouring pads, and fiberfill for pillows, vests, and sleeping bags)
- Industrial strapping
- Engineering plastics
- Film and sheet for thermoforming
- Automobile distributor caps
- Bottles for cleaning products and other nonfood items
- Egg cartons

Five recycled PET bottles make enough fiberfill for a man's ski jacket; it takes thirty-five to stuff a sleeping bag.

HDPE (HIGH-DENSITY POLYETHYLENE)

Most of us know HDPE as the plastic used for milk and water (and sometimes fruit juice) jugs. Although these containers represent the most common uses of HDPE, there is another variety called mixed-color HDPE. This plastic is found as antifreeze, cleanser, or detergent bottles. Most recyclers will only accept the "natural" HDPE (milk, water, juice jugs), but it is certainly worth asking. As more and more products are being packaged in mixed-color bottles all the time, the potential for increasing the recycling of HDPE plastics by accepting mixed-color bottles is good.

Have a look at the bottom of your bottles: the code for HDPE is 2.

As with PET, HDPE can be confused with other plastic resins. Polypro-pylene may look similar to HDPE, but its code is 5.

Currently some manufacturers are endeavoring to include recycled HDPE in their plastic bottles. Procter and Gamble, for example, use approximately 20 to 30 percent recycled HDPE in their containers of certain laundry products. Likewise, some Spic and Span containers are made with 100 percent recycled PET.

Recycled HDPE can be transformed into many end products:

- Lumber substitutes (used for boat piers, livestock pens, shipping pallets, outdoor furniture, litter receptacles, and signs)
- Base cups for soft drink bottles
- Flowerpots
- Pipe
- Toys
- Pails and drums
- Traffic barrier cones
- Golf bag liners
- Kitchen drain boards
- Milk bottle carriers
- Soft drink bottle carriers
- Trash cans
- Signs

An astounding amount has been written about plastics and their im-pact on the environment in the last few years, and opinion on either side is usually extreme. Few people appear to be lukewarm about plastic; they either think of it as a wonder material or they see it as one of society's worst creations.

The Proliferation of Plastics

The proliferation of plastics over the last several decades is the result of the development of low-priced petrochemicals and new technologies. One of the main areas in which the use of plastics has dramatically increased is packaging.

The well-known two-liter bottle was introduced in 1978, but the popularity of plastics as packaging began some time before. In fact, the EPA reports that the use of plastics in products and packaging has increased over 10 percent annually since 1950. Packagers who previously resorted to glass, paper, or metals are now using plastic. Plastics can be lightweight, unbreakable, flexible, and strong—qualities that clearly appeal to packagers.

Combining different types of plastic lends different attributes to a product, also. A squeezable ketchup bottle, for example, is made up of six layers of plastic, each designed for a different purpose, such as bottle shape, strength, flexibility, or impermeability. Plastic can also be combined with other materials to further increase its range of attributes. Food packagers recently developed a material called aseptic packaging, for example, which combines layers of aluminum foil, paper, and plastic. The trouble with these combinations, however, is that the more layers involved, whether they are composed of different materials or different plastic resins, the more costly and difficult recycling becomes.

Aseptic packaging is one example of a multimaterial product that has been criticized for the difficulty involved in recycling it. The packaging, used commonly for single servings of juice, is composed of approximately 70 percent paper, 23 percent polyethylene, and 7 percent aluminum. Over 3 billion aseptic boxes are sold in the United States annually, according to *Recycling Times* (14 August 1990, p. 15).

To counter charges of nonrecyclability, manufacturers have been trying to find uses for the multimaterial packaging. To date, the only known market for the aseptic boxes is in very small amounts in the manufacture of plastic lumber. The *Recycling Times* article quotes Kevin Brown of National Waste Technologies, one of the companies using the aseptic boxes, as saying that the packaging represents 1 percent or less of the material used in making the lumber—at this low level, he indicated, the mixed materials do not seem to affect the quality of the finished product. Widespread recyclability of mixed materials does not seem likely in the near future, however.

Obstacles

There are numerous obstacles standing in the way of the further development of plastics recycling. These range from practical concerns, such as the lack of a well-developed infrastructure, to environmental questions about the wisdom of recycling petroleum-based products.

NONRECYCLABILITY

Plastics recycling is not well developed in comparison to that of paper, aluminum, and glass. The EPA reported in the spring of 1990 that only about 1 percent of all plastics are recycled in this country and that PET and HDPE account for almost all of it. There are several reasons for this. One is the relative inability to distinguish plastic resins from one another visually, which makes them more time-consuming and hence more expensive to recycle. This is becoming less of a problem, though, due to the gradual adoption of the plastics labeling system explained earlier.

There are other problems with recycling plastics. Plastics recycling is not a closed-loop system, as is the case with aluminum or glass. This means that a PET beverage container cannot be recycled into another PET beverage container. The industry has to find *new* uses for the recycled plastics, rather than using the material again and again for the same product. It is worth noting, too, that even those plastics which do recycle can only become another product once.

Recycling PET poses no problems technically, but the quality of the end product is not good enough to use again for bottles. So PET bottles become stuffing, HDPE bottles become flowerpots and toys, and mixed plastics may become plastic lumber.

Other uses are being developed constantly. This trend does not mollify the opponents of plastics recycling, however, who believe that by finding other uses for the recycled plastics, we are simply increasing our reliance on a nonrenewable, polluting material. Opponents of plastics recycling would prefer to see plastics replaced by other products whenever possible, but particularly for one-time uses such as packaging. Closed-loop materials could be used instead, thus reducing the need to recycle plastics.

Plastics are replacing other products that are easily recyclable, thus reducing the amount of those materials available for recycling. As manufacturers switch from glass packaging to plastic, for example, they gradually increase the amount of nonrecyclable (or at best one-time recyclable) materials in the world while reducing the number of 100 percent recyclable materials. Clearly, many people are concerned by this development.

It is no secret that plastics are not popular with most environmentalists. This unpopularity is based on a number of reasons—from the depletion of a nonrenewable natural resource to concerns about the pollution from their manufacture and their nondegradability.

Plastics represent a highly visible part of the waste stream. In recent years complaints of plastic debris on our beaches and floating in the oceans have escalated. A large number of bird, turtle, and seal species have been harmed by becoming tangled in it or ingesting it. The EPA also reports that some communities have been adversely affected by loss of tourist revenues and cleanup costs from plastic wastes washing onto their beaches. Of course, plastic is not the only material that is littered or can endanger animals, but it has taken much of the heat over the last few years.

Even when plastics reach the landfill, they are not popular. While the plastic industry focuses on the fact that plastic makes up only 7 or 8 percent of the waste stream *by weight*, this figure is of course irrelevant when talking about landfills, for it is the volume—the actual space that a material takes up—which counts. The National Solid Wastes Management Association notes that plastics represent approximately 20 percent of the waste stream *by volume*, a much more significant statistic.

Pollution. One of the most often cited criticisms of plastics is that their production is a heavily polluting process (more so than other materials). Of the six most polluting chemicals on an EPA list of chemicals whose production causes the most hazardous waste, the plastics industry uses five.

Many people have been angered recently by the plastics and packaging industries' claims that plastic is environmentally safe or environmentally friendly. This simply cannot be true, the critics argue, for two major reasons. First, almost all plastic, whether it is supposed to be degradable or not, is made from a nonrenewable, polluting source: oil. Second, the technologies used to make plastics from crude oil produce large quantities of hazardous waste.

The one place plastics do seem to be popular is in waste-to-energy plants. This is because they burn the hottest of any significant waste material and thus provide an excellent source of energy. There is considerable debate about the safety of burning plastics, however, even with all the modern pollution control devices on today's incinerators. Observers are concerned that as more plastic is produced, more and more will end up going to these incinerators.

Polyvinyl chloride (PVC) is currently being targeted by those concerned about the possible dangers from burning this particular resin. PVC is used to make shower curtains, vegetable oil bottles, and food wrap. There is concern that when PVC is burned, the chlorine in it may contribute to dioxin and may also combine with hydrogen to form hydrogen chloride gas, which creates a strong acid when it comes in contact with moisture.

Ozone. The process used to manufacture the foams used in much of our food packaging today has come under severe criticism because it may be affecting the ozone layer. Roughly one-half of all foam packaging is inflated with chlorofluorocarbons (CFCs). When these compounds reach our upper atmosphere, atoms of chlorine are released by the sun's rays. The concern is that this chlorine may eventually destroy the ozone layer that keeps us protected from ultraviolet radiation. Many people have grave concerns about the increased cancers and crop deficiencies that could result.

Degradability. Degradable plastic is both new and controversial. The degradability (or nondegradability) of plastic is a subject of much debate, both among environmentalists and throughout the plastics industry. It is a subject about which it is safe to say that just about everyone disagrees. Some people think the deterioration of plastics would be a good idea while others do not. The division is not along traditional lines, either: people within the plastics industry itself and the environmental sector debate the issue.

Recently consumers have been inundated with advertisements pro-
claiming a new series of "environmentally conscious" degradable plastic
products. This innovation has created a lot of discussion as to what
harm, if any, plastics do to our environment and how environmentally
safe these new products actually are. Meanwhile, consumers are buying
these degradable plastic products even though they typically cost more
than regular plastics.

Basically there are two types of "degradable" plastics on the market.
Photodegradable plastics are supposed to disintegrate into small pieces
when exposed to sunlight. (Manufacturers add a sun-sensitive component to the plastic to trigger degradation.) The other type is intended
to be *biodegradable,* which means it should break up when exposed to
microorganisms. (A natural ingredient such as cornstarch or vegetable
oil is added to achieve this result.)

Proponents of degradable plastics see the new development as a par-
tial solution to both our litter problem and our solid waste problem.
They believe that plastics which are typically thrown on the roadside
or end up in the oceans would be less obtrusive if they disintegrated.
Plastic bags and six-pack rings are often cited as good target products
for degradable plastics. Some think that degradable six-pack rings
would also help reduce risks to the wildlife that gets entangled in them.

Garbage bags are an example of the recent proliferation of degradable plastic products. Almost every manufacturer of garbage bags now
sells a "degradable" alternative. Manufacturers say that not only will
these bags disintegrate in the landfill, but their breaking up will allow
the garbage in them to mix in the landfill and biodegrade as well, thus
leaving more room in landfills and helping to curb our nationwide landfill disposal problems.

On the other side, there are strong arguments against degradable
plastics. One argument is simply that they do not exist—the idea is no
more than a marketing ploy. This opinion was stated very clearly by
Debra Lynn Dadd and Andre Carothers in "A Bill of Goods? Green
Consuming in Perspective" (*Greenpeace,* May/June 1990):

You are being duped. Most of the products hailed as biodegradable
in the marketplace today are little better than their "non-

biodegradable" counterparts. Biodegradability means one thing: the material is capable of being broken down by natural processes into pieces small enough to be consumed by microorganisms in the soil. Plastics, as petrochemical products, are not the outcome of biological evolution, so living things lack the enzymes that can break them down to a molecular level where they can be taken and reincorporated into living things.

For many, then, no further discussion is necessary. But for those who believe that degradable plastics do exist, there are still arguments against them.

Opponents say that degradable plastics will not help either the litter or solid waste problems. Litter is a social problem, it is argued—our solid waste will not be reduced either, because degradable plastics will not reduce the volume or toxicity of plastic waste. Even if the plastic did degrade, it is still the same volume, just in smaller pieces. These smaller pieces allow more plastic surface area to be exposed to the surrounding soil and introduce a higher danger that the toxic organics used as colorants, plasticizers, and stabilizers could leach out. Moreover, it is feared that degradable plastics will in fact be made thicker (with more plastic) than normal plastic to compensate for the comparable weakness of degradables. The irony here is obvious.

As for helping to protect wildlife with degradable six-pack rings, opponents argue that we still do not know what effect the degraded plastic parts could have on the oceans. Degradable plastics have new additives and we are not clear as to their potential harm to the environment.

One response to the suggestion that degradable garbage bags will allow general disintegration in the landfills is that, in fact, very little breakdown takes place in a landfill anyway due to lack of oxygen and sunlight. Introducing degradable plastics could increase the risk of leaking hazardous chemicals (enclosed in the plastic bags) into the landfill and then out the bottom.

Some of those who encourage degradable plastics have been criticized as having ulterior motives. For example, biodegradable plastics that would require cornstarch additives have been strongly supported by many from agricultural states who would benefit from the additional sales of corn. Senator John Glenn (D–Ohio) is one politician who has been criticized for actively supporting the cornstarch variety of degradable plastics. He has been accused of being more interested in helping the corn farmers in his state than in plastics.

Opponents also feel that degradables work against recycling plastics. Not only would the widespread introduction of degradable plastics complicate the collection and sorting of plastics, but recycling supporters worry that the existence of degradable plastics will instill complacency among consumers who will feel no need to recycle plastics if they believe it can all break down in a landfill. Moreover, recyclers see degradable plastics as taking away materials for their markets.

One final argument against degradable plastics is that they encourage a "use it and toss it" mentality. Many feel that it is important to teach consumers to think about reusing products as often as possible rather than just disposing of them, even if these things might disintegrate.

Basically, the jury is still out on degradable plastics. As with many things, studies have been conducted showing that certain plastics do degrade and studies have been conducted showing that these same plastics do not degrade. When referring to such studies, one must consider the source and imagine what might be the benefit to the funders of such a study.

Those who have opposed degradables so vehemently have had some cause for celebration recently. A *Wall Street Journal* article (22 March 1991, p. B4) states that many manufacturers now regret promoting degradable products. In fact, some have been forced to pull their products from the shelves. Mobil Chemical Corporation (makers of Hefty bags), for example, has been sued in seven states for false advertising. Despite these setbacks, most manufacturers still claim that their products do degrade. Clearly the debate will continue for some time.

The plastics industry believes that plastics have become the scapegoat of our country's solid waste problem. Because plastics are not understood, companies claim, many people wrongly believe that plastics cannot be recycled or safely incinerated. The incineration of plastics does not cause pollution, these proponents argue. Properly incinerated, they say, plastics can be as safe to burn as paper or leaves. The industry also cites many instances in which plastic provides new, improved applications for problematic situations. Plastic lumber, for example, is desirable for many applications because it resists rotting. Fences and pier supports require much less maintenance when made of plastic.

How to Prepare Plastics for Recycling

Take a minute to prepare your plastic containers for recycling. These few steps will help those who handle the plastics further along in the recycling process.
• Empty the containers.
• Remove the aluminum lid. (Check with your recycler.)
• Rinse them. (Labels and plastic cups need not be removed.)
• Flatten them.

The Mechanics of Recycling Plastics

Once plastic containers have been collected, they must be sorted and packaged for sale. Sorting involves separating the plastic from aluminum (the caps), other metals, glass, and miscellaneous debris.

Most buyers prefer to receive used plastic containers baled. A community may choose to invest in the machinery required to bale the plastics or it may hire a contractor who has the facilities. Plastic can also be granulated before being shipped to buyers. The process is just as it sounds: the plastic is washed and then ground into pellets.

Most methods of recycling plastics involve separating out contaminants and other plastic resins. There are two standard ways of recycling generic resins: wet reclamation and dry reclamation.

Wet reclamation uses a flotation tank to separate the ground bottles into the various generic resins. The final recyclable products of this process are aluminum scrap and pellets of the generic resins ready to reuse.

Dry reclamation, on the other hand, separates the ground bottles into generic resins by an air separation method. The materials are then washed clean of dust and debris and are ready to reuse.

Another technology being developed is called mixed-waste processing, or commingled recycling. Plastic lumber is made using this technology. This method deals with unsorted plastic that is usually mixed to a certain extent with other materials such as paper, glass, or wood. Here metals can be pulled out magnetically and lighter materials, such as paper, are blown out in an air separator. A float tank can also be used to let the dirt and heavy metals sink to the bottom. The recyclable mixed plastic that remains is then combined with other materials to meet the specifications of particular end products. Finally, the processed material is fed into an extruder, heated, and molded into the desired product.

The recycling of mixed plastics is still in its infancy and causes serious problems to the manufacturer. In 1990, Rubbermaid Inc. canceled a proposed line of recycled plastic bins, even after national advertising campaigns, citing problems with recycling mixed plastics at a competitive rate and with consistent quality.

COMPARING PAPER, GLASS, METALS, AND PLASTICS

Having looked at the major recycled materials individually, it's useful to think about how they compare against one another as packaging and with regard to their impact on the environment. It is not always easy to decide which is the best to buy. In stores the choice of products can be overwhelming, let alone the many differences in packaging.

There are several factors to consider: one material might be lighter, one more recyclable, and another more readily available. So which is the right choice? There isn't one right choice for all circumstances. Availability, environmental impact, and of course personal choice all have to be factored into our decisions.

Our purchases do make a difference. When we buy products with a high recycled content, we encourage the manufacturers to make more and we aid the development of markets for recycled materials. Likewise, we can discourage overpackaged goods by writing to the manufacturers and explaining why we won't buy their products.

As shoppers we have to be as responsible as we can with whatever options we have. While no one can stand for hours in the grocery store pondering the pros and cons of aluminum over glass, we can go better prepared by understanding the impact these materials have on the environment. This section is designed to give you food for thought and help you decide which packaging is best.

Environmental Impact

If you have a choice of more than one type of packaging, think about how the production (and disposal) of each affects the environment. Clearly, all production has at least some effect, but which will have the least? As a general rule, plastics are considered to be the most polluting, but paper too has its drawbacks (bleaching with harmful chemicals). Likewise, aluminum made from raw bauxite expends the most energy. (If only we could tell whether the can is from recycled or virgin materials!) Finally, glass is heavy and thus uses up more energy in shipping.

This isn't to say that we can't buy anything, but it demonstrates how everything we use has an effect on the environment. The criticisms cited above are the kinds often used by the makers of competing packaging materials to persuade you to buy theirs, so it's difficult sometimes to know what is right. As a general rule, the following order of preference is considered sensible:

1. Glass: Despite its weight, glass is transparent, impermeable, and inexpensive to produce.

2. Aluminum: Although aluminum can recycling rates are already relatively high, if we can increase them even more we can avoid the energy-intensive use of raw materials.

3. Paper: The things to look for in paper are simple: recycled content (as high as possible) and unbleached.

4. Plastic: If the manufacturing of plastic were limited to products with a long life, it would be much more popular. Despite its drawbacks, plastic can be acceptable as long as we cut back its use as disposable items.

5. Multimaterial: Because of the difficulty inherent in recycling multimaterial products, it's best to avoid them whenever possible.

Availability/Practicality

Sometimes the material you'd like to buy just isn't available or isn't recycled locally. If you can't find a local store that sells milk in glass bottles, for example, you may have to choose between HDPE and waxed-paper milk cartons. Let's say HDPE is recycled in your area and milk cartons aren't. Although plastic is not your first choice in packaging, then, in this instance it makes the most sense.

Another example is margarine tubs. These too are plastic, so normally you might steer clear of them. They are reusable, however, and you have a genuine need for storage containers, so you buy them in preference to double-wrapped sticks of margarine.

Closed-Loop vs. One-Time Recycling

Whether a material can be recycled in a closed-loop system or not is very important. Glass and aluminum, for example, can be made into the same product over and over again, with very little, if any, additional material required.

Newspaper is sometimes recycled on a closed-loop basis, but not nearly enough yet. Other paper grades get recycled into new paper products, too, which must qualify as an almost-closed-loop process.

Currently, all plastics that are recycled have to be made into new products. This means that recycling one PET container does not stop the production of another PET container using raw materials. Manufacturers have to find new uses for the recycled plastic. So in a way, recycling plastic just furthers our dependence on plastic, because we will eventually establish constant markets for these new uses of the recycled plastic.

Alternatives

Look at the alternatives. Sometimes we have none: there are times when we simply have no choice but to buy an environmentally unfriendly product or package, to pay for a very expensive alternative, or to do without. In those cases when we can't or won't do without, we're stuck with the bad product.

A case in point is soap. Most soap comes individually wrapped but attached to four or five other bars by more paper. Some comes in boxes—one box for one bar of soap. Most of these boxes are clear white on the inside, which means they do not contain recycled paper and have been bleached. There are also soaps that are individually wrapped in plastic. Some choices! The alternative is buying individual, unwrapped soaps at some kind of specialty store, but these are much more expensive and usually heavily scented.

Personal Choice

There is certainly room for personal choice in this decision-making process. As you will see throughout this book, distinctions between what is good and bad for the environment are not always clear-cut. Go with what you feel is right.

For example, it can be debated that although aluminum is 100 percent recyclable, and recycled in high numbers, it is nonetheless one of the more energy-intensive materials to make. If you happen to buy a can that comes from mainly virgin ore, you have a product that took a lot of energy to make.

Similar arguments can be made for plastics. Some people feel that although plastic is more harmful to the environment during production and disposal than other materials, its significantly lower weight cuts down on the energy expended to transport it and hence saves energy.

Overpackaging

Whatever the material, try to avoid products that are overpackaged. Even if you can recycle it, you are having to recycle more than should be necessary. Look for a product that is simply wrapped—or better yet, not wrapped at all. Bread is a good example: Europeans buy unwrapped bread every day and they are not concerned about getting it dirty. This is just one example of how we have become used to everything being overpackaged.

Given all the different packaging choices and the implications they each have for our environment, deciding what products to buy can be daunting. The trick is not to get overwhelmed. Overpackaging and environmentally unfriendly products are a big problem today. Anyone who thinks about packaging and tries to make sound decisions is part of the solution.

COMPOSTING

Composting is a natural process in which plant and other organic wastes are broken down biologically to produce a nutrient-rich material. The resulting compost can be used for soil improvement in individual gardens or on a larger scale in communities.

Between 20 and 30 percent of our waste stream is made up of organic materials that have no business ending up in landfills. This amount more than doubles in the fall when leaves and garden trimmings are added to the municipal waste stream. Over 24 million tons of leaves and grass alone are thrown out each year. Yard and kitchen waste takes up a large amount of space in landfills when it could be used effectively to improve the quality of soil in our own gardens and on public land.

How does composting work? Basically it is the action of microorganisms decomposing organic materials. These microorganisms eat the carbon in the waste, turning it into carbon dioxide, water, and humus—an activity that heats up the compost pile and kills any organisms that may be harmful. The by-products from this process then become food for other microorganisms. This sequence continues until the waste disintegrates into what we call compost.

Composting on a Small Scale

Composting at home is a means of recycling yard and kitchen waste such as leaves, grass clippings, fruit and vegetable scraps, and other materials into a nutrient-rich soil supplement for your garden. By combining your organic wastes in a pile or container, they will break down biologically and eventually produce a mixture you can use to improve the quality of your soil.

Leaves, lawn and flower clippings, coffee grounds, apple cores, nuts, seeds, carrot ends, eggshells, any fruit and vegetable scraps—in fact just about all organic kitchen waste—can be used in a compost pile, in addition to horse and cow manure. Certain materials should be avoided, however, when making your compost pile: animals will be attracted to meat, bones, cheese, and grease, for example, and pesticides should not be included either. Paper should be limited in backyard compost piles (tear it into small pieces), but it degrades relatively well in larger systems.

You do not need to live in the country, nor do you need to have a large garden, to compost. Anyone with a garden of any size can designate a small section to begin a compost pile. The process sounds a bit complicated at first, but once a compost pile is established, it provides a simple and efficient way to cut down your garbage and improve your garden. There are several types of compost piles you can use, depending on the area you want to use, how quickly you want your compost, and the time you want to devote to the project.

THREE SAMPLE METHODS

If you have a large garden and a lot of waste, windrows function well. Windrows in your garden will be miniature versions of the same piles used in large, municipal waste composting systems. Depending on the space available, make your rows 2 to 5 feet high, several feet wide, and as long as required. For best results, larger is better: smaller piles won't decompose so quickly. Simply layer your yard waste—about half green materials and half dry waste. Add kitchen scraps as often as possible and a little soil. Turn the pile from time to time to aerate it. Alternating layers of green material, dry material, and soil and turning the mixture every few weeks will result in a faster rate of decomposition.

A cylindrical pen made of some kind of woven wire, like chicken wire, is another method. This approach is suited to gardens with less space and less waste. The holes in the sides of the cylinder are essential to let air to pass through. The walls should be arranged to allow you to add materials and turn the pile.

A third method is to use a perforated steel drum or some other kind of bin. This setup is useful if you are concerned about animals bothering your pile. Make sure the holes in the side are sufficient to let enough air circulate, and don't fill the drum much more than half full. To mix the compost, just roll the drum.

Whichever method you choose, the ideal compost pile requires a good mixture of carbon-rich materials such as dry leaves or straw and nitrogen-rich materials such as green grass clippings, certain kitchen wastes, or manure. Adding soil introduces the necessary microorganisms to the pile. The compost pile should be as moist as a wrung sponge, so sprinkle it periodically with water during dry weather. The mixture is ready to use when the compost is dark and crumbly and has an earthy smell. The whole process can take a period of weeks or months depending on the care the compost pile receives. When it is ready, add a 1-inch to 3-inch layer of compost to your garden. Spread it around individual plants or use it as potting soil.

A FEW HINTS

Keeping a flow of air through your compost pile is important because it's needed by the bacteria during the decomposition process. Turn the pile often to allow air to reach all parts.

The compost pile should stay moist but not dripping. Normal (not too heavy) rainfall should do this. Cover the pile in heavy rain. Sprinkle water on it during dry spells.

You may notice steam or other evidence of heat from your compost pile. Don't be alarmed. This is normal because heat is released when organic material decomposes. Natural temperatures in your compost pile can reach as high as 160 degrees Fahrenheit, killing weeds and pathogenic bacteria.

Chopping and shredding large items before adding them to your compost pile will help speed the decomposition process.

Your compost pile will shrink as it progresses. The various larger pieces, as they decompose, will eventually turn into a soil-like material.

BENEFITS OF BACKYARD COMPOSTING

Taking the organic materials from your waste stream and making compost with them has several benefits. The first and most obvious is the reduced amount of garbage you have to throw away. If you recycle everything possible and then compost, too, you'll be amazed by how little you put in your garbage can each week.

Not only is composting good at diverting your waste from landfills, it is an excellent source of nutrient-rich matter for your garden. You won't have to purchase soil nutrients from the nursery and your fruits and vegetables will be much healthier. A family's organic wastes can make up to 300 pounds of compost in a year.

Composting on a Large Scale

Composting a community's organic waste makes sense for a very simple reason: up to 75 percent of our household waste is organic—that is, carbon-based materials such as food wastes, garden clippings, and paper. Most of these carbon-based materials are ideal candidates for compost piles.

Some communities across the nation use composting on a large scale and the practice is rapidly becoming more popular. Fairfield, Connecticut, opened a $3 million composting center in 1989 to create topsoil for parks, playgrounds, and public landscaping. Likewise, University City, Missouri, began a leaf composting program in 1983 when the city discovered that leaves represented about 15 percent of its waste stream. University City collects approximately 11,200 cubic yards of leaves annually. The material is turned several times during the winter and spring, using an aerator/pulverizer that grinds up the material. The total process takes about six months—by this time the compost is reduced to between 20 and 25 percent of the original volume. The city sells the compost for $4 a cubic yard to nurseries, landscaping companies, and individuals.

In 1989 there were eight municipal composting facilities across the country taking all kinds of mixed solid waste straight from our garbage cans. The largest and most sophisticated of these plants, in Delaware, processes 250 tons of waste per day. Several other facilities are either under construction or in some phase of development. As well, more than a thousand sites handle just yard waste and leaves.

Many communities are being forced to look seriously at yard waste composting. Landfills across the country are beginning to refuse to accept leaves and yard waste—particularly in the fall months when this portion of the waste stream is so large. Moreover, the latest EPA targets—which now urge municipalities to reach a recycling rate of 25 percent—have stimulated more interest in the process.

Composting on a large scale falls into two categories. The first, yard waste composting, takes leaves and other yard wastes only. The second, municipal solid waste composting, takes a much wider variety of the organic wastes found in our garbage.

There are several ways to handle a large-scale composting system. The first is called static pile, or high-rate windrow, composting. With this method you make long piles, each 5 or 6 feet high and about 15 feet wide at the base, with a flat area next to them to control any runoff liquids. The temperature and moisture levels are controlled by injecting air through blowers and piping. The piles are turned regularly with machines equipped with paddles. This method takes approximately four to six weeks for initial composting, followed by a couple of weeks more for curing.

Low-rate windrow composting takes longer, up to three months. With this system, you make the same piles, but don't use the aeration equipment. Although this keeps the costs down, the drawback of this system is that you must pay more attention to potential rodent and odor problems. The piles still must be turned regularly.

Finally, composting can be done by a mechanical process in huge, enclosed barrels called digesters. This method is often called "in-vessel" composting. The digestion portion of this method only takes three to ten days because it uses heat, moisture, and mechanized aeration to speed up the composting process significantly. Most programs then leave the compost to cure for up to four months in windrows to kill off any remaining harmful ingredients. At the end of the process the compost is considered to be as safe as ordinary backyard dirt.

The costs involved in this method are obviously considerably higher than windrow operations because of facility and technology requirements. But in-vessel composting does offer a workable system in cases where land is in short supply. (The EPA cites an estimate of 1 acre needed for every 3,000 to 3,500 cubic yards of leaves collected when digesters are not used.)

What are the benefits of composting on a large scale? Avoided disposal costs and additional landfill space are immediate benefits. The EarthWorks Group estimates that, whereas it costs up to $65 per ton to dump solid waste in a landfill, it only costs about $35 per ton to create municipal compost. The compost that you make will save money in other areas, too: community parks and roadside plants will benefit from the nutrient-rich mixture, and you will have saved the cost of buying compost from outside sources.

A compost system designed to take all the organic and compostable wastes of a community of 1 million people is estimated to be able to create up to 600 tons of finished compost a day. Multiply that figure by the millions of people in this country and the amount of potential compost from our waste stream is overwhelming.

There are many markets for such enormous quantities of compost. American farmers have a serious problem with soil erosion: it's estimated that up to 65 tons of compost would be needed to add just 1 inch of compost to an acre of land. The nursery and landscaping industries are another potential market. Moreover, landfills need to be capped with several feet of dirt when they are sealed, and the dirt is often hard to come by and expensive.

Composting can be accomplished, then, on any scale, from a small backyard pile to a huge community project. Whatever method you use, you will be helping to keep up to 30 percent of your area's waste stream out of landfills and putting the organic matter to good use at the same time. With the support and encouragement of individuals across the country, the practice of composting our organic waste can be developed on a national scale.

Concerns About Composting

Some environmentalists are concerned that any toxic waste in our garbage will mean high levels of heavy metals in the finished compost, rendering it unsafe and unusable. Most municipal waste composting programs are screening the garbage for toxic materials, but this is still a matter to be studied. Pesticides, on the other hand, seem to break down with the compost and are found in finished compost in quantities similar to normal soil.

Another concern is that composting on a large scale will not allow for separating recyclables. Currently, some programs do and some do not. Clearly it would be preferable to remove these valuable materials before beginning the composting process. It appears to be a matter of economics: it costs too much to pay people to manually pull recyclable items from the waste.

Another less urgent, but nonetheless important, concern is the odor caused by massive composting projects. Some sites are smellier than others, but this problem must certainly be a consideration when composting facilities are anywhere near residential centers. Sites that compost leaves and garden clippings are much less bothersome than those that compost all kinds of organic waste. Composting inside, turning windrows often, and keeping sites as far away as possible from towns help minimize these problems.

Even with these concerns, however, the potential for widespread composting as a valuable part of our solid waste management policy seems excellent. Not only can large portions of the solid waste stream be diverted from landfills and incinerators, but a valuable commodity can be made from the waste.

4 Uncommon Recyclables

When we think about recycling, most of us automatically think of newspapers, plastics, glass, or aluminum. This is natural, as these are the materials we see being recycled most often. But recycling involves a wider number of materials which, although not as visible, play an equally important role in protecting the environment from pollutants and reusing materials that would otherwise be headed for a landfill or incinerator.

Some of these materials are more suited to domestic recycling; others have been recycled by industry for years. Around the house we can now recycle motor oil, tires, and batteries, all items that are potentially very harmful to the environment. And although most of us aren't aware of it, industry has recycled such things as car bumpers and asphalt for years.

MOTOR OIL

Recycling motor oil results in many benefits:

• Re-refining oil takes only about one-third the energy required to refine crude oil to lubricant quality.

• Recycling all the used oil in the United States would save 1.3 million barrels of oil per day.

• One gallon of used oil contains about 140,000 Btu of energy.

• Recycling keeps hundreds of millions of gallons of used motor oil from polluting our land and water.

State and local authorities are slowly becoming aware of the consequences of haphazard disposal of used motor oil. As a result, recycling programs that include motor oil are being developed across the country. The situation is critical, however, and needs immediate, comprehensive action. Used motor oil contains heavy metals like lead and cadmium as well as many other toxic elements (arsenic and benzene)—substances that create havoc with the natural environment. We only recycle about 30 percent of the automobile oil we use. The rest is discarded . . . and our current methods of disposal are causing serious environmental problems.

Over 300 million gallons of used motor oil are generated annually from privately owned cars and small trucks. Approximately two-thirds of this comes from do-it-yourselfers who change their own oil and dispose of it in a variety of ways, very few of which are safe. Commonly, when oil is changed at home, it is either poured down a storm drain, put in the trash can to end up eventually in a landfill, or even poured directly onto the land or a road.

Only about 10 percent of the oil changed from people's cars actually gets recycled. In fact, it has been estimated that the amount of used motor oil that is dumped in the United States annually equals ten to twenty times the amount that was spilled from the *Exxon Valdez* tanker in Alaska in 1989. The Coast Guard has estimated that sewage treatment plants discharge twice as much oil into coastal waters as do tanker accidents and that a major source of this oil is backyard mechanics dumping into storm drains and sewers. The need to collect this oil and stop its improper disposal is clear.

The consequences of incorrect disposal methods are dire for the local environment. Motor oil does not just break down and disappear into the environment: oil poured into the sewer can go straight into our waterways, disrupting treatment plants and harming streams, rivers, and the ocean. When it is put in the trash and ends up in a landfill, there is a real danger of the oil seeping out and affecting ground and surface waters. Oil containers in the trash can also harm sanitation workers if they pop open when compressed by garbage trucks. Finally, oil poured out on the road or directly on the land will invade the local ecosystem and kill plants, reduce soil productivity, and eventually work its way into local water sources.

The EPA notes that it takes only 1 gallon of used motor oil to contaminate up to a million gallons of fresh water: that's a year's supply of water for fifty people. When motor oil reaches freshwater sources, even the thinnest film on the water surface blocks sunlight, prevents the replenishment of dissolved oxygen, and impairs photosynthetic processes.

And by not recycling used motor oil we are not only harming our environment but wasting what is a valuable energy source in its own right. Motor oil doesn't lose its effectiveness permanently, for example, it just gets dirty. Used motor oil can be cleaned and used again and again for the same purpose. It is heated, the impurities are separated out, and then it is ready for reuse. In fact, 2.5 quarts of "new" motor oil can be extracted from 1 gallon of used oil, whereas it takes about 42 gallons of virgin oil to make that same 2.5 quarts of motor oil.

The recycled oil can also be used as fuel. The EPA estimates that if all the motor oil that is disposed of improperly by do-it-yourselfers were recycled, it could produce enough energy to power 360,000 homes each year or provide 96 million quarts of high-quality motor oil.

Despite the advantages of recycling motor oil, however, not nearly enough is being done. According to the EPA, two factors have played an important role in creating the current situation: the marketing of motor oil and the fluctuation of oil prices. Certainly the distribution pattern of motor oil sales changed dramatically during the 1960s. In the early part of the decade, service stations accounted for about 70 percent of all sales of lubricating oil for passenger cars. During the decade large quantities of motor oil began to be sold through retail outlets, however, because the high sales they generated allowed strong price discounts. This trend developed to the point where today mass marketers outsell service stations eight to one. As people began to buy the oil at retail outlets instead of service stations, the number of do-it-yourselfers soared.

Energy prices have also influenced the situation. The EPA notes that in 1983 crude oil prices were around $29 per barrel and service stations and even retail outlets could earn up to forty cents per gallon for used motor oil. Naturally, then, it was in their interest to collect it and return it to the processing chain.

When oil prices are low, used motor oil may have no, or even negative, market value. With a negative market value, service stations and other outlets have to pay someone to take the used oil from them. In the past, this situation has led to a variety of illegal means of handling the used oil. Trucking firms have been known to deliver used motor oil directly to apartment buildings instead of proper heating fuel. When burned, this untreated oil is a very toxic air pollutant. Moreover, Superfund sites across the country are often a result of the illegal dumping of used oil.

So when the market for used oil is bad, there is no economic incentive either for an individual or for a service station to recycle. Indeed, there's an incentive to dispose of the oil by illegal means. Today we have a situation in which the majority of motor oil changes are being done by backyard mechanics who, on the whole, don't dispose of the oil in a safe or useful manner: they don't recycle it. And even when it is disposed of properly, we can't be sure that it ends up being recycled anyway.

The good news, however, is that the tide is beginning to turn and states across the nation are establishing responsible recycling programs for used motor oil. The EPA estimates that by 1988 half of our states either had a recycling program operating or were considering one.

States are reinstating the old practices in which do-it-yourselfers take their used oil to central locations such as service stations or automotive supply stores. As the owner of the service station does not bear the burden of disposing of the oil, most are willing to serve as collection centers. Actually, used motor oil fits very easily into a recycling program. Virginia, Washington, and Alabama have all reported successful recycling projects that include used motor oil.

Alabama's Project ROSE (Recycled Oil Saves Energy) is generally considered to be the most successful recycling program for used oil in the country, proving that this useful resource can be recycled efficiently on a large scale. The program includes a combination of curbside collection, collection centers, and drum placement in strategic locations statewide. Curbside collection has been successful in predominantly urban areas. The collection center program involves many garages, service stations, and automotive service centers that voluntarily collect the oil and make a small profit from its sale. Finally, drum placement is used in urban areas where there are few service stations or garages.

It's easy to recycle used motor oil. The most important thing to remember is that it must not be mixed with any other substance as this will render the oil unsuitable for recycling. Just drain your oil into a reusable, sealable container such as a milk jug. Take it to a center in your area that recycles oil, and they'll tell you where to pour it. Then take your container home for the next time you change your oil. With a curbside program, disposal is even easier. Most programs will provide you with a container you can leave out with your other recyclables. In most cases, when you leave a full container, the collection agents will leave you an empty one. Speak to your recycling coordinator for details on how your program works. (If you get your oil changed at a service station, ask them first if they recycle the oil. If they don't, consider finding one that does.)

Most re-refined oil is used as fuel for ships and industrial boilers, but consumers can purchase it also. Many of the motor oils on the market have some recycled content, although this is not always marked on the label. Ask the store owner which brands have recycled content and support these products. You will be helping to complete the recycling loop.

BATTERIES

Recycling batteries is essential because it:
- Prevents millions of pounds of toxics from escaping into the environment
- Avoids chronic health problems
- Saves natural resources (lead, mercury, and more)

Household Batteries

Americans use approximately 2.5 billion disposable batteries annually (3 billion, if you include rechargeable batteries), according to the Environmental Action Coalition in New York. These include all the batteries we use to power our clocks, radios, flashlights, calculators, and a number of other things around the house. When thrown away like normal garbage, batteries create a serious health and environmental risk. Along with pesticides, household cleaners and solvents, enamel and oil-based paints, and used motor oil, they should not be put out with your regular trash.

The reason batteries are hazardous has to do with their contents. Household batteries typically contain mercury, zinc, manganese, nickel, and cadmium, which are harmful to our health and to the environment—especially when batteries are disposed of through incineration, as the heavy metals contained in them are then released directly into the environment, despite emission control devices. The number of household batteries put into municipal incinerators is strongly suspected to affect the level of mercury, cadmium, zinc, manganese, and nickel emissions from those incinerators.

Despite these dangers, very little is being done to recycle household batteries. Recycling them is not economically feasible in this country due to the difficulty of collecting sufficient quantities and separating the various types. The technology for removing mercury and other metals from batteries does exist, however, so try to find a recycler in your area.

Despite this general apathy, a few small programs are beginning to appear. A joint project between New Hampshire and Vermont sells used batteries containing mercury and silver to recyclers and stores the remaining batteries for household hazardous waste collection. Minneapolis residents can put household batteries in a clear plastic bag with their regular recyclables. In New York City, the Environmental Action Coalition has enlisted approximately thirty jewelers, camera stores, hearing aid centers, and a few general stores to begin collecting small "button" batteries for recycling. Minnesota is investigating the possibility of establishing a household battery management program.

State and local authorities should be urged to include batteries in their recycling programs because of the serious environmental dangers of leaving them to be thrown out like other household garbage. The best thing to do with these items, if your recycling program doesn't accept them, is to save them until your community has a household hazardous waste collection . . . or to find out from your community where you can take them.

Although there is no substitute for automobile batteries, solar power and rechargeable batteries are acceptable alternatives to standard dry cell batteries. Solar-powered items are becoming much more common. Solar-powered calculators, in particular, have been around for years. Buying a solar-powered product eliminates the need for batteries at all.

Rechargeable batteries are another option. Although more expensive initially, plus the cost of the recharger, the batteries and charger will pay for themselves in no time and you're avoiding the necessity of throwing away toxic products. If more people would switch to rechargeable batteries we could avoid the serious environmental problems associated with their current disposal.

Lead-Acid Batteries

Americans are exposed to more than 400 million pounds of highly toxic lead each year from discarded lead-acid batteries from our automobiles, boats, and farm equipment. We use over 70 million of these batteries (containing 1.25 billion pounds of toxic lead and at least 70 million gallons of sulfuric acid) annually—and discard approximately one-third of them in landfills, incinerators, and even on the roadside. (The other two-thirds are usually recycled.) The number of discarded batteries increases by approximately 5 percent annually due to increases in the number of vehicles on the road. So the problem is getting worse, not better.

Apart from the obvious waste of a natural resource, these discarded batteries pose a dangerous health and environmental threat. As many as twenty-five facilities on the national register of Superfund sites are associated with battery recycling. Even in minute amounts, lead is a very toxic substance responsible for many debilitating conditions. Especially in children, lead can build up in body tissue and cause severe damage. Lessened muscular coordination, brain damage, mental retardation, and loss of hearing are just some of the effects known to result from lead poisoning. In its most severe forms, victims can die from exposure to lead.

Long-term, low-level exposure to lead is considered much more dangerous than immediate, treatable exposure. Long-term exposure occurs when lead enters our drinking water or the air we breathe. Batteries buried in municipal landfills can leak the lead into groundwater. If batteries are incinerated, the lead remains in the ash (which may then be buried and cause the same problems) or escapes into the air.

Because of these problems, efforts have been made over the last few years to eliminate lead from as many products as possible. It has been almost completely phased out of gasoline in this country, for example. Likewise, it is now banned for most paint uses (although the Centers for Disease Control estimate that up to 50 percent of all residential homes still have paint containing lead in unsafe quantities). The problem is that no viable alternative has been developed to replace the use of lead as an energy storage medium in batteries. Approximately 78 percent of lead used today is in these batteries.

As is the case with motor oil, the success or failure of recycling the lead from storage batteries to date has largely been determined by the price of virgin materials. When the price of virgin lead is low, there is little economic incentive to recycle batteries for their lead: it becomes more expensive to transport and reprocess the lead than to mine virgin lead. Illegal dumping and other forms of inappropriate disposal occur in this climate.

As a comparison, in 1960 when lead prices were at forty-three cents per pound, 83 percent of lead-acid batteries were recycled. In 1986, however, when lead prices had dropped to nineteen cents per pound, recycling rates had dropped as well—to 70 percent. The good news is that lead prices climbed back up to around forty cents in 1988, but programs must be in place to take advantage of the increased recycling this trend encourages.

Recycling lead is a relatively simple process. Batteries are collected by automotive repair or supply stores and then sold to someone who can crush the batteries ("battery breakers"), drain out the sulfuric acid, and separate the lead from the rest of the battery. The lead is then remelted and used again.

Clearly an organized program must be developed to overcome the fluctuations of the market and establish reliable, regulated channels for lead-acid battery recycling. Otherwise we will continue to be exposed to over 400 million pounds of lead each year.

Various legislative initiatives have been proposed to deal with the problems associated with hazardous recyclables such as lead-acid batteries and motor oil. Most of these measures involve the use of financial incentive programs to encourage proper recycling and treatment of these materials. The final chapter suggests possible solutions to these problems.

TIRES

Recycling tires is sensible for several reasons:
- Making a pound of rubber out of recycled materials saves about 75 percent of the energy needed to produce 1 pound of virgin rubber.
- Retreading requires only 30 percent of the energy needed to produce a new tire.
- Recycling creates six times as many jobs as landfilling does.
- Recycling saves landfill tipping fees of up to $2 per tire.

Scrap tires have traditionally been classified as a "special waste" because of their size, shape, and chemical makeup and because they are not generally collected with normal household waste. Thus tires have always presented a special problem of disposal and reuse.

Today, in stockpiles around the United States, there are estimated to be over 2 billion used tires. Each year this number grows by approximately 200 million passenger car tires and another 40 million truck, bus, and tractor tires. It is estimated that we are recycling only 40 million tires each year. Tire recyclers cite both the limited uses for tires and the lack of affordable yet high-quality equipment to cut up the tires and separate the structural components like fabric and metal as prime reasons for the lack of widespread tire recycling. Moreover, a strong lobbying campaign from tire companies in favor of incineration is smothering recycling efforts. Once again, by missing the opportunity to recycle tires, we are creating environmental and safety problems and wasting precious natural resources.

At one time tires went into landfills like most other waste. But for a variety of reasons, this is no longer the case. Once buried in a landfill, waste tires have an uncanny way of working their way back to the top of the pile, or "floating." In fact, they can break through the clay cap built over the waste pile to prevent water infiltration, destabilizing the landfill and making eventual reclamation of the area virtually impossible.

Another reason why tires stopped being sent to landfills was simply because of their size and bulk. They took up too much space, so the landfill operators began charging more to accept them, making this method of disposal much less appealing. Although tires represent only a little over 1 percent of the solid waste stream by weight, they take up a disproportionate amount of space in the landfill.

So tires began to be left anywhere and everywhere in piles, called tire cemeteries. Indeed, there are unsightly tire stockpiles somewhere near most communities today. The problem is that these piles are not just unsightly but pose serious risks to the surrounding communities.

The problem of fire is perhaps the best known of these risks. Over the past several years, tire piles burning out of control in several parts of the country have made headline news. One tire fire in Virginia burned for seven months. These fires burn very hot and can take weeks to control because 75 percent of the tire pile is air, which feeds the fire. Meanwhile harmful fumes and unpleasant black smoke envelop the surrounding neighborhoods and then are carried by the wind for miles. If water is used to put out the fire, it mixes with the oily liquids created by burning and it all runs off and can contaminate both surface and groundwater supplies. Once tire fires are finally put out, the cleanup costs millions of dollars and can take years.

Apart from the fire hazard, piles of tires have proved to be an ideal breeding ground for both rats and mosquitoes, once again creating a dangerous environment for the surrounding communities. Not only do the tires serve as a protective haven for the rats, but when the tires are discarded with other solid waste, the piles provide ample food for the rats as well. Raccoons have also been known to inhabit tire piles.

Mosquitoes couldn't ask for a better place to live. Because of the shape of the tires, water collects in them easily. Then, as the tires absorb sunlight, the water warms and creates the perfect mosquito breeding ground. Concern is growing that certain types of mosquitoes that carry viruses harmful to humans are thriving in these stockpiles. As well, recent reports speculate that nonnative species of disease-carrying mosquitoes have come into the United States with new tire shipments.

So what do we do with all these tires if we can't put them in landfills and we can't keep stockpiling them? Waste tires have always been used for certain purposes, but never in volumes large enough to deal with the whole disposal problem. Both retreading and rubber reclamation (recycling the rubber) have been used as traditional methods of waste tire utilization.

Retreading extends the life of a tire, resulting in fewer tires overall being discarded. Retreading also conserves resources (one tire has as much as 2.5 gallons of oil in it) and energy (using only about 30 percent of the energy of new tire production). It is estimated that currently about 10 percent of passenger car tires (and between 50 and 70 percent of truck and bus tires) are retreaded. Retreading is much less common today than it once was, however, for several reasons.

Tires have become cheaper, relatively speaking, over the years, particularly with the introduction of Asian manufacturers into the market. The price of new economy tires is often not much more than that of quality retreads. With little or no difference in price, most people will buy new tires. Also, with each new year come new models of cars, some with brand-new tire sizes, so there are no retreads to fit the new models. Public perception of retreads works against them too: many people feel that retreads are inferior to, or not as safe as, new tires.

Truck and bus tire retreading, however, is still common. Truck tires, for example, are often retreaded numerous times. As each tire on a big truck bears a much smaller portion of the load than does a tire on a passenger tire, they are less likely to be worn down to the core and thus can be retreaded. The expense of new truck tires also encourages retreading.

Certainly the possibility for using retreads still exists. A program of education—along with the public's commitment to use retreads whenever possible—can ensure the continuation of this practice.

Rubber reclamation has traditionally been another method of utilizing waste tires. As with retreading, however, the amount of reclamation is declining. Tires were originally made from natural rubber, which was relatively easy to recycle. But modern tires have begun to use various synthetic rubbers, which are more difficult to recycle and thus result in less tire reclamation. Glass- and steel-belted radial tires have aggravated the problem.

Owing to the high performance of the new synthetic tires compared to traditional tires, the market for natural rubber tires has suffered dramatically. As the percentage of synthetic tires in the market increases, the cost efficiency of recycling tires declines severely. This has resulted in the decline in rubber reclamation as a method of waste tire utilization.

When a tire is recycled to reclaim the rubber, it is first cut up into small squares. These are then crushed into tiny pieces. After all the steel is removed, the rubber pieces are packaged and sold to manufacturers who can use the rubber again. The recycled rubber can be used to make a number of products from new tires to adhesives, hoses, and carpet padding.

Pyrolysis—the thermal separation of tire ingredients into their premixed state—has been used with rubber products for a long time. Although significant resources have been devoted to research, no viable commercial applications have come to fruition, seemingly because of a variety of cost and quality problems. The opposite extreme—freezing tires to aid in more efficient shredding procedures—has also been researched, but without much commercial success to date.

Currently, several million tires annually are cut up and used to make other products: sandals, floor mats, washers, insulators, and dock bumpers are some of the most common. Rubber chips from tires have also been used to replace wood chips in processing sewage sludge and as landscaping mulch. (It holds moisture better than traditional mulches.) Experimental uses include using tire chips for absorbing oils and hazardous wastes and as a fill material for road construction. At present the number of tires needed to supply these various markets is not large enough to significantly alter the problem of the remaining millions of tires. But experimentation may lead to the development of permanent uses for a large enough number of tires to solve our current crisis.

New uses for waste tires are being sought constantly. While some techniques involve transforming and reducing the tire somehow, research is also being done into possible uses of whole tires. Once again, the number needed will not eliminate the mountains of tires in scrap piles. Any use that is genuinely practical and keeps the tires from landfills, incinerators, and scrap piles, however, is a good use.

The use of scrap tires for artificial reefs has had some success in salt-water applications. Tires are bundled together, weighted with cement, and placed in the ocean. As marine growth eventually attaches itself to the tires and provides food for fish, the structure slowly evolves into an artificial reef.

Another use of whole tires is as highway and erosion barriers, two ideas promoted by the Goodyear Tire and Rubber Company. As highway barriers, whole tires are stacked together and attached securely, enclosed in fiberglass, and placed in front of fixed objects like bridge abutments, divider strips, and support posts. Tires can also be used as breakwaters. Goodyear proposes that tire breakwaters could save coastline that is at risk of being washed out to sea—and at a significant cost savings. The company estimates that a breakwater of tires might cost approximately one-tenth as much to build as a conventional breakwater.

Architect Michael Reynolds, known for the innovative use of recycled materials in his work, has designed homes that use several thousand used tires in the exterior walls. They are packed with earth and mortared with bricks, then covered with a coat of stucco so the tires are not seen. The walls provide enough insulation to keep the inside temperature comfortable year round.

There is much debate about the use of tires in incinerators as a source of energy. They are used as fuel in power plants, tire manufacturing facilities, cement kilns, and in paper production. Burning rubber has a heat of combustion of approximately 15,000 Btu per pound, which is similar to that of petroleum and much higher than that of paper, wood, or ordinary combustible materials.

The first plant in the United States to operate solely on burning tires is located in Modesto, California, next to what is thought to be one of the country's largest tire stockpiles. The tires are burned whole and the heat is captured to generate steam that powers an electric turbine. The Modesto stockpile is already thought to have enough tires to keep the plant working for up to ten years.

According to Frank Stark of Rubber Research Elastomerics in Minnesota, no states are supporting tire recycling programs currently. A lobbying campaign by tire companies to encourage tire incineration instead seems to be taking its toll. Minnesota canceled a tire recycling program in 1989 in favor of incineration, and many other states are doing likewise. Any tire recycling efforts under way today in this country are strictly private enterprises.

Proponents of using tire-derived fuel claim that the tires can be burned without harming the environment, while others disagree. Critics of incineration also argue that the raw materials should have a better use than for a one-time spurt of energy. For more on the environmental debate surrounding incineration, see the section entitled "The Alternatives" in Chapter 1.

An encouraging application of discarded tires is their use in asphalt rubber, a substance being adopted to surface many roads, runways, and playgrounds across our country and in many European nations. The Asphalt Rubber Producers Group estimates that in 1990 some 2 million tires were used in the production of asphalt rubber. Another 1.5 million were used in crack-sealing materials.

In this process, scrap rubber is ground or granulated into crumb rubber. This crumb rubber is then mixed with asphalt cement and the two elements react and form a gel known as asphalt rubber. By varying the percentage of granulated rubber in the mixture, various types of asphalt rubber can be created to suit different requirements. For example, different proportions are used to restore a road, to waterproof it, or to reduce or repair cracking.

Asphalt rubber has been used in thirty-five states, although its most widespread use has been in Texas, Arizona, and California. Texas, with trials dating back to 1976, was a pioneer in the study of asphalt rubber on roadways. Over the years, more than 60,000 tons of asphalt rubber have been used on over 2,500 lane miles of roadway throughout the state. Over 2 million scrap tires have been used there thus far. In Phoenix, Arizona, over 1,000 miles of roadway have been paved with rubber asphalt.

Proponents of the testing in Texas are very pleased with what they say are positive results. In that state, which was particularly well suited as a testing ground because of its variety of climatic conditions, studies claim that asphalt rubber outperformed conventional pavements in all conditions.

Noise reduction, increased pavement life (it is more flexible and hence resists cracking), and optimum skid surface are some of the benefits associated with asphalt rubber surfaces. Advocates cite long-term cost savings because the method reduces maintenance costs by its resiliency, flexibility, and ability to seal against water damage. If one also takes into account the cost of tire disposal, which is as much as $2 per tire in a landfill, a savings of at least $33,000 per mile (up to 16,000 tires may be recycled for each mile of rubber asphalt) makes the overall costs of using rubber much more appealing. The up-front costs have been quoted as being anywhere from 10 to 100 percent higher than conventional methods, however, and this is currently a serious drawback to the development of this type of surface recycling.

The process has been criticized for other reasons, also. First, critics cite the uncertainty about whether the introduction of rubber into the asphalt will impede the recycling of conventional asphalt surfaces. Moreover, these critics say, no one knows whether adding rubber to asphalt will affect the emissions from an asphalt plant. Apparently only limited testing has been done to determine any changes in emissions due to rubber's introduction into the process.

Several reasons can be cited for the slow development of asphalt rubber. Certainly the high up-front costs seem to have kept public funds from being allocated to this method of resurfacing to date—and government entities are by far the largest consumers of asphalt. Since public funds are usually allocated year by year, the higher up-front costs would mean much less road being paved each year—even if in the long run the roads last longer. Less road being surfaced each year also means less asphalt being bought in general and this concerns firms that pave with conventional asphalt.

Current methods of public spending do not appear to allow for the benefits of long-term savings from reduced maintenance or avoided disposal costs. Perhaps changes in public spending policies will allow this apparently viable way of reducing our scrap tires the opportunity to prove itself.

ASPHALT

Recycling asphalt results in several benefits:
• Saving natural resources
• Lower costs
• Preventing huge amounts of used asphalt from entering landfills
In addition to using scrap tires in road paving, technologies have been developed to reuse existing asphalt. Since approximately 93 percent of the 2 million miles of paved road in this country have asphalt on them, according to *American City and County* (July 1990, p. 42), the potential economic and environmental benefits of recycling are enormous.

Studies have shown many advantages associated with surface recycling: the elimination or retardation of reflective cracking; the maintenance of drainage patterns; and the provision of improved surface conditions such as skid resistance, smoothness, and resistance to weather. On a very practical level, recycling the surface instead of layering new material on old allows clearances under bridges and through tunnels to be maintained.

The environmental benefits of asphalt recycling are clear. Instead of throwing away all the torn-up road and replacing it with virgin materials—which creates a disposal problem and uses unnecessary raw materials—recycling simply repairs the existing asphalt and relays it. Recycling can also prove very cost-efficient when one considers the avoided expense of all-new materials. Not only are natural resources preserved, but faster completion times and public convenience are also incentives.

Recycling asphalt has developed as a practice largely because of economic concerns. The need for road repairs grows every year as more traffic and heavier trucks pound the surfaces of our roadways. As the need for repairs grows, however, the budgets to carry out the repairs do not. Moreover, the materials used for asphalt paving have risen significantly in cost in recent years. So governments have begun to look for solutions that will allow more repairs for less money. Recycling fits the bill.

Recycling asphalt is just what it implies: old asphalt is scraped off the road, crushed, and used again. As the components of asphalt pavement—asphalt cement, mineral aggregates, and mix—change with age because of traffic, standing water, and oxidation, for example, other materials are usually mixed in with the old asphalt to improve it or give it different qualities.

There are several different methods of asphalt recycling, each suited to certain road conditions or certain desired results on the roadway in question. The Asphalt Recycling and Reclaiming Association publishes guidelines for five different types of asphalt recycling: cold planing, hot-mix recycling, hot in-place recycling, cold in-place recycling, and full-depth reclamation.

Cold planing involves cutting up the asphalt, processing it, and respreading it to a specified grade and slope, free of humps and ruts. With this method the road can be used again immediately following the resurfacing. No smoke or flames are generated from this recycling method and it offers significant energy savings in comparison to hot methods.

Hot-mix recycling is the most commonly used asphalt recycling method today. With this technique the asphalt from the road surface is typically scraped up or crushed and then taken to a plant to be processed with new heated aggregates. Then it is returned to the road as a new surface.

Hot in-place recycling uses the same idea as hot-mix recycling, but the whole process takes place on site. The asphalt is pulled up from the road, fed into a mixer (perhaps with liquid additives), mixed and heated, and then respread on the road. Doing the work on site avoids the time and cost involved in transporting materials from site to plant and back. Some concerns exist, however, about air pollution caused by the heating of the asphalt materials in the open air, particularly when an open flame is used.

Cold in-place recycling uses certain stabilizers, emulsions, and other additives to treat the asphalt rather than heating it. The surface is scraped, the asphalt is screened and crushed, and then it is mixed with new materials before being replaced on the road surface.

Full-depth reclamation, as its name implies, recycles not only the asphalt pavement but a portion of the underlying material as well. The materials are crushed and prepared as in the earlier methods, but because the base level has been resurfaced also the result is a more fully stabilized surface.

The advantages to recycling road surfaces rather than throwing them away are many. In addition to saving natural resources and energy, the community can realize significant cost savings. There is every reason to believe that this industry will continue to develop vigorously in the years to come.

CAR BUMPERS

Recycling steel car bumpers results in these benefits:
- 74 percent savings in energy
- 90 percent savings in virgin materials used
- 97 percent reduction in mining wastes
- 105 percent reduction in consumer waste

Automobile bumpers certainly rate among the more unusual recyclable materials. This industry shows again, however, that almost anything can be recycled with some thought, effort, and organization.

Today's bumper recycling industry had its humble beginnings in the mid-1960s in southern California. The idea for recycling bumpers came about when a man from the electroplating business noticed, on his annual trips to Palm Springs, that the combination of heavy winds and sand in the Palm Springs area severely damaged the chrome finish on car bumpers. Thus he began taking with him a supply of reconditioned bumpers to replace those that were damaged—and was so successful that he started a business which eventually grew to become an international industry. Various businesses then gradually began collecting damaged bumpers from body shops in the Los Angeles area and developed techniques of repairing them.

According to the Bumper Recycling Association of North America, transforming a damaged bumper into a "like new" replacement is a multistep process. It begins when a body shop asks the recycler for a specific type of bumper. The first step is removing the old chrome on the replacement bumper by submersing it in a strong solution. Repairing the bumper could include welding and straightening, depending on the extent and type of damage. Then templates are made to ensure that the bumper is of the exact shape as the one it is replacing. The bumper then goes through a series of grinding and polishing operations to ensure that all of the nickel is also removed. This is followed by electroplating, which involves washing, rinsing, nickel plating, and finally chrome plating. Finally, the reconditioned bumper is delivered to the body shop for installation.

While this method is still used today, it is now much less common a practice than it used to be because over the years car bumpers have changed from metal to urethane. Today it is mainly pickup trucks, and other large trucks, that still require steel bumpers. Yet many other steel parts, such as those found on boats, antique cars, and household fixtures, lend themselves to recycling, particularly where electroplating is involved.

The bumper recycling industry has adjusted with the times. While still recycling steel products as described above, it has also developed techniques to repair and recycle urethane bumpers. Although not one of the largest recycling industries, this unique enterprise provides a valuable service.

SCRAP

There are two major benefits of recycling scrap:
• Preservation of natural resources
• Space saving in landfills

Scrap recycling involves a variety of commodities including ferrous and nonferrous metals, glass, paper, textiles, and plastics. The collection, processing, and reuse of these materials constitutes an aboveground mining industry for scrap recyclers. Indeed, although not particularly well known, the scrap recycling industry is large and substantial. The Institute of Scrap Recycling Industries (ISRI) has over 1,800 member companies.

The recycling of scrap materials has been happening for many centuries in one form or another. It is thought that as early as people started working with metal they took obsolete pieces and remelted them for reuse. In more recent times, scrap collectors with their horse-drawn carts have collected old implements, rags, and used appliances for years. In fact, this practice is still common in many cities around the world, particularly in less developed countries. Today, scrap processors have sophisticated, multimillion-dollar facilities to sort and process used materials.

The volume of scrap materials processed in this country each year is significant. ISRI estimates that the following volumes were recycled by scrap dealers and processors in 1989: 45.9 million tons of scrap iron and steel; 1.4 million tons of scrap copper; 2.4 million tons of scrap aluminum; 891,000 tons of scrap lead; 227,000 tons of scrap zinc; 659,000 tons of stainless steel scrap; and 21.4 million tons of wastepaper. The role of this industry in helping to preserve our natural resources and reuse whatever materials possible is clear.

Most processors in the scrap industry tend to specialize in one particular material because of the unique equipment and different collection and handling processes for each material. Specializing allows more efficient and therefore profitable handling of the scrap materials.

Ferrous metal dealers handle scrap iron and steel. The scrap is either left over from foundries and steel mills (the equivalent of pre-consumer wastepaper) or collected from a variety of used items. Scrap steel can come from used vehicles (cars, trucks, farm equipment—even ships), household appliances like refrigerators and stoves, steel construction beams, and anything else made of steel. The dealer must collect the scrap and divide it according to up to eighty different specified grades before steel mills and foundries buy it back for remelting.

Nonferrous metal dealers handle aluminum, stainless steel, copper, zinc, lead, titanium, nickel, and precious metals (gold, silver, platinum, palladium). While the amount of nonferrous scrap metals recycled is not as high in volume as that of ferrous metal, it is more valuable. (Some dealers store it in bank-type vaults.) It comes from any number of sources. Copper can be found in an automobile's pipes, lead in its battery, and nickel in stainless steel appliances, for example.

Wastepaper is another specialization of scrap dealers. The amount of

wastepaper in this country is prodigious in comparison to other countries. ISRI estimates that while Americans use up to 600 pounds of paper
annually per capita, that figure is as low as 25 pounds in the former
Soviet Union and only 2 pounds in China. Paper waste is collected from
homes, offices, and industry through recycling programs or comes in
the form of pre-consumer waste (cuttings from the paper mills themselves that never make it to the consumer in the first place).

Glass recyclers are part of the scrap industry as well. Although most
glass collected for reuse comes from beverage containers, it can be used
in glass for all kinds of purposes. Recycled glass ends up in perfume
bottles, medicine vials, and, of course, beverage containers again.

The recycling of plastics constitutes the smallest sector of the scrap
recycling industries, according to ISRI. Only about 1 percent of all plastics used annually are recycled. Given our estimated annual consumption of nearly 14 billion pounds of plastics, there is clearly room for
expansion.

Textile recycling is perhaps the least-known aspect of scrap recycling, but the industry is larger than most people realize. ISRI estimates
that 13 percent of all textile fibers used are on a repeat trip through the
mill. Even fur cuttings are recycled.

The way in which textiles are recycled is actually not too dissimilar
from how paper stock is recycled. Cotton, wool, synthetic, and
synthetic-blend waste textiles are sold to a dealer by clothing and furniture manufacturers, textile mills, and individual consumers. After the
waste textiles are sorted for type, a processor cuts, washes, and packages
the materials for sale to a textile garnetter. The garnetter further sorts
the material and then begins the shredding and combing process that
produces fibers ready for sale to the textile manufacturers.

Recycled textile fibers can be found in a surprisingly wide-ranging
variety of products. Bleached denim and pure cotton wastes, for example, go into making fine-quality stationery and document paper, as
well as U.S. currency. Recycled cotton and synthetics are ground to
produce compounds for manufacturing vulcanized fibers, roofing, and
flooring products. Wiping cloths and other materials are made from
recycled cotton cloth. Natural and synthetic wastes are used in making
flock and filler and in plastic materials that require additional tensile

strength. These wastes are also used in batting and padding for toys, upholstery, and cushioning products. Recycled wool and other textiles are shipped to manufacturers, both in the United States and abroad, for reweaving into new fibers and fabrics. These recycled materials then are made into clothing, blankets, carpeting, and hundreds of other consumer products.

As this chapter has shown, recycling can involve all kinds of materials. These examples of less common recyclables should lead to ideas for other products with the potential to be recycled. Innovative thinking and the cooperation of industry and consumers are necessary, however. All such projects are working toward the ultimate goals of saving energy, reducing waste, and promoting environmental responsibility.

5 What You Can Do: Reduce . . . Reuse . . . Recycle . . . Reject

Few people would deny that as a society we are much more wasteful than we need be. As we have become more affluent, we have demanded more "things": to own, to use, to wear, to eat. Unfortunately most of the things we buy are not made with durability in mind. "The throwaway society" is an overused, but nonetheless true, description of America and many other developed nations around the globe.

No one wants to be denied the possessions and comforts to which we've become accustomed . . . and there's no reason why we should be. We simply need to take the time to think more carefully about the way we lead our lives. By considering the *consequences* of our purchases, and the disposal of these purchases, we can drastically reduce our effect on the waste stream.

Follow the simple steps of *reducing* the amount of waste you create in the first place, *reusing* things as much as possible before throwing them away, *recycling* what you have no further use for, and finally *rejecting* items with too much or inappropriate packaging. If, as a society, we can make this commitment, we will be well on our way to solving our garbage and environmental problems.

REDUCE

Reducing the amount of waste we generate involves looking at products with an eye to their packaging and their overall useful life. How long will the product be useful to you? How long will its container be useful to you? If one product comes in a reusable container and another doesn't, all other things being equal, the first product is the best choice because you will be throwing away less and getting a useful, long-lasting container out of your purchase.

One-use-only products are some of the worst environmental offenders. Products designed for one use only are cropping up on shelves everywhere. Diapers, razors, pens, paper towels, lighters, single-serving containers, paper cups and plates, and even cameras are made to use and toss. The irony is that there are almost always less costly alternatives.

The key word is convenience. We have all been fooled into believing that these one-time products are so "convenient" that we cannot live without them. This is simply not true: it is a marketing ploy to make us spend more money. What possible attraction can there be to buying a whole new camera each time you want to take photos, rather than simply buying film?

Admittedly, a little bit of thinking is involved. You do have to remember to take your camera with you when you want to take photos, but is this so difficult? Likewise, avoiding paper towels means planning ahead and keeping cleaning-up rags in the kitchen or bathroom. Avoiding one-serving packages of food means you might want to make stews and the like in larger quantities and freeze individual servings. Planning ahead like this and avoiding the marketing traps will save you money and help you regain control over your own life—while helping out the environment at the same time.

REUSE

Remembering to reuse things instead of automatically throwing them away takes a little bit of relearning for most of us. Once you do get back in the habit, however, you'll be amazed at how much you can avoid throwing out.

We have probably all heard our parents talk about how they saved and reused everything while they were growing up. They saved lengths of string, reused wrapping paper, and had reusable shopping bags (an idea that is just beginning to catch on again), just as a few examples. In our parents' day this was a matter of economics as well as an understanding that commodities were scarce.

Today we forget that reusing products before we throw them away saves us money. Not only that, we take the availability of anything and everything for granted. It simply doesn't occur to many of us not to run down to the store and buy whatever we want, but today it still makes sense to reuse everything we can. We must see through the marketing ploys and understand that reusing things saves us money. Equally, we must realize that many of the earth's resources are nonrenewable. Indeed, our blatant disregard for our natural resources over the past decades is bringing their eventual disappearance much closer to our lifetime than originally expected. Today it also makes ecological sense to reuse whatever products we can.

Can you find another use for that piece of paper you're about to throw away? If you've gotten tired of a dress, could someone else use it? Does your car have to have *new* tires, or would retreads do? The answer is almost always yes.

RECYCLE

Recycling is one of the best ways to notice a huge difference in the amount of garbage you throw away. Anyone who has recently begun to recycle will understand this. Think of how many newspapers, glass bottles, plastic containers, and cans you throw away each week. Now think how empty your garbage cans would be without them. If your area doesn't offer curbside collection of your recyclables, there are sure to be local charities who will take them from you. See Chapter 2 for the different collection methods available.

REJECT

When you go shopping next, take a few minutes to look carefully at the packaging on the products you buy. Try to imagine how they could be presented with less packaging and still be appealing and safely sealed.

It isn't difficult. Try to buy products with the least, or most responsible, packaging.

Toothpaste is only in boxes so they can sit on the shelves in neat little piles. But how many of us would object to having the tubes loose in bins, with the caps safety-sealed? Do potato chips really need to be sold in two individual bags inside a third bag? Are plastic tampon applicators really necessary? Why do bars of soap sold in groups need to be individually wrapped as well as wrapped up together? And do we really need to buy our fruit in molded cardboard containers and covered in plastic wrap?

All this excess packaging contributes to the waste stream by creating an unnecessary amount of garbage. So select your purchases according to which manufacturers are the most responsible packagers. And, importantly, write to the others to tell them why you're not buying their products any more.

You don't have to change your life drastically or suffer terrible inconveniences in making these adjustments. The suggestions discussed throughout this book are easy to implement with only a little forethought and planning. Just a moderate change on the part of everyone would mean an enormous drop in the amount of garbage we produce, a significant energy savings, and a reduction of pollution, just to name a few benefits. Realistically, we know that not everyone will participate, however, so the work of those who do recycle becomes all that much more important.

This chapter details specific things that everyone can do—at home, while shopping, and at work—to help cut down the amount of garbage in the world and give today's recycling movement the push it needs.

AT HOME

Your home is a great place to begin. Take a quick look around and you'll be amazed at the number of ways you can make some easy, "environmentally friendly" adjustments to your lifestyle.

Reduce

Reducing the amount of products you use and throw away is much easier than you might think. It simply involves learning to avoid marketing ploys which tell you that you need things you don't, thinking about alternative uses for everyday items, and developing other less wasteful habits. Start out with some of the following ideas and then come up with your own.

AVOID PAPER DISPOSABLES

• Don't use paper cups, paper plates, paper napkins, and plastic knives and forks when you can just as easily use proper dishes, cloth napkins, and silverware.

• Don't use paper towels, tissues, or toilet paper to wipe up spills. Have a rag—one that can be washed and reused—handy in the kitchen, bathroom, nursery, and wherever else you might need one. The rags don't take up much space in the washer, but you'll save a lot of space in your garbage can.

AVOID ONE-USE-ONLY ITEMS

• Don't use plastic wrap when you can store something in a reusable container. If you don't have any containers free, find a spare plastic bag and use that.

• Don't buy plastic bags specifically for lining wastepaper baskets, for example, unless absolutely necessary. Use some of the bags you already have around your house, or only line the garbage cans that get wet garbage.

• Use disposable diapers as little as possible. Diaper services are no more expensive and sometimes are quite a bit cheaper than using disposables. The cloth diapers can be used 100 or so times and are then used as rags before they are thrown away or recycled. Not only do disposable diapers constitute a large part of our waste, they can release toxic elements into the land and water table because human feces may carry infectious germs.

• Use as few disposable products as possible. So many baby products today are disposable—just try to see how many of them you really need. Use an electric razor and remember to take your camera on trips so you don't need to buy a disposable one.

• Most women's sanitary products are disposable, too, but look for alternatives. Women can now buy washable (reusable) menstrual pads made out of absorbent cotton.

• Try using a refillable ink pen rather than disposable plastic ones. You can impress people while helping out the environment.

JUST USE LESS

• Buy good-quality products that will last a long time. When you buy less expensive items, you often save money in the initial purchase price, but you may have to replace them two or three times in the time you'd use a good-quality alternative. This can be said for working gloves, clothes, furniture, and any number of other products.

• Use slightly less detergent than the manufacturer recommends unless you are washing a really dirty load. You'll probably find no difference in the cleanliness of your laundry, and you'll be saving detergent. This is particularly true for loads you are washing to make them fresh again rather than to remove any particular stains. By using less detergent, you replace the container less often (and have to throw one away less often).

• Reduce the amount of water, detergent, and energy you use by being more careful about laundry. Run the machine only when you have a full load—and don't automatically throw things in the laundry if they aren't dirty. Do you really need a fresh towel for each shower? Do you really need to wash something you've only worn for one or two hours? If you're the person who does the laundry at your house, you'll also notice the added benefit of more free time by cutting back on unnecessary laundry.

• Use rechargeable batteries.

• Don't use a full page of paper to write yourself a three-word note when you can use a corner or half of that page, a piece of scratch paper, or the back of an old envelope.

• Reduce the amount of junk mail you receive. Write to the Direct Mail Marketing Association (see Appendix A), and tell them that you don't wish to receive unsolicited mail. It may take a month or two to notice the effect, but you will notice. You can also reduce your junk mail by telling your organizations not to sell your name to other companies.

• Consider stopping subscriptions to magazines or newspapers that you don't really read. If you only read a magazine occasionally, just buy it from the newsstand when you really want it.

• Don't buy a product when you can make the equivalent with things you already have at home. Wood polish can be made with mineral oil and lemon juice, for example, hair spray can be made from boiled lemons, and baking soda can be used instead of many cleaning products. There are many books on the market describing hundreds of alternatives—usually less harmful to the environment—for unnecessary products.

• Begin to pay attention to everything you buy and use. You may discover places to cut back that would benefit you in other ways, too. Do you buy too much junk food? Do you take too many medications? Are there some products that you waste more than others? Noticing will help you reduce your waste—and may improve your health.

• Use less aluminum foil. It is made from a nonrenewable source (bauxite) and isn't easily recycled. Use a baking tray instead of foil for cooking, wrap your sandwiches in wax paper instead of foil, and try to think of other ways you can cut down on your usage of foil.

Reuse

Not only can you learn to buy less, but you can get more use out of what you do buy. Previous generations didn't have the abundance of products available to them that we enjoy today, and we can learn a lot from their example. Before automatically throwing something away, just take a minute to think about how you might be able to use it again. This section offers some ideas.

CONTAINERS/WRAPPING

• Wash and reuse plastic containers—they're perfect substitutes for plastic wrap. If you have no plastic containers at home, don't buy any—

just start collecting margarine tubs and similar containers. You can use these containers in the refrigerator and freezer and for lunches.

• Line wastebaskets, if you have to line them, with plastic or paper bags that you already have instead of buying bags specifically for that use.

• Use plastic vegetable and fruit bags (the ones you brought home from the store filled with mushrooms or peaches) to cover food in the fridge if you don't have plastic containers.

• Save the aluminum or plastic pie plates that come with some foods. You can hang them in the vegetable garden to keep the birds away or use them to sit houseplants in. You may also be able to use them in your own cooking, or to store leftovers. The aluminum may be recyclable with your regular aluminum cans—check with your collector to be sure.

CLOTH

• Make rags out of old clothes, sheets, towels, and other cloth. They can be used for wiping up spills, polishing wood, silver, or brass, and dusting. Think of the products you buy specifically for these purposes and then think of how much money you will be saving.

• Old stockings can be used to stuff homemade dolls and puppets, or to stuff into a weatherproofing roll to put in front of a drafty door.

• Don't throw away clothes without getting some other use out of them: family or friends might want them, or they could go to a charity shop, homeless shelter, or women's crisis center.

• Save baby clothes for the next baby in the family. If you're not planning any more, what about your brothers, sisters, cousins, friends? If you don't know anyone who needs them and you aren't going to save them, any local charity would be very pleased to accept them.

• Use pieces of cloth to make sacks for birthday or Christmas presents. These can be used over and over again and reduce your need for wasteful wrapping paper.

• Try handkerchiefs instead of paper (nonrecyclable) tissues.

• Use cloth napkins at meal times so you can wash them and use them over and over instead of throwing away paper napkins each meal.

PAPER PRODUCTS

• Get a reusable coffee filter instead of using disposable ones.

• Brown paper bags: if they aren't recycled near you, charity shops and other stores can use them. Some day-old bakeries give a small discount to customers who bring in old brown bags.

• If there's a particular type of paper that is not easily recycled in your area (such as glossy paper or colored paper), why not save it up to light fires (instead of using recyclable newspaper) or shred it to use for packaging?

• Save wrapping paper. This is easy if you take a little care in opening presents. Then just fold the paper carefully and it will be in excellent condition for its next recipient.

• Give your old magazines to hospitals and rest homes if they're not recyclable in your area.

• Donate (or sell) books you no longer want to a used book store.

• Have you ever considered using a paper shopping bag as wrapping paper? Many people have done this for years. Cut out a few pictures from a magazine and attach for decorations. Children will have fun doing this.

• Don't use a fresh piece of paper to make a shopping list or a note to yourself when you can use the back of an envelope or a piece of scratch paper. The trick is to keep a pile or a tray of scrap paper somewhere easily accessible. If you have a home office, keep the scrap near your desk for scratch paper. And when you've used one side of a piece of paper, don't throw it away—just run a diagonal line down the used side and then put it, blank side up, in your scratch paper tray. You'll be amazed at how much paper you can save this way. Soon you won't need new sheets of paper for anything but your final copy of something. Then recycle the paper, don't throw it away. (To start your scratch paper pile, just go through one day's junk mail.)

• Save the reply envelopes that come with your junk mail. You can put a label over the printed addresses and use the envelopes yourself. Likewise, large envelopes (full-page size) can easily be reused by putting a label over the first address. If you open envelopes with a letter opener or knife, you can easily seal them back up again with a strip of tape.

• Save cardboard boxes of various sizes for a variety of uses: to store files, accounts, or photos, to use for wrapping a present. Store them inside each other so they don't take up much space.

MISCELLANEOUS

• Boxes, old sewing spools, scrap material, buttons, and all sorts of other leftover items make wonderful toys for children. Encourage them to use their imagination.

• Donate old appliances to charitable organizations who can use them themselves or sell them.

• When a sponge is too dirty to use with the dishes, why not use it to wipe up spills on the floor, thus getting just a bit more use out of it?

• Cleaning out the fireplace? Small amounts of ash can do wonders for your garden. (Caution: Small amounts! Don't overdo it.)

• Dishwashing: if you don't use a dishwasher, how about filling a bucket in your sink rather than the sink? That way, when you've finished washing the dishes you can throw the water out on the plants instead of just wasting it!

• If you are doing any construction or handyman projects around the house, save scraps of wood and materials to use for the next project.

• And finally, if you can't find a use for it yourself, return it to where you got it. Dry cleaners are only too pleased to get their wire hangers back. Garden stores will also gladly take back the plastic pots, crates, and plant labels you get when you buy plants. They can use them over and over, so don't throw them away.

Recycle

Many things we would have thrown away in past years are now easily recyclable. Most of these materials are discussed in more detail elsewhere in this book, and Chapter 2 explains the different places and methods of disposing of your recyclables. This section, then, is just a brief reminder of the many things that belong in recycling bins rather than in your garbage cans.

• Aluminum cans and mixed metal cans: Depending on your collector, these are collected either together or separately.

• Plastic beverage containers: PET (the two-liter soda bottles, normally) and HDPE (waxy-colored milk jugs, usually) are the most commonly recycled plastic containers.

• Newspapers: This is probably the material most commonly recycled by households. You should be able to find somewhere locally that recycles newsprint.

• Brown paper bags: These shopping bags can be recycled too and are usually accepted with cardboard. Ask your recycler.

• Cardboard: Cardboard is usually made of recycled materials. Stores have been recycling their cardboard boxes for years, so if your recycler won't take them, try asking your grocery store.

• Glass: Since glass is one of the more commonly recycled materials, you shouldn't have much difficulty finding a place to recycle it. Depending on your recycler, you may have to separate colors.

• Plastic bags: Some Safeway and Thrifty stores are now collecting any kind of plastic bag for recycling. Maybe you can encourage your grocery stores to do the same.

• Office paper: Both white and colored office paper can be recycled, although it usually has to be separated and the white is much more in demand. The collectors that take domestic recyclables don't often take office paper, but it is commonly recycled. Check with your county or a few big companies in your area.

• Computer paper: Computer paper is high-grade recyclable paper. Again, check with your county or local companies.

• Motor oil: Do-it-yourselfers cause severe damage by pouring used motor oil away incorrectly. With this in mind, many cities and counties are including motor oil in their recycling schemes. If yours doesn't, chances are a local automotive shop does.

• Tires: When it comes time to replace the tires on your car, try to find a dealer who will recycle (or, better yet, retread) them.

• Batteries: Because batteries leak toxics into the groundwater system, they should not be included in your normal garbage. County landfills and garbage collection programs are beginning to accept such hazardous garbage and in turn dispose of it properly.

• Food scraps: Compost! (See Chapter 3.)

AT THE STORE

Once you have whipped your home into environmental shape, think about what you can do when you are out shopping. This isn't quite so easy: whereas at home you are free to change things at will, this isn't true at the store. Shopping more responsibly involves not only changes on your part, but on the part of store management and personnel. But the more you encourage environmentally preferable alternatives, the faster things will change.

Reduce

You can reduce the amount of garbage a shopping trip creates before you even leave your house. Then, at the store, think about packaging and bulk purchases. Here are some guidelines to help you get started.

SHOPPING BAGS

• Take your own shopping bags to the grocery store and department stores. (Store the bags in your car so you don't forget to take them with you.) Likewise, keep a few plastic bags in your car so you can put new vegetables in them. Then just save them and use them again. Surely, millions of Europeans can't all be wrong.

• Even if you don't have your own shopping bag with you, you don't need a new bag when you're only buying one or two things. When you buy a book, a birthday card, a CD or record, for example, or when you rent a video, you're almost always given your purchase in a bag. You don't need this bag! Just tell the clerk, "No thanks." Nine times out of ten the clerk will think it's a great idea.

• If you are shopping in many stores and have already bought one item that's in a bag, put all your future purchases in the same bag. There's no need to take a bag from every store. Better yet, remember to take your own bag to start with.

• In the grocery store, don't put your lettuce in a plastic bag. And if you're just getting a couple of apples (or carrots or peppers . . .), don't put them in a bag either. Just keep them together in your shopping cart so the checker doesn't have to search it for runaway carrots.

WRAPPING/PACKAGING

• Is there a bakery in your area that sells bread the European way— that is, with no wrapping? If so, consider making an extra stop and buying your bread there and eliminating some wasteful packaging.

• Ask your dry cleaners not to put plastic coverings on your clothes when you pick them up. (Or just get one to cover the whole load.)

• Try to buy products with the least packaging. Packaging is usually just thrown away, anyway. So if a product you usually buy has layers of unnecessary packaging, consider buying a competitor's product that is more simply packaged. And don't forget to write to the manufacturer of your old brand to explain why you're no longer buying their product. If enough people do this, the message will get through. Just ask yourself if the manufacturer really needed to use so much packaging to get the product safely from his place to yours.

• Buy concentrates whenever possible. Why pay for (and waste) all the extra packaging when all you need to do is add water?

• Buy large or family sizes of everything you can. Nonperishables are obvious candidates, but you can also do it with foods you think you'll use up. This way you are requiring much less packaging for the same amount of product—anything from laundry detergent and coffee to breakfast cereals and rice. But don't buy normal-sized packages that have been wrapped together in plastic to sell as a bulk purchase, as is often the case at big discount stores. You are not cutting down on pack-aging here—you're using more.

• Buy in bulk (unpackaged in bins). You can get all kinds of things this way: beans, granola mixtures, cereals, candy—even hardware. Then save and reuse the bags.

• Consider replacing your light bulbs with fluorescent bulbs as they burn out. The longer-lasting fluorescent bulbs are more expensive to purchase, but they're more energy efficient, they produce less garbage because they last so much longer, and they're cheaper in the long run when you consider that you have to replace them much less often.

• Buy a live Christmas tree so you'll have nothing to throw away after the season. (If you must buy a cut tree, be sure to cut it up and use it in your compost heap after Christmas.)

Reuse

Reuse everything possible from a shopping trip, whether on your next trip or around the house. You'll find that most things can be used again and again.

• Reuse your plastic and paper bags. Plastic bags can be used to store food, and small paper bags make great lunch bags.

• Save the tissue paper the stores wrap your clothes in. How often have you wanted some for wrapping a present? Better yet, if you already have some tissue paper at home, ask the store not to use it.

• Likewise, things you buy often come in boxes. These boxes can be reused for wrapping a present or for storing files or old photos.

• Save margarine tubs, candy tins, and other containers for storage around the house.

Recycle

When shopping there are two ways to foster recycling: first, use your purchasing power to encourage manufacturers to use recycled materials in their products; second, buy products that you can recycle yourself. This section gives you a few ideas.

• Buy products that are made of (or packaged in) recycled materials.

• Keep in mind which materials are easily recyclable in your area. Buying a particular product because it is recyclable doesn't actually do any good if your area does not have a collector that accepts it. Something must be recyclable in *practice*, not just in theory. You may want to buy fruit juice in glass jars rather than in waxed cartons or frozen containers, for example, because the glass is very easily recycled. You may want to buy meat and fish from a butcher counter where they wrap it for you in strong white recyclable paper rather than buying it prepackaged in plastic and styrofoam that you cannot recycle.

• Shop at rummage and garage sales. This is a form of recycling, too.

• Need new drinking glasses? It's very easy to find recycled glass products in most department stores today. It's light green in color.

• Many household products made with recycled materials can now be purchased. Paper towels (if you really need them), toilet paper, computer paper, and stationery are just a few examples.

• Check the packaging on everything you buy. Is it made from recycled materials? If not, try to find a product that is.

• Remember to check over everything you bring home from the store to see if it's recyclable or not. If it is—recycle it.

Reject

Shopping gives you the opportunity to show manufacturers what you think of their goods. By refusing to purchase irresponsible products and packaging, you are sending an important message.

• Try to avoid single-serving foods. Think about how much more plastic is used to package six individual yogurt servings than to package one large tub (or to wrap individual cheese slices). Many snacks and single-serving lunch and dinner items are available today, supposedly for convenience. Plan ahead and don't fall into this trap.

• Don't buy overpackaged products. Potato chips that are packed in two single bags—and then in a larger one—are a good example. Chocolates and beauty products are other examples of items with much more packaging around them than is really necessary.

• Avoid disposable products whenever possible. Use a razor that only needs changeable heads rather than throwing the whole razor away each time—or use an electric razor. Reconsider the sense of disposable diapers. Buy a pen with refillable cartridges instead of throwing away a plastic pen each time it runs out of ink.

• Buy in bulk. Reject single servings and unnecessarily packaged items. The larger the item, the less packaging needed to deliver it.

AT WORK

The workplace is an excellent target for waste reduction and recycling policies. While the types of materials you handle are probably quite different from those you have at home, the sheer quantity of paper and other products used in an office on any given day represents an enormous opportunity to make significant changes.

Reduce

Routines are common in every work environment, but these routines are not always efficient. These suggestions show how office policies can be adjusted to reduce waste significantly without harming productivity.

• Write to the Direct Mail Marketing Association to have your organization's name and address removed from their list (see Appendix A).

• Have a look at your office's magazine and newspaper subscriptions. Does anybody read these? Consider stopping any that don't get much use.

• Send one memo around the office for people to initial rather than giving everyone their own copy. The same principle can work for many things. For example, company reports don't always need to go to everyone. Consider having one reference copy in each department that everyone there can share.

• If your office uses paper plates and cups at meetings or in the kitchen area, consider encouraging people to bring in their own mugs at the very least. (A lot of meeting places and office complexes have cleaning services that will wash cups and dishes for little or no extra charge.) In the long run, having your own dishes and silverware will be cheaper than buying paper plates and cups all the time.

• If your printer uses a tractor feeder—which usually requires one blank page to be wasted when you pull a document off the printer— consider ways to avoid wasting that sheet. If you're going to be printing lots of things, just leave them all attached until you really need to remove them from the printer. Then you only lose one sheet instead of one sheet per document. And remember to *use* that blank sheet—don't throw it away.

• Can you use electronic mail to send someone a message rather than waste paper? Since everyone's computers are usually switched on in an office anyway, you aren't wasting any more energy.

Reuse

It's very easy to throw things away without thinking, particularly when one is busy. But by taking a few minutes to change certain wasteful habits, you can save an enormous amount of paper and other supplies.

• Keep a scratch paper container near your desk and use the paper for rough drafts, brief memos, notes to yourself, and the like. If people take notes at your meetings, this is a great place to use some of the scratch paper you've been storing up. To start your scratch paper pile, just take a day's worth of junk mail.

• Save containers and try to find another use for them. If your building has a day care center, for example, it could probably use some containers to hold toys or crayons. Boxes are good for keeping accounts and old papers also.

• Having a clearout day at work? Any papers from your desk or files that are headed for the recycling bin can first be used as scratch paper. Old business cards you no longer need? These are the perfect size for little reminder notes.

• Could you use shredded or scrunched paper for packing and shipping things instead of styrofoam packing pellets?

Recycle

Finally, offices are a great place to recycle. Enormous amounts of high-quality paper and other materials that are thrown away unnecessarily can be recycled.

• Set up recycling containers around the office for any materials you generally throw away, such as office-quality paper, aluminum cans, glass, or newspapers.

• Take turns delivering the full containers to a center that pays for recyclable materials and you'll earn your organization a little money on the side.

• Try cutting down on your use of colored paper in the office, particularly if it's not recycled in your area. White or light-colored paper is more easily recycled and has less harmful inks.

• For detailed information on how to recycle at your office, see Chapter 6.

6 How to Set Up a Recycling Program

This chapter outlines ways to organize a recycling program at work, in your community, at school, and at home. While each of these situations requires a separate approach, they clearly have many points in common. In fact, the suggestions found here are applicable to any volunteer, social, or service group interested in earning money from recycling.

To avoid repetition, the first section on recycling at work is the most detailed. Thus subsequent sections can focus on aspects unique to that particular application without reiterating every point previously discussed. Read through all the different sections to see the scope of possible programs. Use this chapter to get your group thinking about the issues involved in establishing a successful recycling program, and adapt these suggestions according to your individual needs.

AT WORK

Organizing your office's recycling program can be a very rewarding experience. Offices are notorious wasters, particularly of paper, so every day you'll be able to see the amount of garbage you are diverting from our landfills and incinerators.

This section suggests points to consider when organizing a recycling program in your workplace. Every office requires an individual program based on its own specific situation. The availability of collectors for different recyclables, the amount of waste you generate, and the degree of support from your company are just a few of the factors that will shape your recycling program.

Keep in mind that your program's success will depend to a very large extent on the enthusiasm of your employees and their willingness to exert themselves for the cause. Try not to make it a chore. Emphasize the benefits of recycling—and then watch your waste decrease and your profits increase.

Initial Organization

The initial work you undertake in establishing an office recycling program is very important. A solid, organized foundation will make future stages fall into place much more easily.

SETTING IT UP

The wide variety of activities you must organize will take a certain amount of planning. Bringing together an enthusiastic group of people to help get things moving, as well as making an accurate assessment of your office's particular needs, are both vital.

Step 1. Set up a development team to handle all aspects of your program. Responsibilities may include initial investigations and analysis, acquisition of any necessary equipment or materials, liaison with collection contractors, education, quality control, and, perhaps most important, generating initial enthusiasm for the idea. It is a good idea to appoint or hire one person as a "recycling coordinator" to ensure coherence. Your group's first job might be to present a proposal to senior management to get approval for a recycling project. Use the following suggestions to help you with your proposal.

Step 2. Analyze your waste output. What does your waste stream consist of, and in what proportions? (For example: computer paper, general office paper, corrugated boxes, brown paper bags, aluminum, glass, and various grades of plastics, wood, and metals.) Some waste haulers and recycling companies offer relatively inexpensive "waste audits" to help you determine these things. In addition, they can offer advice on how to improve your recycling program by changing wasteful practices, for example, and purchasing recyclable or reusable items.

Step 3. Choose which materials you will recycle. To decide this, you will need to know which materials can be disposed of most easily in your area and which are the most profitable to recycle. The choice of which materials to recycle will depend on your company's priorities.

Step 4. If cost is a factor, analyze your current waste disposal costs versus the potential savings from lowered standard collection costs plus the potential profits from selling your recyclables. You'll also need to factor in the collection costs, if any, of the recyclables.

Step 5. Work within your current waste disposal structure whenever possible. This will help things run more smoothly, and the people who currently manage your disposal can provide you with useful information.

It is important here, if you work in a large office building, to understand your current disposal costs. Probably your building management pays a regular fee for the disposal of the whole building's waste. If this is the case, you can try to negotiate a discount on your portion of the waste disposal costs, as your recycling efforts are going to dramatically reduce your contribution to the building's waste. Likewise, if a recycler's cost to pick up from your building is a bit steep for you, see if your building's management will contribute to the cost with some of the money you're saving them by recycling.

Recycling waste can be a very profitable project. Hyatt Hotels, for example, earn $3 million per year in saved disposal costs and income from recycling a variety of materials throughout the hotel chain. But don't be dismayed if your program isn't profitable at first. Cost isn't the only reason to recycle. Even if you don't see immediate profits from your recycling efforts, there are plenty of other benefits. Instilling an environmental ethic in employees, lowering pollution, and conserving non-renewable natural resources are all valid reasons to recycle.

Step 6. Set goals for an initial period of perhaps four or six months. What percentage of your current waste stream can you eliminate? What are your target amounts of chosen materials to recycle each month?

CHOOSING A METHOD OF DISPOSAL

You need to get your recyclables from your office site to a place where they can be recycled into new products. You may choose to transport it yourselves, or, more likely, you'll make arrangements with a recycler, waste hauler, nonprofit program, scrap broker, salvage company, or your city's own recycling program to come and take it from you.

There are three general markets, with many variations, for your recyclables: end-users, brokers, and internal markets. You may choose to deal directly with one of these, or you can go through a group or program that deals with one of them. Your choice of partner may affect such things as the price you receive for your materials or the condition in which you must deliver them. See Chapter 2 for detailed descriptions of the roles of these buyers.

Step 1. Search out potential contractors in the area. Check out their past history. Learn what materials each one accepts, and find out their cost/payment schedules. Talk to other clients to learn how everything operates. You may find that you must arrange for collection of certain materials with one contractor and deal with another for further materials, or you may find one single source that can handle all the materials you have chosen to recycle.

Step 2. Determine what services your collector will provide. Does the company charge for transportation of the recyclables? Does it charge for providing bins and other containers? Will its schedules match those of your current waste disposal people, or will it be on separate days and at separate times? Will your collector give you a confidentiality agreement (to guarantee the security of any proprietary information)?

Establishment

Once the groundwork has been laid, you are ready to put your plans to work. This involves putting collection bins in place and then making sure all employees are educated and ready to participate.

SETUP

It is important to study the layout of your workplace before deciding where to put collection bins. Receptacles must be in convenient places to encourage full participation in your program.

Step 1. Determine where to place the collection bins for your recyclables. Containers should be visible and conveniently located. Look at where your garbage is thrown away currently. Glass and aluminum may be mainly cafeteria waste, for example, so you should consider setting up collection bins for these materials in the cafeteria next to the garbage cans. Computer paper may be centralized in one printer room or it may be dispersed throughout your office. Can you get by with one container in the printer area, or should each desk, or area, have its own paper recycling bin? Answers to such questions will help you determine the best places to situate recyclable collection bins. Remember that your success rate will be higher if people don't have to go out of their way to recycle.

In a large office, it will probably work best if every desk has its own recycling bin next to its regular waste bin. When the recycling bin gets full, the employee can carry it to a central location to dump it.

Step 2. Understand your collector's requirements. Does he require that you centralize the materials before he'll collect them? If so, how will this be accomplished? You may need to designate a space for central collection. Will your regular garbage collectors add this new collection responsibility to their workload, or will you need new personnel?

Step 3. Encourage employee participation. How will you initially get employees to participate? (See the following section on education.) Will participation be voluntary or mandatory? If mandatory, how do you intend to enforce it? If voluntary, how do you plan to encourage participation? Either way, it's essential that your program is seen to be endorsed—and actively encouraged—by senior management.

You may find that, despite your careful planning and detailed explanations of how beneficial recycling is, people still grumble about the burden that has been placed on them. If this is the case, just tell them about Japanese recycling practices: in some parts of Japan (a nation with a big waste disposal problem due to its size) office workers are expected to separate recyclables into seventeen different types!

INITIAL EDUCATION

For employees to take part in your recycling program, they have to understand what is expected of them. A few simple steps can assure their thorough understanding and guarantee higher participation rates.

Step 1. Distribute information sheets to all employees. It's a good idea to introduce people to the idea of recycling before they actually have to begin doing it. From the moment you make the decision to establish an office-wide or building-wide recycling program until the day you begin, start preparing employees for the changes they'll be expected to make. You might consider beginning with relatively general information sheets telling everyone about the overall project. Then slowly get more specific and eventually explain the project's exact requirements. Some information on the actual mechanics of recycling your target materials might be useful also. People will more readily accept a concept if they fully understand it. Stress the benefits of recycling early on.

Step 2. Arrange classes. Depending on the size of your organization, this may or may not be practical. If you are a relatively small company, consider getting everyone together for a couple of hours one day. If your company is very large, this may be more difficult unless your firm already has a schedule of training classes organized. If you do have regular training sessions, a section on your new recycling program might fit in well (and be a welcome reprieve from regular work).

Step 3. Use newsletters. If your company already has a newsletter, get in touch with the editor and make sure your new recycling program gets a lot of coverage. Take the time to explain what you are doing and you can be assured of a place for your program in the newsletter. If you don't have a newsletter, you may want to consider establishing one. It could be a useful way of educating people about recycling, and then of course it could eventually include other corporate issues.

Step 4. Make posters. A few bright posters strategically placed around your building will serve as a friendly reminder to recycle. Particularly important will be signs directly over your recycling containers clearly stating what can and cannot be recycled—especially important in the case of plastics, for example, because there are so many types and your collector will only want specific resins, such as the most common PET and HDPE plastics. Get instructions from your contractor and pass them on to your employees. He may also be able to provide you with posters and other educational materials.

Step 5. Plan speaking engagements. Offer to speak at a company or departmental meeting—anywhere that will get the attention of the right people and help spread the word.

Continuation and Development

If people aren't kept apprised as to how their efforts are having an impact, they may lose interest and become discouraged. We all like to know that what we do is useful, and if we can see concrete results it makes it more pleasant to continue working toward our goals.

PROGRESS REPORTS

Progress reports will provide the necessary encouragement for participants. There are several ways to make sure everyone is aware of how your program is faring; you might try some of these.

Step 1. Use visual signs. There are many ways to keep everyone aware of the progress you're making. The familiar thermometer symbol—the mercury rises as the goal is approached—is one example. If your company initially sets six-month targets, you can have a thermometer for this period. Start a new one each time you raise your targets or begin a new period. Instead of a thermometer, you might choose a symbol more closely associated with your project, such as a garbage can. Show how it fills up as you reach your targets. Better yet, use a mini-landfill and show how it *empties* as you reach your targets. The more innovative your ideas, the more you'll keep people's interest and the more successful your project will be.

Step 2. Get more coverage in your newsletter. As the weeks and months go by, don't forget the newsletter as a communication medium. Keep in touch with the editor and make sure your project still makes the news. If you're reaching your targets, make sure everyone knows about it. And if you're not, everyone should know that as well (and why).

Step 3. Get a mention in your annual report. If your company has taken on recycling in a big way, chances are the financial news may be worthy of the annual report. You may have some very good news to report about the cost savings from your recycling program. Even if the numbers aren't taking over the balance sheet yet, establishing a project like this should still be big news. Remind the more cynical individuals that even if they don't care about recycling, society does: a company that is recycling its waste looks good.

Step 4. Use the posters you already have. With a system of bright "news flash" sheets or something similar, you can post news items or small progress reports next to the posters that people already associate with the recycling project.

QUALITY CONTROL

Someone will have the responsibility of assessing your program's effectiveness. Are you reaching—or even surpassing—your targets? Are you having trouble with a particular material or with a particular department? Are things going smoothly with your collection contractor? Is there a need to reassess any key factors in your program?

The person monitoring these issues should report any problems to the committee. No program runs perfectly at first; you'll need to make adjustments as you go. Learn from your mistakes and improve your program.

INCENTIVES

Whether you make recycling voluntary or mandatory, you may want to include some kind of incentive system to encourage employees to participate. Offices are more often than not competitive places, so why not use this characteristic to your advantage? How far you are able to take the incentive idea will depend on the overall orientation of your company and the budget you wish to devote to it. You may also want to consider whether competition will be on an individual or departmental level.

The possibilities are endless, but clearly the prizes must be decided by those who are going to pay for them. A few suggestions: lunch for two (or the department); entitlement to leave work early; theater or movie tickets; free vacations.

If your organization gets to keep the profits of your recycling efforts, another incentive is to let the employees decide how to spend the money. They may choose to have parties or formal dinners, or to donate the earnings to local charities.

CONTINUING EDUCATION

Whether you do it through refresher courses or simply by sending out flyers with updated or repeat information, you must remind participants of what is expected of them. After all, they are there primarily to do their job and cannot be expected to make your recycling project their number one priority. Therefore it will be your responsibility to occasionally, and gently, remind them what to do.

FEEDBACK

As you cannot be sure your message is being received if you don't hear from the other side, consider ways to let the employees ask questions and make comments about your program. This could be done through newsletters, at meetings or classes, or through suggestion boxes, whichever you feel is the most effective method of communication.

Ultimately, the goal of this exercise is to help you improve your recycling project. People may be confused about certain aspects of the program or they may have suggestions about improving it. Either way, at best you will learn a few things and at the very worst you keep people talking and thinking about recycling.

In addition to these suggestions, there are a few final points to consider: buy products made from recycled materials. It's not enough simply to recycle; you must help create and maintain markets for recycled products. This means buying products made from recycled materials. In an office, your paper supplies will be the easiest place to start. Call your local suppliers, check the yellow pages, and call the businesses listed in this book. Your location in the country will dictate how easily recycled paper can be obtained. But even if it isn't produced locally, there is no excuse not to buy it elsewhere and have it shipped to you.

Try to get the highest percentage of recycled materials in your paper as possible. Paper from 100 percent recycled materials is perfect, but if you can't get that, shoot for the highest percentage you can. Just 10 or 20 percent is really not good enough. And don't let anyone tell you that recycled paper can't be as good quality as paper from virgin materials—it just isn't true. Ask the supplier whether the percentage quoted is pre-consumer or post-consumer waste. Pre-consumer waste doesn't really count. Also try to buy recycled *and* unbleached paper. (See Chapter 3 for more details on post-consumer waste and paper bleaching.)

Discourage the use of colored paper such as yellow legal pads or pink telephone message pads. Not only is white paper easier to recycle but the colored paper obviously has inks in it—and when these are recycled the inks have to go somewhere. We all need to get away from the feeling that bleached white paper is the only proper paper. Unbleached, recycled paper is usually a golden brown or light gray color and is perfectly acceptable for any business use; it's just a question of getting used to it.

When buying recycled paper products, don't forget file folders, envelopes, toilet paper, and paper towels (if you need them). These products are becoming relatively easy to find now, both in our local stores and through wholesale distributors.

Once you have found your sources of recycled paper, begin looking around the office at other items that might have alternatives made out of recycled materials. A little research might be required, but what are research departments for? Furniture, cafeteria trays, glasses, and carpeting are just a few suggestions. The rest of this book will give you other ideas.

In addition to teaching workers to recycle their waste, it's important to emphasize cutting down on the waste they create in the first place. This topic is discussed in detail in the previous chapter, but here are a few ideas suitable for the workplace: use two-sided photocopies; pass one memo around the office and have everyone initial it rather than making one copy per person; keep used paper for scratch pads; and use proper coffee mugs instead of paper or polystyrene cups.

Finally, know that what you are doing is really helping cut down our solid waste disposal problems. Commercial garbage is thought to be the largest portion (about 50 percent) of a city's waste stream in places with large commercial areas. The irony is that a very high percentage of this commercial waste is recyclable. It is imperative that businesses, along with schools, government buildings, and other institutions, make recycling a part of their daily routine.

IN YOUR COMMUNITY

Although the initiative to develop a recycling program should come from the individuals in a community, you'll find the task much easier if you have significant cooperation from your city or county officials. This is not said to be discouraging—many communities all across the United States have developed highly successful recycling programs on their own. Local government support does make life easier, however.

Community programs vary tremendously in scope, but you can learn a lot from studying others who have gone before you. In fact, there is so much variety that you can easily find a community whose recycling needs are similar to yours and which has struggled through the initial stages your community will also go through.

If possible, your recycling program should be implemented as part of your community's overall waste management plan. Programs added haphazardly or outside a developed waste management structure are less likely to succeed. There's one way to ensure good integration between your program and the county: when you have the budget, hire a full-time recycling coordinator. Having such a person at the local and state levels is ideal.

To find out how other communities have developed their recycling programs, contact one near your town and talk to the recycling coordinator. If you don't know of any nearby communities currently recycling, contact your state recycling coordinator, who will be able to refer you to someone closer to home. Chapter 7 describes several communities with successful recycling programs. In developing your recycling program, a lot depends on the size and location of your community and the local market for recyclable materials. In this aspect, particularly, neighboring communities will be able to share their own research with you.

Several important factors will influence the success of your community recycling program. Good planning and organization are essential, for example. Run the program like a business and focus on efficiency and productivity, even though it may be a volunteer organization. Publicity is another key: get as many people as possible informed and involved. The more who know about it and encourage the program, the more successful you will be.

Initial Organization

As with office recycling programs, the early work you do requires careful attention. But because a community is clearly much more difficult to organize than an office, your first steps will be even more important in this larger arena.

DEVELOPMENT TEAM

You will need to have one key person who is in charge of organizing your program. This person can work alone or as part of a development team. Having a group makes everything much easier and helps the program develop faster. The key here, however, is to have one very dedicated person who can serve as energizer, organizer, and supervisor.

Working in conjunction with established community groups is a good idea. Charitable organizations, service groups, social groups—all are possible candidates. The benefit of working with these groups is that they will already have established connections with the community, lines of communication, and methods of publicity. They can also provide a source of labor and materials and possibly even an office to use as your headquarters. Becoming involved with established community groups also ensures a supply of workers over a period of time. Often programs suffer when initially enthusiastic volunteers lose interest.

Lines of communication with your local government are essential if you plan to work closely with them. Administrators and those involved in the city's waste management services are key contacts. You'll need to understand how the city waste disposal service functions, and you'll need these officials' help and support. It is best to solicit the help of local government at the very beginning. Only if you're unable to gain their support or if special circumstances apply should you consider designing an independent program.

ANALYSIS

Help from city officials in preparing an initial analysis for the project will be most beneficial. Most local governments will have records or at least good estimates of the kind of information you'll be gathering during this phase.

The first thing to do is conduct a waste analysis of the community. What does your garbage consist of? This is the key to understanding the kinds and amount of recyclables you may recover. A variety of factors may come into play here. If you are located near a plastics factory, for example, it stands to reason that you'll have a higher than average proportion of plastics in your waste stream—assuming that plastic packaging holds a higher than usual market share in the immediate area because of the factory.

Next comes market analysis. What recyclables would you be able to sell if you collect them? Again, the presence of a local plastics factory implies that you may have a very good market for collected plastics. (The factory is selling plastics, so it also needs to buy the raw materials back to make more.) Talk with recycling contractors, city officials (who may have looked into this issue before), and neighboring communities with established recycling programs. You need to know what materials are currently being accepted in your area and what price you can get for them.

Costs must be considered also. Clearly, your city government will be more receptive to the idea of a recycling program if you can show potential savings or even earnings. Look at traditional collection and disposal costs versus those for collecting recyclables. What will new equipment, if required, cost? Don't forget to add in the potential earnings from selling the collected recyclables. A recycling program may not start out being profitable, but point out to city officials the other benefits such as additional landfill space, more jobs, and reduced pollution.

Once you have a good understanding of these issues, establish goals for your program. What recyclables will you collect? How much do you hope to collect? What participation rate do you expect? Are you interested in instilling an environmental ethic in your community or in saving precious landfill space?

Do you expect the program to be a profit maker, or will you set up a nonprofit organization? This financial consideration is crucial. Both systems have their benefits and drawbacks, and the one you choose will depend on your overall goals. Nonprofit organizations have tax-deductible fundraising abilities but are more closely watched by government than regular businesses. If, on the other hand, you decide to try to make a profit you may be limited to only recycling materials for which there is a healthy market at any given time.

METHOD OF DISPOSAL

Curbside collection, drop-off centers, and pay-back centers are all options for a community recycling program. What you can do will depend on the local contractors and the resources you can commit to the project.

Talk to local contractors and haulers. Check into their history and talk to some of their clients to find out how reliable they are. Find out what they charge for their services and what their requirements are. How must the recyclables be prepared for pickup to avoid contamination? What recyclables do they accept? Will collection be cheaper if you separate glass colors first? What services do they provide? Do you provide containers or do they?

Establishment

Once you have concluded the initial research, you're ready to begin putting your program together. There are financial, technical, and educational issues that need attention.

SETUP

Prepare for the financial aspects of the program. Open a bank account, establish bookkeeping and accounting methods, and assign the relevant responsibilities. Depending on the city's resources, you may need to hire labor. Drivers, site attendants, and quality control personnel may have to be found.

You need to know how all aspects of the program are going to function. A good understanding of the local government's workings is essential now, as is knowledge of the contractor's requirements and schedules. Get help from your local government's solid waste office.

By now you will have selected a method of collection. Depending on your community's demographics, this may be curbside collection, drop-off centers, or even block collection. If you use drop-off facilities, you must decide if you will pay residents for the collected recyclables or if they will be donating to the city fund.

You must also arrange for the equipment needed for each of these programs—ranging from collection and storage containers to waste processing units like balers and crushers. The size of your program and the materials being recycled will determine your equipment needs. For example, many rural communities are beginning to used shredded newspaper for livestock bedding. In such a case, a shredder and baler may be wise purchases.

You may need to select a site as a transfer station where curbside collections can be taken if your contractor does not haul the recyclables directly to a reprocessing center. You may also need sites for drop-off centers. Convenience is the key. Choose locations near a high volume of traffic and make sure they are well marked and easy to find and access. Security is another issue. Will the sites be staffed or secured to prevent scavengers? Remember: recyclables are valuable commodities today.

PUBLIC EDUCATION

Informing and educating the public about your program and the benefits of recycling is absolutely essential: community involvement is the key to a successful program. There are a number of ways to achieve this. Remember that recycling may be a new idea to many residents and that you will need to explain it clearly and perhaps many times to obtain any kind of success rate. For this part of the process, it's helpful to have someone with public relations experience on your development team.

Free spots on radio and television are an excellent way to spread the word. Certainly the project should merit an article or two in the local newspapers. At this stage your connections with community groups can come in handy, too. Try to arrange speaking engagements with as many groups, service organizations, neighborhood associations, schools, and even churches as you can. These groups have good communication infrastructures you can use to your advantage.

Depending on your budget, you may also want to send out leaflets and flyers. If you are working with the city, you may be able to have notices enclosed with residents' utility or waste disposal bills. Posters and notices in public places will also help. Likewise, door-to-door contact by recycling program representatives can be very effective. If you are beginning your program any time near an election, see if you can get local politicians to take up your program as part of their platform.

Be sure to include certain basic information in any publicity you use. Explain the benefits of recycling—people need to know why they should bother. Clearly state what materials you will accept, how to prepare them, and where to take them (curbside or drop-off). This information should be sent out well before your recycling program begins, once again just before its inception, and then several times as reminders once the program is running.

Continuation and Development

Particularly in the beginning, you'll need to keep a close eye on the workings of your recycling efforts to make sure everything is being done properly. As it is a new procedure for everyone concerned, there are bound to be errors at first.

It's a good idea to have observers from the development committee who can check on procedures. For example, in a curbside program someone can drive around with the collection truck to ensure that only the proper materials are being collected and that they are not contaminated. Likewise, someone can work at a drop-off center to make sure residents are only leaving proper recyclables.

This quality control is very important. The price you get for your recyclable materials will depend on how well you separate them and how little contamination you are able to ensure. These are key factors in the establishment of a long-term, successful program.

Let the public know how things are going. First of all, a reminder now and then will keep them recycling. Also, let them know how successful your program is and what benefits you have reaped. How much money has been earned? Is there noticeably less litter since the recycling began? How much are you diverting from landfills or incinerators?

Finally, try to gain feedback from residents. A drop-off center may be a good location for a suggestion box. You can also encourage the use of the "letters to the editor" section in the local paper as a forum for discussion of your project.

All these suggestions will give you a basis on which to build your community's recycling program. With preparation and organization and enthusiasm from organizers and participants alike, you should be well on your way to a successful program.

AT SCHOOL

Recycling at school is not only another way to divert valuable materials from landfills or incinerators: it's an excellent way to educate students about environmental issues while raising money for important school activities. Hundreds of schools around the country have active and successful recycling programs, and yours could be one more.

Initial Organization

Again, getting the basics right at the beginning will make life easier as your project develops. The establishment of an enthusiastic steering committee and a careful analysis of your recycling potential are important tasks, keeping in mind issues particular to a school environment.

DEVELOPMENT COMMITTEE

As with any new project, you'll need a group of people to organize all the details, with one person (or student/teacher pair) assigned overall responsibility. A mixture of students and teachers, and perhaps administrators, on this committee will ensure that all voices are heard when making decisions.

If you have no administrators on your committee, try to get at least one teacher with good connections to the administration. Just as in a community where you need to work with the local government, at school you'll need to work with the administration and school board to get your proposal approved and operational.

The development committee's responsibilities will be many, so it's a good idea to assign duties to individuals or to student/teacher pairs. You'll need to determine what recyclables are best to collect, the most efficient and inexpensive way of collecting them, how you will structure your program, and how you will encourage participation. You will also need to get approval from both the principal and the school board, so prepare a strategy for approaching them, too.

Important: your county and state may have specific regulations concerning school activities that you need to investigate. Such matters as fire and safety regulations and proper insurance for off-site contractors must be determined before you begin a recycling program.

ANALYSIS

One of the first things to determine is what recyclables are readily available for your program. Will you just collect what's on campus? Or will you encourage students, families, and community members to bring their recyclables to school? The answers to questions such as these will help you decide what materials to collect.

If you're just going to collect materials that are on campus, for example, beverage containers and disposable food trays (if you can find a dealer to accept them) are likely to form a large part of your program. Newspapers will probably not (other than those coming from classes that have subscriptions as part of their curriculum). If you decide to collect materials from the community as well, the number of recyclables available to you will be that much greater. Accepting recyclables from the community will have important implications for your collection methods, however, as we shall see.

Another factor in determining what you'll recycle is the practicality of recycling certain materials. If you have lots of aluminum food trays, for example, but cannot find a dealer locally to accept them, there's not much point in collecting the trays. You need to talk to local dealers to learn what they'll accept and, if you hope to earn money from your program, how much they'll pay for each material. Either your local government or other schools with established programs can point you in the right direction for this information.

Additionally, you may want to discuss the goals of your program. Are you trying to raise money to help with extracurricular activities? If so, how much? Are you just happy to cut down on garbage, or are you doing this as an exercise in environmental education for the students? The answers to these questions may help shape the overall focus of your program.

METHODS OF COLLECTION AND DISPOSAL

You will need to investigate the possibilities of collection and disposal available in your community. Find out which contractors have been doing it for a while and if they have a good reputation. Will they take all the materials you've decided to collect? What services will they provide (containers, delivery schedules, payment options)?

The dealer or collector you eventually choose will tell you how to prepare the recyclables for collection. Cans may have to be rinsed or the caps removed from PET bottles, for example.

Finally, you'll need to work with your contractor or dealer to determine methods of collection. Will the contractor pick up from various sites around your campus? Or will you need to collect the materials periodically and centralize them? Is there a charge for collecting?

Establishment

Having conducted your initial investigations, you should have a good basis for the actual establishment of your program. Now you must find the most convenient locations and hours for collection and educate the faculty, staff, and students about the program.

SETUP

The equipment and site for your program will have to be chosen. If providing containers is your responsibility, you may need to raise some money first to purchase them. The site (or sites) for collecting and storing the recyclables will depend on several factors. Above all, how much space do you have available for the project? You'll need a clean, secure place to store materials.

Will you have one central room for all recyclables or will you have containers where the various recyclable materials are likely to be thrown away? If a recycling bin for aluminum cans is left next to the soft-drink vending machine, for example, you'll have a higher collection rate than if the students and faculty have to take the cans somewhere else. Likewise, putting recycling containers near wastebaskets in classrooms will raise your paper collection rate.

If you have a room that serves as a drop-off center, will it be staffed? Organizing student and teacher volunteers to staff the room will be very important in this case. You must determine how much free time—after school and studies and extracurricular activities—the students actually have to devote to your program. Teachers will have similar constraints on their time.

If you accept materials from parents and the community, you may want to have containers at the entrance to the school where they're most convenient for the general public. If you're only going to accept materials during certain hours, it makes sense to do this when students are being brought to school and picked up.

At some point before beginning your program, you'll need to have official approval from your principal, the school board, or both. When you've worked out all the details, write a short proposal outlining your planned activities, the facilities you will use, and what you hope to achieve from the recycling program. The proposal should include mention of the recycling dealer you will be using, your target recyclables (and why you chose them), the collection schedule, and any other information that may be important. Try to speak to the principal or a board member first to learn what kind of information and assurances they will want from you.

Once you've received approval, you can get the actual mechanics of setting up your recycling program under way. Put the containers around the school. Organize your central collection area and establish staffing hours (if required). You may want to consider some brief training for those who will be staffing the drop-off center.

At this point you'll also want to build up enthusiasm for your program. Think about how you'll encourage participation and educate everyone about what materials will be accepted and how they must be prepared.

EDUCATION/AWARENESS

To benefit from maximum participation, you'll want all the various groups who make up your school's community to participate. Each of these groups—students, faculty, families, the community—will have to be targeted separately. This will involve several different awareness campaigns. The key things to tell everyone are why you want to have a recycling program, what materials you will accept, how to prepare them, and the hours of operation at your drop-off center.

Students can be informed about the program through their classes, through flyers and posters around the school, and in assemblies. Sending a flyer to teachers and asking them to read it and discuss the program with students is one method. Brightly colored, informative posters on the walls around the school will help spread the word. If you don't have a general assembly planned near the debut of your program, perhaps you can organize one specifically to tell everyone about the recycling campaign.

Present your recycling plan to teachers at one of their regularly scheduled meetings. As the plan may affect their classrooms and involve changing some of their habits, you'll need their strong support for the program. Stress the benefits. Explain the changes they'll need to make (containers for recycling and so forth), and try to sign up any really enthusiastic members for duty at the drop-off center.

You can inform parents and families by sending flyers home with students. You may want to do this several times to ensure that they reach their destination. If possible, provide the phone number of a faculty member or the school office so that parents can call with any questions.

To inform the community, try to get as much local publicity as possible. The local newspaper and local television stations may be interested in your program. Prepare simple press releases for anyone who may be interested. Send these to local community groups, businesses, and churches and ask them to tell their members and post the information.

Continuation and Development

To ensure continued participation, you must keep the students—the backbone of your program—informed as to how you are doing. If you're raising money for a specific project, let everyone know how close you are coming to the target amount.

PROGRESS REPORTS

Use a student newsletter, notices through teachers, or posters to keep everyone informed about your progress. You may also need to remind everyone occasionally about the correct materials to bring or how to prepare them properly.

One of the original committee members should have responsibility for quality control. After the initial rush of enthusiasm, quality may drop off somewhat, so you'll need to ensure that your recycling collector is still receiving high-quality materials in the form he requested. If not, you may find yourself earning much less money for your recyclables.

To ensure maximum participation, be reliable. Once you have set hours for your drop-off center, stick to them and make sure the center is staffed properly at all times. Participation will drop off sharply if people cannot rely on your schedule.

For reasons of both health and appearance, you'll need to keep the containers and the collection area clean and attractive. Regular cleaning must be a part of your schedule. If the recycling agent changes your containers for you, you won't have to worry about those, but the general collection site must be tidy and hygienic.

Once your program is up and running smoothly, you may be able to take advantage of everyone's awareness and participation to teach about other environmental issues. You have the perfect forum and, if all goes well, eager participants. The success of your program will depend on the enthusiasm you can create among the school's community. By running an organized program and keeping everyone informed of your successes, this should be easy.

IN YOUR HOME

How you decide to set up your home for recycling depends on a number of factors. The amount of free space you have, the kinds of recyclable materials your household uses, and what is practically recyclable in your area are all important considerations.

With just a little organization, you can begin recycling a large amount of your waste stream and realize real benefits. You can achieve lower garbage pickup costs, a little extra income, and a great sense of accomplishment from knowing you are doing something that helps both your community and your environment.

Analysis

The first step is to look at the kinds of recyclable materials you use. Determine how much recyclable waste your household produces on a weekly (or monthly) basis. This is important primarily for the matter of storage: how much space you require depends on how much of the various recyclable materials you use. Get an idea of the variety of materials, too. If you drink a lot of soda, for example, you'll probably have a lot of aluminum cans or PET containers to recycle.

Materials to Recycle

To determine what you can recycle, you need to find out what materials are accepted locally. If you have curbside collection, the county or the private firm in charge will be able to tell you precisely what is accepted in their program. Ask specific questions: what *types* of plastics or metals, for example, or what *grades* of paper.

If you do not have curbside collection, your investigation will be a little bit more involved. Try looking in the yellow pages for recyclers. You can also ask any charitable organizations running recycling programs and look for drop-off or buy-back centers in supermarket parking lots.

Methods of Disposal

Curbside collection is certainly the most convenient disposal method. If your community has such a program, you'll probably have been supplied with bags or bins in which to put your recyclables. All you have to remember is to put the materials out for collection on the proper day.

If you don't have curbside pickup, you will need to take the recyclables to a drop-off center of some kind. Find out if they require you to separate the materials, clean them, or prepare them a special way. Is there one drop-off center near you that takes everything, or will you have to go to two or three places to dispose of all your recyclables?

Start Recycling!

Look around your house to find the most suitable place to store your recyclables. The space you choose doesn't need to be large but it should be clean, dry, and convenient. Your garage or a closet near the kitchen are possible places.

If space is limited, arrange your various containers so that they stack one on top of the other. Containers should be relatively sturdy so they'll last some time—cardboard boxes are useful. If you have curbside collection, you'll probably be given sturdy plastic bins that are marked for the various recyclables you can donate. These are usually designed to stack for easy storage.

Decide on the most convenient place for the recycling bins. Keeping the bins near your other garbage simplifies matters by eliminating the need for many trips to different parts of the house to dispose of garbage. As with an office recycling system, it will only be successful if it is convenient.

Whether your recycling bins are provided for you or you use your own, try to mark them clearly for recycling. This serves as a constant reminder to the household of what you're trying to do. It will also help house guests who might confuse the bins with garbage cans.

Decide how often you'll take a trip to the drop-off center. If you rinse your containers, you should not have a problem with smell or with attracting scavengers no matter how long you wait between trips to the drop-off center. If you don't rinse them well or live in a rural area with raccoons and other animals who may be interested in sticky containers, you'll want to take the recyclables more often.

Depending on your household's size and structure, you may want to have one person designated as an informal recycling coordinator. It isn't a bad idea to have one person make sure everything runs smoothly: reminding everyone to recycle, seeing that the curbside bins are put out on appropriate days, or seeing that your storage area doesn't start getting messy.

Establish Goals

While establishing goals may sound unimportant, it can really help. If no one in your household understands *why* you are going to the trouble to separate, rinse, and deliver recyclables, everyone will tire of it very quickly.

You don't need particularly grandiose reasons, and it doesn't matter what they are. Most people recycle because of their concern for the environment, to earn a little extra money, to make their garbage fit into just one can each week, or just because it seems a natural thing to do. Take a minute to think through your own motivations—if for no other reason than because the kids will inevitably ask, "Why?"

If your goal is to earn extra money, remember to keep track of how much you collect from each trip to the pay-back center. In time, you will see the amount increase. If you are trying to squeeze your garbage into one can or teach your children about waste reduction, make a point of showing them how much space your recyclables would take up in the garbage can. You can also take advantage of your household project to teach your children why recycling benefits the planet.

7 What's Being Done?

While the last two chapters have focused on what an individual can do, a lot is happening on a larger scale across the country too. Increasing demands on our solid waste disposal systems have made government officials and industry members alike stand up and take notice. The result is a nationwide trend toward recycling as a viable option to help solve our waste problems. This trend can be seen both in increased legislation and in the voluntary efforts of industry and other elements of society to focus on developing recycling programs.

LEGISLATION

The resulting laws and programs are wide-ranging. From mandatory recycling programs to specific product bans, all kinds of programs are being tried, all toward the same ultimate goal: to drastically reduce our waste. More than 100 individual laws on recycling were passed nationwide in 1989 alone. These range from general, statewide regulations to very specific ones.

Federal Legislation

It is worth noting at the outset that there is very little legislation at the federal level which deals directly with recycling; most of it has been assigned to the state level. And almost all of that federal legislation focuses on waste reduction or minimization, of which recycling is just an optional method. The EPA, although involved to a certain extent, does not contribute as much to the development of recycling as many think it should. The most specific treatment of recycling has come about in the last several years through the publication of federal procurement guidelines.

THE EPA

The Environmental Protection Agency was created in 1970, absorbing several existing agencies, to coordinate government action and research on environmental issues. The agency's responsibilities are wide-ranging, and recycling plays a relatively minor part in its overall agenda. The EPA does have an important role, however, in gathering statistics regarding solid waste management throughout the nation. Moreover, it has started gathering information on recycling over the past several years.

Despite an overall focus on other issues, the EPA has recently been involved with the development of several projects relating to recycling. The first of these is a nationwide database listing surplus materials from one company that may be suitable as raw materials for another. The idea is to put industrial waste to good use. This Pollution Information Exchange System (PIES) database, established in 1990, is part of the Pollution Prevention Information Clearinghouse of the EPA. Anyone can access the number with a computer and modem and see what materials are currently available for sale.

A second project is called the EPA's Agenda for Action. It is here that the EPA set its goal for the nation to reduce and recycle 25 percent of our waste by 1992. To achieve this goal, several projects have been undertaken: market development studies for aluminum, glass, paper, tires, and compost; educational and outreach media; grants to various organizations to fund research into source reduction opportunities; and the establishment of the Recycling Advisory Council. This council, organized by the National Recycling Coalition, has the mandate of exploring recycling and market issues.

Finally, the EPA has been developing government procurement guidelines for the purchase of recycled materials. These guidelines cover a variety of materials from paper products to building materials.

Any discussion of the EPA's role is bound to be controversial. Regarding its efforts toward recycling, it has often been claimed that it doesn't do nearly enough. While the projects cited here do show some concern, many would prefer to see the EPA take a much stronger role in leading the nation's efforts to develop recycling.

THE RESOURCE CONSERVATION AND RECOVERY ACT OF 1976 (RCRA)

The most important legislation in terms of solid waste management today is the Resource Conservation and Recovery Act, usually referred to as RCRA, which was passed by Congress in 1976. RCRA is really an amendment of the first national solid waste act, the Solid Waste Disposal Act of 1965, which established minimum federal guidelines for waste disposal. This act was then amended in 1970 by the Resource Recovery Act and then again in 1976 by RCRA. RCRA itself has been amended several times since its inception; the most important additions are the Hazardous and Solid Waste Amendments of 1984. Although this act and its subsequent amendments focus directly on the regulation of solid and particularly hazardous waste management, it mentions recycling as an option for waste minimization. (RCRA's regulations regarding hazardous waste will not be discussed here.)

In particular, two aspects of RCRA deserve mention. The first is a division of the bill known as Subtitle D. Subtitle D encourages the individual states to develop comprehensive solid waste management plans. A state plan should include, among other elements, a strategy for encouraging resource recovery and conservation activities. RCRA directed the EPA to provide technical and financial assistance to the states for these plans, but the funding lasted only a few years. The EPA says that Subtitle D wanted states to be autonomous, preferring to leave to the states the impetus for waste minimization and recycling since each state knows its own needs and situation.

The second important aspect of RCRA was that it directed the EPA to produce federal procurement guidelines for government agencies and contractors to buy materials and products with a recycled content. Their purpose was to develop markets for recycled materials. To date, five procurement guidelines have been issued. These cover paper and paper products, retread tires, re-refined oil, building insulation, and fly ash.

The procurement policies set the minimum content of recycled materials to aim for when buying the specified products. RCRA named four criteria for establishing these minimum content standards: the intended end use of the item, availability, technical performance, and

price. For example, the EPA recommends minimum content standards for certain papers and paper products:
- Newsprint: 40 percent post-consumer recovered materials
- Toilet tissue: 20 percent post-consumer recovered materials
- Paper towels: 40 percent post-consumer recovered materials
- Paper napkins: 40 percent post-consumer recovered materials
- Corrugated boxes: 35 percent post-consumer recovered materials
- Note pads: 50 percent wastepaper
- Book papers: 50 percent wastepaper
- Envelopes: 50 percent wastepaper

The EPA also recommends minimum content standards for recovered materials in certain building insulation products: (percentages are by weight of the material in the insulating core only)
- Cellulose loose-fill and spray-on: 75 percent post-consumer recovered paper
- Perlite composite board: 23 percent post-consumer recovered paper
- Rock wool: 75 percent recovered material
- Plastic rigid foams:
- Foam-in-place: 5 percent recovered materials
- Glass fiber reinforced: 5 percent recovered materials

Regarding re-refined oil, the EPA recommends that procuring agencies set a minimum re-refined oil content standard for purchasing engine lubricating oils, hydraulic fluids, and gear oils at 24 percent of base stock. For retread tires, the guideline recommends that agencies obtain retreading services for their used tires and purchase retread tires. This does not apply to the purchase of new vehicles.

Procuring agencies—the entities to whom these guidelines are directed—are federal or state agencies or contractors with such agencies. The procurement guidelines apply to any purchase by one of these bodies of an item costing more than $10,000 or when the body bought $10,000 worth of the same or equivalent items during the preceding fiscal year. Implementation is usually expected to begin within one year from the guideline's date of publication.

Further procurement guidelines are in varying stages of development. This is the timetable at the end of 1991 according to the RCRA procurement hotline:

• Building construction products: draft guidelines (including specific guidelines for fiberboard, geotextiles, plastic pipe, and hydromulch) by the end of 1992

• Asphalt rubber: summary of the status of testing and current knowledge due by the end of 1991; further action unclear

• Paper: guideline revisions (including minimum-content standards for copy paper) by the end of summer 1992

• Fiberglass: revisions to building insulation guidelines being considered but no determination of a standard for fiberglass

RCRA is considered by many to have been a disappointment as far as recycling is concerned. Not only was recycling not specifically encouraged but many say it was actually discouraged for years because of the government's emphasis on incineration as a waste disposal option. Although RCRA directed the EPA in 1976 to publish guidelines for federal procurement of recycled materials, the first guideline did not appear until 1983. The remaining four came out in 1988 and later. As a result, the market for recyclable materials that should have begun to expand in the mid-1970s has only recently begun to develop. The limited number of materials addressed by these procurement guidelines is another source of disappointment to many. Finally, many people think the EPA guidelines are far too low. It has been suggested, for example, that the recycled content of paper or paper products should be targeted well above the 20 to 50 percent range currently recommended.

Although RCRA was originally scheduled for reauthorization in 1990, no such action was taken. Reauthorization bills were introduced in both houses in late 1991, and committees were scheduled to review these bills in early 1992. According to the RCRA procurement hotline, a vote on its reauthorization is not assured in 1992 because the Bush administration opposes the bill. However, environmental organizations are still working hard to lobby Congress for an improved, expanded, and effective national waste law with a focus on reducing waste in the first place and lessening our reliance on incineration and unsafe landfills.

State Legislation

To discuss all the recycling legislation enacted or being considered at the state level would require a book of its own. Because new legislation is being passed all the time, pending legislation will not be discussed here. Instead we will survey some of the recycling laws that have been enacted recently.

Legislation regarding recycling at the state level is not new. The first bottle bill was passed in Oregon in 1971. Comprehensive statewide legislation first appeared in 1986 in Rhode Island. Since then the scope and variety of state legislation have increased substantially.

Each state is having to take a close look at the issue of recycling and the result is a wide variety of recycling programs, some mandatory and some voluntary, nationwide. This section will look at three specific states—Florida, Washington, and New Jersey—to show what overall legislation may look like. Then we'll take a look at several other states' regulations.

FLORIDA

Florida has passed what is considered by many to be very bold recycling legislation. Mandatory separation from the waste stream of many recyclables and hazardous waste, public education, and reasonably high target rates are all part of the program. Industry, state agencies, and consumers are all affected. Thirty percent waste reduction and recycling by 1994 is the state's current goal.

Florida's law requires all counties to establish recycling programs (with the aid of state funds) and to enforce them once they're in place. The state treasurer has the right to cut off all state funds to any county that does not comply with the law.

Items such as newspaper, glass, aluminum cans, plastic bottles, and yard waste must be separated from the waste stream. Whole tires, lead-acid batteries, and used oil are banned from landfills. In addition, materials such as white goods and construction debris must be separated and recycled whenever possible.

Industry has been given an incentive to work toward waste reduction by the threat of an "advance disposal fee." A charge of one cent per container will be levied on glass, metal, or plastic containers if the re-cycling rate for these items has not reached 50 percent by October 1992. In October 1995, a standard container deposit system of five cents per container kicks in.

Florida has banned or limited the use of several materials. Since January 1990, plastic carry-out bags are required to be made of degradable plastic. Similarly, food packaging made from polystyrene foam or plastic-coated paper is banned unless it is degradable within one year. Research into degradable projects is being jointly funded by government and industry.

Under the new law, state agencies are required to separate materials for recycling. Various agencies will also have new responsibilities directed at the successful implementation of Florida's new laws. These responsibilities include maintaining a directory of recycling businesses, publishing standards for compost production and use, undertaking a study to identify packaging that is "unnecessary" and "nonrecyclable and nonbiodegradable," developing information on recovered materials markets and preparing a strategy for market development, initiating statewide waste reduction and recycling promotion and education campaigns, and offering technical and planning assistance to local governments in establishing recycling programs.

Toward the goal of developing the markets for recycled products further, the state is offering tax credits to businesses for the purchase and use of recycling equipment. Recycling education grants are also being offered to local governments. State agencies will promote recycled product use among business and industry in addition to testing the use of specific recycled products. These include compost, mixed plastics, and rubber asphalt. In fact, Florida has used recycled rubber asphalt on its roads for years and the state Department of Environmental Regulation estimates that Florida is one of the leading states with regard to the use of recycled rubber asphalt.

Florida has considered imposing a per-ton disposal fee on publishers and producers using nonrecycled newsprint. Currently, however, it is experiencing voluntary compliance by the states' newspaper publishers in their efforts to increase the amount of post-consumer newsprint in the state's newspapers.

Several steps have been taken to deal with difficult waste items such as tires, used oil, and lead-acid batteries. A comprehensive used oil collection program is being established statewide with the use of grants to counties to help them establish collection centers. The law also mandates the establishment of a scrap tire management program. To this end, a dollar-per-tire fee has been implemented to establish a waste tire fund to finance processing facilities and tire recycling research. Finally, battery retailers must now accept old lead-acid batteries for recycling.

WASHINGTON

Washington state's recycling bill, which came into effect in 1989, established a waste reduction goal of 50 percent by 1995. This is one of the most ambitious targets announced by any state legislature in the country, but when one considers that Washington was already reaching a recovery rate of 28 percent in 1989 it certainly does not seem unrealistic. It is worth noting that other states which have set targets of 50 percent are allowing up to five years longer to reach that goal.

Under Washington's new regulations, each county and city is required to have a comprehensive solid waste management plan (including recycling and composting). After the plans were approved, the municipalities had one year to begin source separation and collection programs. In general, counties feature curbside collection in urban areas, drop boxes and buy-back centers in rural areas, and yard-waste collection programs wherever feasible. To fund the programs, counties can add a disposal surcharge and there's also a 1 percent statewide tax on solid waste collection services.

All solid waste disposal sites are required to provide recycling opportunities to the public. Facilities must accept cans, bottles, paper, and any other material for which markets exist. To foster market development, the recycling law mandated the formation of a recycling markets committee responsible for recommending new markets. Among the materials being studied for new applications are mixed wastepaper, scrap tires, yard debris, and plastics.

Washington also plans to give industry and the public incentives to recycle by imposing advance disposal fees on many products in order to help in the cost of administering litter control. Products affected will probably include food (for human or pet consumption), beverage containers, newspapers, magazines, glass containers, metal containers, and plastic or fiber containers made of synthetic material. A portion of the funds raised from these fees is to be used for public education and awareness programs to foster private local recycling efforts. Other features of the law: state and local governments must educate residents about the need for waste reduction and recycling; state agencies must provide employees with the opportunity to recycle and must increase their use of recycled paper; schools must implement recycling programs.

NEW JERSEY

New Jersey is one of our nation's most highly urbanized and most densely populated states. Its approximately 8 million residents live in an area of 7,836 square miles. In recent years these factors have contributed to the state's serious problems with air pollution and toxic wastes. New Jersey has also had a problem with waste disposal, having to dump over 50 percent of its waste in neighboring states and paying a high per-ton cost to do so.

New Jersey is also one of the first states to implement a statewide, mandatory recycling law, which went into effect in 1987. The state's initial goal, by law, was to recycle 25 percent of its solid waste by 1992, but early indications have shown it will easily reach and exceed this goal. In fact, a Solid Waste Task Force in 1990 even recommended upping the goal to 60 percent.

All of New Jersey's twenty-one counties have mandatory programs in place. No fewer than 500 municipalities have curbside recycling programs, while the rest use some sort of drop-off program. Newsprint recycling from the residential sector and corrugated and office paper recycling from the industrial sector are required statewide. Leaves have been banned from state landfills since 1988. Over 200 municipalities provide used motor oil collection sites. Some 277 municipalities are collecting plastics for recycling.

Financial considerations play an important role in New Jersey's recycling scheme. One program has loaned over $10 million since 1985 to recycling businesses in the state. Tax credits of up to 50 percent are also available to companies who purchase recycling equipment.

Market research is under way to look at materials such as dry cell batteries, used tires, glass, and newsprint. The Department of Transport is looking at crumb rubber and crushed glass for use in asphalt, and the Department of Corrections is using newsprint as animal bedding at three prison farms.

It appears that New Jersey will have no trouble meeting its initial recycling goal of 25 percent. In fact, the state looks well on its way to having one of the highest recycling rates of any state nationwide.

CALIFORNIA

California's most recent—and most important—measure in a string of recycling laws, signed in October 1989, is AB 939. Under this new law, cities and counties had to turn in source reduction and recycling plans by June 1991 with the threat of stiff fines for those who didn't. Moreover, cities and counties must divert at least 50 percent of their waste stream from landfills by the year 2000 (25 percent by 1995 is an interim target).

California's new recycling laws strive to create markets for recycled materials. To this end, the state will give preference to such products as recycled oil, compost, used rags, desks, cars, reloaded ammunition, and recycled glass and will begin to buy retread tires for state-owned vehicles. Tax credits and development bonds for those who buy recycling machinery are in the final stages of approval.

MAINE

Maine also passed a series of recycling bills recently. LD 1431, the most comprehensive of these, established a statewide recycling goal of 25 percent by 1992—which jumps to 50 percent by 1994. There are several important aspects to Maine's new recycling legislation.

The state now requires wastepaper and cardboard recycling by any firms in the commercial sector with fifteen or more employees. (They must begin by mid-1993.) State agencies are also required to purchase recycled paper.

The new laws also impose several packaging bans. Aseptic packaging (juice containers with plastic, paper, and aluminum layers), plastic cans, and plastic beverage "yoke" connectors are all banned. Plastic containers must be labeled by resin type.

NEW YORK

In New York state, all municipalities are required to have mandatory source-separation legislation in place by September 1992. The state's current recycling and reduction goal is 50 percent by 1997. The state will provide substantial funding (up to 75 percent) for the start-up costs of recycling programs. This grant program has paid for the salaries of eighty-nine recycling coordinators in counties and towns around the state. It also pays for public education programs.

New York's recycling legislation stresses the importance of waste reduction. The state has developed a commercial and industrial waste audit program designed to help businesses reduce the amount of waste they create. A newly established Bureau of Waste Reduction and Recycling will help implement the campaign.

TRENDS IN STATE LEGISLATION

Even though each state has designed a program to fit its unique situation, there are common themes to all the legislation that has been passed recently across the country. Financial incentives, procurement policies, education, and bans on certain products and materials are just some of the methods chosen by individual states to achieve their waste reduction goals. Here we consider some of the more common themes in state legislation.

Mandatory recycling programs basically come in two different forms: mandatory recycling by residents and laws that require local governments to establish recycling programs. States requiring citizen participation include Connecticut, New Jersey, Pennsylvania (in municipalities of a certain size), and Rhode Island. States where local governments are required to establish programs include Florida, Oregon, North Carolina, and Washington. Still other states, including Wisconsin, New Mexico, Maryland, Minnesota, and Missouri, require recycling within their state agencies.

Most states are setting specific recycling targets to be met over the next several years. These range from cautious to very ambitious. Maine is thought to have one of the most ambitious targets: 50 percent by 1994. The District of Columbia is aiming for 45 percent by 1994, and the state of Washington has set 50 percent by 1995 as its goal. Other states with set targets include Iowa and California (50 percent by the year 2000), Michigan (30 percent by 2005), Louisiana (25 percent by 1992), Ohio (25 percent by 1994), and West Virginia (30 percent by 2000).

Financial incentives to recycle are part of the legislation in states like California, Florida, Iowa, Maine, Minnesota, New Jersey, Oklahoma, Oregon, and Wisconsin. These typically come in the form of tax reductions or loans for organizations that purchase recycling equipment. New Jersey offers a 50 percent tax credit; California, a 40 percent credit with a cap of $250,000 per taxpayer; Maine, a 30 percent credit; Minnesota, loans of up to 50 percent of capital costs.

Banning certain materials from landfills is another common element in recycling legislation. Yard wastes, tires, oil, batteries, and construction materials are often refused. Such bans are part of an effort to force the development of markets for these materials. Minnesota, Oregon, and Wisconsin are among the many states that impose such bans.

Many states have enacted product bans or restrictions. Plastic beverage containers (unless recyclable), beverage containers with detachable rings or tabs, and polystyrene packaging made with chlorofluorocarbons have been common targets. Florida, Louisiana, and North Carolina have enacted such laws.

Requiring or encouraging state agencies to buy products made from recycled materials is one of the key aspects of recycling legislation. Many states have passed legislation regarding procurement. Paper products are usually the prime subject. California, Illinois, Iowa, Maine, Missouri, Pennsylvania, Tennessee, Wisconsin, and Vermont are among the states to have set percentage requirements for the amount of recycled products that must be purchased. Maine and Missouri also include a 10 percent price preferential—which means the state must purchase recycled paper products when the price is within 10 percent of the price of the same items made from virgin materials. Vermont has a price preferential of 5 percent for certain products.

Public education is another common ingredient. Funds are being set aside for education in the schools as well as to educate the general public. Public education plays a role in the recycling programs of more than twenty states.

Many programs concentrate on recycling and other methods while skimming over the vital first step of waste reduction. New York, however, has a law requiring annual analysis of the packaging portion of the waste stream—the idea is to help businesses evaluate ways of reducing the amount of waste they generate. A good program of waste reduction at the state level—involving government offices and agencies, educational institutions, and industry—would make the overall goals of all these programs much easier to achieve . . . and do it in a more effective way.

STATE AND LOCAL SOLUTIONS

Recycling programs don't have to be mandatory to be popular and effective. In fact, many of the most successful programs are organized on a purely volunteer basis. No matter what the size or location of a community, successful recycling programs can be established. Across the country, from rural communities to inner cities, citizens are working together to collect and recycle whatever materials are best suited to recycling in their area.

The Institute for Local Self-Reliance, in its book *Beyond 40 Percent*, studies communities with higher than average recycling and composting rates. Their top seventeen communities, listed below, show that the community's size is not the determining factor in the amount of reduction that can take place when people are organized and dedicated.

Rank	Community	Population	Recovery Rate (1989)[a]
1	Berlin Township, NJ	5,629	57%
2	Longmeadow, MA	16,309	49%
3	Haddonfield, NJ	12,151	49%
4	Perkasie, PA	7,005	43%
5	Rodman, NY	850	43%
6	Wellesley, MA	26,590	41%
7	Lincoln Park, NJ	11,337	41%[b]
8	West Linn, OR	14,030	40%
9	Hamburg, NY	11,000	40%
10	Wilton, WI	473	40%
11	Seattle, WA	497,000	36%[c]
12	Cherry Hill, NJ	73,723	35%[c]
13	Upper Township, NJ	10,870	35%
14	Babylon, NY	213,234	34%[c]
15	Park Ridge, NJ	8,515	34%
16	Fennimore, WI	2,430	34%[c]
17	Woodbury, NJ	10,450	32%[c]

[a]The recovery rate is the ratio of tonnage recycled plus tonnage composted to the tonnage of municipal solid waste generated (residential, commercial, and institutional waste disposed and recovered).
[b]Based on 1988 data.
[c]Residential or commercial recovery levels are at least 40 percent.
Source: Institute for Local Self-Reliance, Beyond 40 Percent: Record-Setting Recycling and Composting Programs (Washington, DC: Island Press, 1991).

To show that innovative programs have been established for a variety of situations, we turn now to examples of town, county, and state programs that are all proving successful. From block corner programs to statewide programs, recycling is working all across the United States.

Wellesley, Massachusetts

Wellesley is a residential suburb of Boston with a population of approximately 27,000 people. The town's recycling program is eighteen years old, entirely voluntary, and collects an impressive variety of recyclable materials. It is worth noting that Wellesley residents have never had curbside pickup of their waste: they either take it to the dump (Wellesley's is called the Recycling and Disposal Facility, or RDF) or pay private contractors to collect it. Eighty percent take their own waste to the RDF.

Of the residents who bring their waste to the RDF, approximately 90 percent separate recyclables. In 1989, Wellesley residents were estimated to be recycling 41 percent of the waste stream—considerably higher than the Massachusetts state average. The town's aim is to recycle at least 50 percent. Thirty-nine percent of the residents compost their leaves at home also.

Wellesley's RDF has attained a certain amount of international fame for its comprehensive, popular program, its pleasant, parklike setting, and the unusual features that make it so unique. The current RDF was born years ago when Wellesley's incinerator was shut down for failing to meet federal emission standards. A local group called Action for Ecology then went to work to establish the recycling program. The group waged a public relations campaign that included inserts with residents' utility bills, education in the schools, and coverage in the local papers.

One striking characteristic of Wellesley's program is the impressive number of different materials it collects for recycling. The facility has designated areas for various grades of paper (cardboard and corrugated cartons, newspapers, magazines and mixed paper, brown paper bags), plastic containers, metals (steel or tinned cans, aluminum foil and trays, miscellaneous metals), glass, and yard waste (leaves, grass, brush).

Even within these categories, the items accepted are wide-ranging. At the miscellaneous metals area, for example, the program accepts nonferrous metals like aluminum (storm windows and doors, house siding, cookware, lawn chairs, gutters, TV antennas), copper (pipes and fittings, vehicle radiators), and brass (bed frames, pipes and fittings). Light iron—refrigerators, stoves, hot water heaters, toasters, bicycles, metal desks, and steel piping—is also accepted. Finally, tubs, sinks, sewer pipes, radiators, hibachis, and heavy steel (car parts and heavy piping) can be dropped off, too.

The cardboard and corrugated cartons area doesn't just take corrugated boxes. Detergent, tissue, shoe, and cereal boxes, in addition to toilet paper rolls and cardboard egg cartons, are all accepted. All these items are listed to show what can be recycled if one takes the trouble to collect the items and seek out markets for them.

Some of the unique features of the Wellesley RDF are its book exchange shed, the "take it or leave it" area, and the swap-shop board. It also houses an area for Goodwill Industries. The book exchange, located in a small shelter, is one of the most popular stops. The "take it or leave it" area is like a free flea market: residents bring things they no longer want and take anything that interests them. Items that remain longer than three days are shipped off with the general waste.

The recycling swap shop is the RDF's effort to encourage reuse of household hazardous wastes. Although the facility does not accept hazardous wastes, they provide a bulletin board of "wanted" and "available" hazardous wastes. For example, someone with leftover house paint can leave a card with his name and phone number for anyone who needs the paint. To ensure safety, all items must be in their original containers with full labeling.

Leaves and grass clippings collected at the RDF are composted and available free to residents. Also, any public trees that are cut down are split into firewood pieces and kindling and left for residents to take.

In 1988 and 1989, Wellesley's Recycling and Disposal Facility recycled over 5,400 tons of garbage. This is estimated to have saved the town approximately $350,000. The RDF sells all that it can from what is collected and saves money from avoided dumping costs. (All nonrecyclable waste from the facility is shipped to a nearby landfill.) Commercial haulers, who must pay to dump their rubbish at the site, are encouraged to recycle too: any hauler who separates recyclables and puts them in the proper areas is not charged for those items. All money earned is put into the town's general fund.

There are many reasons for the success of Wellesley's recycling program. An important aspect is its popularity among the community. More than 3,000 cars pass through the facility on a typical Saturday, but people don't just dump and leave. At the book exchange, the most popular venue, people gather and visit with one another. A genuine concern for the environment among residents is another key to the program's success.

Queen Village, Pennsylvania

Queen Village is a waterfront neighborhood about a quarter of a square mile in area with approximately 7,000 residents in central Philadelphia. The voluntary recycling program established here in 1985 was a pioneering method of collection that now serves as a model for densely populated urban areas elsewhere. The Queen Village method utilizes block corner pickup.

Block corner pickup is just what the name implies: residents take their recyclables to designated block corners at assigned times and dates. The materials are then picked up by a truck just as in curbside collection. Queen Village began block corner pickup service when some elderly residents contacted the Village Recycling Committee to ask for help in getting their recyclables to the local drop-off center. When one of the committee members suggested that someone from the committee could pick them up on the corner and take them to the drop-off center, the idea was born.

The program began in 1985 with only twelve participating blocks but had expanded by the following year to over forty-six blocks with more than 1,200 participating homes. It's a very simple system: twice a month residents leave their recyclables on the designated street corners between set hours; a municipal truck comes by and collects them. In Queen Village the drop-off period is limited to one hour to avoid scavenging and limit unpleasantness for the residents who live on that corner.

To organize their program the Queen Village residents first established a recycling committee. The committee has ten members with one designated as chairperson. This group did all the groundwork to set up the program, such as finding what materials could be sold locally and finding someone to collect the recyclables.

The block coordinators in the Queen Village program are key figures. These people take on a lot of responsibility and have to be dedicated to the project. Coordinators choose appropriate block corners, notify residents of the pickup schedule, and oversee the pickup. In Queen Village, committee members are also block coordinators.

Whether or not block corner recycling can work for your community depends on several factors. If block corners are too far apart, if there's no effective social network among neighbors, and if corner property owners are not willing to have recyclables collected in front of their residences, this system will probably not work. Also, neighbors must be willing to walk down the block—to make that extra effort—in order for the program to be a success.

With the proper conditions, however, this system is proving to be a very effective recycling method in dense urban areas. Collection trucks can work much faster than in regular curbside pickup systems because they have many fewer stops—and when they do stop, the driver can get out and help because they're at each corner longer than they would be at individual houses. This saves money in time and labor costs. Money earned can go to community projects. Queen Village, for example, uses its earnings for trees, park plants, and fences for community gardens.

Despite the extra effort required by residents to carry their recyclables several blocks and the difficulty in finding a hauler to work Saturdays (which the committee decided was the best day), the Queen Village program is very successful and is providing similarly satisfactory results in other communities.

Santa Clara County, California

Santa Clara County's recycling takes place at a complex known as The Recyclery. The Recyclery is a combination facility that houses the county's landfill, biomass recovery, MRF, buy-back center, and education center all in the same area. The facility is run by Browning-Ferris Industries. (For more on BFI, see Chapter 8.)

The Recyclery has been operating since early 1991. In its first few months it had already recycled over 829 tons of cardboard, 66 tons of plastics, 80 tons of paper, 1,598 tons of wood, 57 tons of scrap metal, and 231 tons of other materials.

The facility's MRF takes recyclables from curbside collection throughout the county, from individual residents who bring in a wide range of materials that the buy-back center will accept, and from offices and factories. It can process 1,600 tons of waste per day. The biomass recovery project takes wood from demolished buildings and other sources and shreds it into pieces small enough to be used for burning in electric power plants.

Materials collected at the center may end up at opposite ends of the globe. While aluminum cans are usually sold locally, for example, phone books, cardboard, and white office paper are often sold overseas.

One of the key features of The Recyclery is the education program it runs in conjunction with its other functions. The buy-back center also houses the education center—visited by an estimated 5,000 residents in its first few months.

A visitor to the education center first walks past an enormous "wall of trash." Signs on the wall inform visitors that the garbage they are seeing is created by one person in six years, by the County of Santa Clara in three minutes, or by the United States in one second. As visitors walk along the wall they can also read descriptions of how garbage has been handled historically.

The center has an interactive video system through which visitors can see how the various parts of the MRF function. They can also make a metal-separating conveyor belt work. The center has been specially designed with an observation room where the public can watch the MRF in action. They can watch how materials are taken from the tipping floor along conveyor belts to a sorting room and then into balers.

The center also has demonstrations showing the various stages a product goes through when it is recycled: paper, glass, plastic bottles, and aluminum cans. For plastics it shows a PET bottle, then the bottle cut into flakes, then fiber that has been spun from the plastic flakes, and finally a paint brush and a sample of carpet to show the final products.

The education center is an important part of the overall plan at The Recyclery. The combination of various functions at the facility serves Santa Clara County with a carefully considered waste reduction and education program.

Oregon

Oregon's recycling laws take a slightly different focus than those of many states. While it's becoming more common for states to require their communities to recycle, Oregon simply requires that its citizens have the opportunity to recycle.

Despite an almost 30 percent growth in population in the last two decades, Oregon's cities have not suffered from this rapid growth the way other cities have done, particularly in the East. Thus the state has been free to pursue preventive environmental measures rather than constantly fighting current problems. Oregon has been in the forefront of environmental conservation and protection for years. Well before any laws enforced recycling opportunities and education, there were many recycling programs already in existence throughout the state.

Oregon's official recycling history began in 1971, when the Oregon Bottle Bill was passed by the state legislature. Perhaps the most important component of Oregon's solid waste legislation, however, is the Recycling Opportunity Act, passed in 1983 with an implementation date of July 1986. Although this bill has been amended significantly by subsequent legislatures, it forms the basis of Oregon's recycling philosophy.

The Recycling Opportunity Act requires certain minimum provisions. Among these are a recycling depot at every landfill and transfer station (or at a more convenient location), monthly curbside collection of recyclables in cities of 4,000 or more, and public education programs. The act establishes a statewide waste management policy based on the following points (in order of priority): reduce the waste generated; reuse material; recycle; recover energy; and, finally, dispose of anything left.

Since its inception, the Recycling Opportunity Act has had many new recycling programs added to it. These include tax credits for capital investment in recycling, state agency procurement of recycled products, recycling education in the schools, and special recycling programs for special wastes like oil, lead-acid batteries, and tires.

Although the Recycling Opportunity Act requires that certain opportunities be established, it does not require Oregonians to recycle. But they do: the Department of Environmental Quality (DEQ) states that 90 percent of Oregonians participate in at least one recycling program. About 25 percent of the state's solid waste is diverted from landfills annually. In addition, many municipalities go beyond their legal requirements in providing recycling opportunities: a number of smaller towns (of less than 4,000) offer curbside recycling to their residents.

A wide variety of materials are recycled in Oregon. Strong markets exist for ferrous metals, tin, glass, corrugated cardboard, and newspaper. Regarding newspaper, Oregon finds itself in a unique situation: even though 75 percent of all Oregon's newspaper is recycled, the state still needs to import paper from other states to meet the demand from the paper industry.

Oregon has had successful voluntary programs for more than twenty years. According to the state's DEQ, this success can be traced to a strong environmental ethic among its citizens coupled with education programs and convenient recycling collection systems.

INDUSTRY'S EFFORTS

Rightly or wrongly, industry is often the target of criticisms for its general disregard for the environment. When it comes to recycling, once again, businesses are usually considered the big, bad wasters of our society.

No one could deny that in many cases this is true. But it is equally true that many companies, large and small, are taking steps to cut back on their waste by establishing recycling and other waste reduction programs. This is not to say that industry does not still have a long way to go, but we must acknowledge the efforts being undertaken today and encourage more widespread application of successful programs.

It is certainly in any company's best interest to reduce its waste generation. Waste reduction can improve efficiency and productivity which in turn strengthens a company's economic base. Many corporations are equally concerned with losing what autonomy they currently have with regard to waste reduction decisions. As Congress continues to look at waste reduction as a subject for legislation, companies across the nation are getting more nervous. Industry wants to keep waste reduction as a voluntary initiative—and only by doing something about it before Congress acts can it be assured of continued self-regulation.

Whether a company develops an extensive waste reduction program
out of concern for the environment, for its image, or for the bottom
line is a moot point. The fact is that with each business that implements
a waste reduction program our country is better off.

Here we examine what some companies are doing to cut back on
waste and recycle. As in recycling communities across the country,
these programs were developed to suit the specific needs of each company.

3M

Since 1975, 3M has run a program that it calls 3P: Pollution Prevention
Pays. The program's aim has been to create technical innovation that
eliminates or reduces pollution at the source—before cleanup problems
occur—thus saving the company money as well as avoiding environmental problems. The program is coordinated by 3M's Environmental
Engineering and Pollution Control Department, which is in charge of
environment-related activities worldwide.

Participation in the program is worldwide. The corporation's technical employees are encouraged to develop ideas for the 3P program.
Product formulation, modification of the manufacturing process, rede-
sign of equipment, and waste recovery are all targeted. 3M estimates
that since 1975, the 3P program has prevented an estimated 1 billion
pounds of emissions to air, water, and land and saved half a billion dollars through better use of manufacturing resources and avoidance of
pollution control costs.

3M details some of the 3P program's successes. For example, it cites
one case in which its Electronic Products Division in Columbia, Missouri, eliminated a process that caused a hazardous waste. At this plant,
copper sheeting was cleaned with a chemical spray before it could be
used in the production of flexible electronic circuits. The spray created
a hazardous waste. That cleaning method was replaced by a new machine that scrubbed the copper with pumice, leaving a nonhazardous
waste. The investment was recovered in less than three years through
reduced materials, labor, and disposal costs.

Attacking a different problem, the same division cut down on waste and saved money also. After electronic circuitry is photographically printed on copper sheeting, it is rinsed with a developer solvent. Instead of discharging the solvent-tainted water directly, 3M employees developed a way to reclaim the solvent. The wastewater was directed through a decanter system that allowed the heavy solvent to settle and be separated. It was then distilled and recycled into the film developing process. The results of this innovation were cost savings in solvents, a substantial decrease in the amount of solvent being discharged from the facility, and the recycling of what had previously been waste into a useful product.

Recycling is an integral part of 3M's program also. Total savings from recovery operations in 3M facilities in the United States (including heavy equipment and transportation) equaled $22 million in 1989 and climbed to $26.8 million in 1990. The company has a team of six resource recovery experts who counsel the various manufacturing plants and help them find potentially valuable waste materials. They work with different divisions to spot waste reduction and recycling opportunities within the company, find markets for these commodities, and establish market agreements to begin smooth operations of the waste recycling.

All sorts of materials for recycling have been identified over the years: heavy equipment, synthetic fibers, chemicals and solvents, precious and other metals, and paper and cardboard. Heavy equipment might include older company cars or equipment that's sitting idle because of changing processes. The company is making a concerted effort to eliminate the use of solvents wherever possible, and at least to recycle those that cannot for the moment be eliminated. Paper and cardboard are collected mainly as waste from the manufacturing process, although they are also collected from office recycling programs. These recycled materials are either used again within 3M or sold outside the corporation.

Office programs that recycle aluminum, glass, and paper are active throughout 3M facilities. These programs are organized and run independently. Whereas an aluminum can collection scheme was started at the head office two years ago, for example, office paper has been collected in many facilities since the 1970s.

The philosophy of waste reduction at 3M encourages voluntary participation and new ideas. There are no strict rules requiring employees to recycle or cut waste. The company prefers instead to demonstrate how certain practices can cut costs and waste, to set up a program providing staff with any necessary help, and to publicize success stories. From there employee participation develops on its own.

The company has, however, established broad goals for overall waste reduction. Its aim is to reduce waste by 35 percent by 1995 and further to 50 percent by 2000. The company's divisions are not told how to go about waste reduction, but they have the help of both the Resource Recovery and Environmental Engineering departments if needed. Moreover, they have access to their own laboratories to develop methods to reformulate a product, for example. Although no specific regulations are in force regarding these goals, the operating divisions are judged in their performance reviews on whether or not they are attaining these goals.

Gaston Copper Recycling Corporation

Gaston Copper Recycling Corporation is in the business of recycling for profit. The facility, in South Carolina, is a leader in the reclamation and refining of metals, particularly copper. It is a principal supplier of copper, precious metals, and white metal products to the telecommunications and electronics industries.

Basically, the company is in the business of transforming obsolete business and communications equipment into a variety of metal products: old telephone and telecommunications equipment is transformed into reusable materials that are then sold to a variety of end-users. The company is a major manufacturer of copper rod. A variety of other metals, by-products of the refining processes, are marketed from the Gaston plant also. These include aluminum, plastics, iron and steel, nickel sulfate, stripped lead, and lead block.

The existence of a plant such as the Gaston facility has several benefits. Above all, the massive amounts of scrap received at the plant daily are not going to a landfill or being incinerated but are being recycled into needed products. Also, the recovery of copper, precious metals, and other metals from scrap is helping to slow the depletion of these natural resources. This operation demonstrates that recycling can be profitable and beneficial at the same time.

XTree Company

XTree Company, a software house in San Luis Obispo, California, has completely reorganized its business practices to make its activities as environmentally sound as possible. The company has approximately forty-five employees and has taken full advantage of the flexibility inherent in a small company to make the changes necessary to achieve its environmental goals.

The company's environmental program, called Project Green, was launched in 1990. It has four basic elements: the use of recycled and recyclable products; internal conservation and recycling; reforestation; and public awareness of environmental issues. The use of recycled and recyclable products is widespread throughout the company. By carefully researching the environmental impact of the packaging it was using and looking into alternatives, XTree has been able to switch to packaging, software manuals, disk sleeves, and shipping containers and packaging materials that are all environmentally preferable to standard supplies.

There were several considerations in changing products. For such things as manuals, literature, brochures, registration cards, and diskette sleeves the company uses paper with the highest possible recycled content—paper that is itself recyclable. For the inks used in printing it looked for aqueous as opposed to oil-based inks and replaced foil appliqués with the equivalent color in water-based ink. (The company's "Green Pages"—a listing of companies both local and nationwide that can supply the products they use—is available to employees and anyone who requests it.)

In addition to an extensive recycling program (various grades of paper, aluminum, glass, plastics) the company encourages the use of refillable pens and pencils, water-based correction fluids, electronic mail instead of memos, sharing magazine subscriptions, and general reuse of office supplies. Project Green extends to the kitchen and lavatories as well: recycled paper products, proper dishes and silverware, unbleached coffee filters, and nontoxic cleaning products are used. Moreover, faucet aerators and low-water toilet fixtures have been installed throughout the company's facilities. The company estimates that it has cut its water consumption by at least half.

Apart from its own work, XTree also helps support reforestation by planting a tree for every copy of certain software programs registered by the purchaser. This is done through contributions to the Global ReLeaf program of the American Forestry Association.

XTree Company established Project Green to address the environmental concerns of its customers and employees. Employee participation in this entirely voluntary program is estimated to be almost 100 percent; everyone involved strongly supports the company's environmental goals.

NATIONAL PARK PROGRAMS

Assuming that people will be more receptive to recycling while enjoying nature, many of our nation's parks are getting on the recycling bandwagon. Recycling programs are springing up across the country: Pennsylvania, Oregon, Washington, New Jersey, California, and Michigan have all got programs in some stage of development in some or all of their parks.

Throughout the National Park Service (NPS) recycling is catching on, too. Its Integrated Solid Waste Alternative Program (ISWAP) has five major elements: source reduction, recycling, waste combustion, landfills, and outreach. Currently, the NPS encourages its parks to recycle one or more materials but acknowledges that this is more practical in larger parks than in some of the smaller attractions. Recycling works well in Yosemite National Park, for example, but isn't practical at certain historic houses because of the small number of visitors.

In 1989 the NPS did a survey of 215 parks to see how much recycling was being done at that time. At least 50 percent of the parks that responded were already involved in some kind of recycling project—and this was before the Integrated Solid Waste Alternative Program. Although no further surveys have been done to assess the effect of the new program, NPS officials believe the level of recycling throughout the national parks has increased dramatically in recent years.

Recycling programs have developed in some of our national parks due to a joint effort between the NPS and industry. In particular, the Dow Chemical Company and Huntsman Chemical Corporation sponsor recycling efforts in several different parks. They collect plastics, glass, and aluminum, pay for the cost of collection, and produce brochures and displays to inform park visitors about the recycling programs.

Dow and Huntsman approached the NPS in 1989 with the idea for a recycling education program and efforts began in three national parks in 1990. The Great Smoky Mountains National Park, Acadia National Park, and Grand Canyon National Park all participated in the first year of the Dow/Huntsman program. Other programs began in Yosemite and Mount Rainier National Parks in 1991, and plans are under way for programs in The Everglades National Park and the National Mall area in Washington, DC.

The Dow/Huntsman scheme provides for a summer intern at each park whose primary responsibility is to implement the program. In addition to placing recycling bins, this involves preparing posters, brochures, exhibits, ranger talks, radio messages, and other methods of spreading the word about recycling. Initial results show that the programs are extremely successful. The three parks collected over 100,000 pounds of recyclables in just the first two months. The NPS also believes, from discussions with park visitors, that people are taking their recycling habits home with them. Glass bottles and aluminum cans are the most commonly collected items. Some parks, however, like Yosemite in California, recycle more materials than many comprehensive community or business programs do.

Yosemite National Park has been recycling since 1976. The park's program is wide-ranging, involving not only the campers but park employees as well. Campers are given plastic bags in which to collect all their recyclables during their stay; there are recycling centers in the park where visitors can leave their recyclables, and employees are urged to participate also. Collection bins for office paper and newspapers are located near the employees' living quarters, and the park's restaurants and stores are expected to collect cardboard.

Most of the recycling done at Yosemite until recently was organized by the park's concessionaire, the Yosemite Park and Curry Company, which works under contract with the park. Under the concessionaire's program aluminum, glass bottles, some plastics, newspaper, office paper, cardboard, used motor oil, antifreeze, car batteries, shipping pallets, film canisters, laser cartridges, fluorescent lamps, tires, and disposable cameras are among the materials collected and recycled. The concessionaire also makes compost: the stock in Yosemite Valley produces up to 4,000 cubic yards of manure yearly that is used to make compost instead of being sent to a landfill.

The park has a central facility where the various materials are collected, sorted, and then shipped out to processors in the area. In 1990, some 682 tons of recyclables from Yosemite Park were collected. Apart from the variety of recyclables collected throughout the park, the park staff organize swap days. On these designated days, office workers bring any items they no longer need and put them out for others to take.

In 1990 the EPA provided Yosemite Park with a two-year grant to start a comprehensive solid waste reduction program. This grant has helped to expand the recycling activities of the park staff (as opposed to the concessionaire). Among other things, the grant allowed the solid waste foreman at the park to concentrate more strongly on recycling and to hire an assistant to organize recycling efforts. As landfill fees went up by nearly 30 percent between 1990 and 1991, the need for recycling at the park became even more important.

Among the programs developed by the park staff was the inclusion of recycling information and education by the park naturalists in their contacts with visitors. Also, a parkwide recycling education program— as opposed to simple advertising of recycling opportunities—was initiated. The idea was to teach visitors about the benefits of recycling in addition to just encouraging them to recycle the materials they used while at the park.

As many other national parks begin to consider recycling programs, Yosemite National Park's program can serve as an excellent example of what can be achieved. It is protecting the environment and helping to keep the area more beautiful while at the same time educating the park's many visitors.

8 A Look at the Recycling Industry

As we have seen, recycling has been around for a long time in one form or another. It is only in recent history, however, that it has taken on its current multifaceted infrastructure. What began as scavenging or careful reuse of materials developed into neighborhood newspaper and glass bottle collections and ultimately into today's industry.

THE INDUSTRY'S INFRASTRUCTURE

The recycling industry has many different groups participating in it, each with its own important role to play. Government, on a local and national level, institutes or supervises legislation concerning recycling. Industry groups representing the people who actually work with recyclables and waste play a role in the development of legislation, educating the public and providing services to their members. Finally, the recycling industry touches all kinds of peripheral groups such as the media and organizations that are not specifically involved in recycling but do represent manufacturers of recyclable materials.

This chapter introduces a few of the key players in the recycling industry. The purpose here is not to give an in-depth analysis of these organizations but to establish a fundamental overview of the many varied entities who participate in the recycling industry today.

Industry Groups

The individuals and companies involved directly in recycling are represented by several different industry groups. Some focus on the development of recycling in general, while others focus on the work of a particular industry. Three of these industry groups are introduced here.

NATIONAL RECYCLING COALITION (NRC)

The National Recycling Coalition is a nonprofit group, founded in 1978, dedicated to developing the role of recycling and conservation as waste and resource management tools. Members of the NRC represent government agencies, nonprofit groups, grassroots recycling organizations, private businesses, and concerned individuals.

The NRC has a variety of activities designed to promote recycling. Important among these is its role in working with state associations and local groups to encourage recycling at the local level, increasing local communities' knowledge of recycling issues. The group also advocates a national policy on recycling, sponsors a yearly conference, provides educational and technical assistance to members, and publicizes the benefits of recycling nationwide.

The NRC's national policy on recycling covers a wide range of issues to increase the viability of waste reduction, recycling, reuse, and recovery as strategies for resource conservation, environmental protection, and economic development. Among the ideas put forward in the NRC policy are the elimination of tax laws that give unfair advantage to users of virgin materials, the establishment of a national database providing information on recycling rates for recyclable commodities, and the formulation of a national policy for recycling education.

The National Recycling Congress, the group's annual conference, gives delegates the opportunity to meet and learn from each other's experiences. A large number of delegates come from local government: people who up until recently had little to do with recycling but now are responsible for implementing sometimes complicated programs. Expert speakers present information on topics as wide ranging as pending legislation and the role of plastics in today's society.

The NRC gives annual awards in recognition of companies, people, or programs responsible for recycling achievements. Awards are given in such categories as best curbside program, best recycling center, outstanding corporate leader, and outstanding environmental/community group leader.

INSTITUTE OF SCRAP RECYCLING INDUSTRIES (ISRI)

The Institute of Scrap Recycling Industries, as opposed to the NRC, is a much more specific group: it represents the scrap processors and recyclers of North America. More than 1,800 companies—processors, brokers, and consumers of scrap commodities—make up the organization's membership. Commodities represented are metals, paper, glass, textiles, and plastics.

ISRI was formed in 1987 through the merger of the Institute of Scrap Iron and Steel (originally founded in 1928) and the National Association of Recycling Industries (originally founded in 1913). Member companies range from small, family-owned businesses to large publicly held corporations.

The organization's purpose is to provide services to members. These services include education and training, updated information regarding government regulations, and public relations assistance. ISRI also produces several industry periodicals. *Phoenix* is a public service magazine for government officials and others; *Scrap Processing and Recycling* focuses on issues of importance to member companies.

NATIONAL SOLID WASTES MANAGEMENT ASSOCIATION (NSWMA)

This association was formed in 1968 to be a voice for the waste services industry. Its more than 2,500 members represent branches of the industry such as refuse hauling, resource recovery and recycling, waste processing, hazardous waste treatment and disposal, landfill operation, engineering, and street sweeping.

The NSWMA represents the waste industry before Congress, the media, and other organizations. It monitors and addresses key legislative issues affecting the industry and advises Congress with regard to environmental laws. In addition, it produces a series of studies each year reflecting public attitudes toward recycling, garbage disposal, waste-to-energy, and other waste management concerns. It also publishes figures on solid waste recycling in America.

The organization publishes *Waste Age*, a monthly magazine directed at professionals in government, private industry, and academia. It also produces a biweekly newspaper, *Recycling Times,* that covers markets for recyclable materials. Finally, it sponsors an annual convention and trade show called Waste Expo that gives members the opportunity to meet and learn about the latest technology and issues affecting the waste industry.

Apart from the groups listed here, for whom recycling is their main concern, there are many other industry groups that promote recycling—usually related to the recycling of their specific product or material of interest. Among these are the Glass Packaging Institute, the National Soft Drink Association, the Plastics Recycling Foundation, the American Paper Institute, the American Iron and Steel Institute, and the Aluminum Recycling Association. The addresses of these and many more associations are listed in Appendix A.

COMPANIES IN THE RECYCLING INDUSTRY

The diversity of businesses involved in recycling demonstrates the industry's advanced state of development. The technology used to recycle our waste is extremely sophisticated, and a growing number of companies are profiting from providing heavy machinery and specially designed trucks to the industry and from hauling and processing the waste. There are several well-known, national companies and many smaller, local firms ranging from manufacturers of recycling equipment, waste processors, and haulers to recycling consultants.

Equipment and Technology

The variety of equipment and advanced technology being used in recycling is truly diverse. Shredding systems exist for tires, industrial and municipal waste, rubber, wood, glass, plastics, metals, appliances, and paper. There are containers of all shapes and sizes to be used for curbside pickup or in offices or industrial sites.

All kinds of vehicles designed specifically for collecting, sorting, and hauling recyclables are in service across the country. Huge machines are designed to wash and separate different grades of plastic or to crush cans, plastic, glass, or cardboard. Great balers take in loose paper, aluminum, or plastic, crush these materials and form them into compact cubes, and then tie them in bundles for easy transportation. Conveyors and compactors are sold to recyclers everywhere.

This equipment comes in all sizes, for the smallest to the largest job. Some companies specialize in one or two products, while others have developed a range of products to cover almost every aspect of recycling. Whatever a company's scope, recycling equipment is big business, and the recycling magazines are filled with equipment updates and new developments in machinery.

One company that provides equipment and technology to the recycling industry is American Recovery Corporation. This company—formed in 1988 as a joint venture between Potomac Capital Investment Corp. and Sorain Cecchini of Italy—has exclusive rights to design and market Sorain solid waste recovery equipment in the United States and Canada.

Sorain Cecchini technology is considered by many to be among the most sophisticated waste processing systems available. A full-scale Sorain facility could offer the following recovery systems: waste receiving; primary processing system; plastic film (polyethylene) recovery; HDPE and PET container recovery; corrugated recovery; newsprint recovery; mixed-paper recovery; office/computer paper recovery; aluminum recovery; ferrous recovery; organic material recovery; and combustible material recovery. Moreover, refining systems could be installed for composting mixed organic and yard waste, for processing LDPE and HDPE film plastic into plastic pellets, for cleaning and densifying recovered ferrous materials, for densifying recovered aluminum, and for baling recovered paper.

One of the unique features of the Sorain system is its patented "bag breaker," a machine that mechanically opens garbage bags to empty the garbage. This is done by pushing the garbage through a series of stationary jaws that tear the bags open.

The equipment used in all these processes is wide-ranging. Cranes lift and transport waste, and conveyor belts move it from one processing station to another. Mechanical sorters of many types are used: waste is passed across a series of screens to sort it by size; through air classifiers that separate light from heavy waste (paper from metals, for example); and magnetic separators to separate ferrous metals. A variety of shredders may be used also—to handle metals or plastics, for example.

The recovery and refining processes described here can result in any number of end products. These include various paper grades as feedstock for the paper industry; plastic pellets for plastic trash bags, pipe, or molded objects; compost for soil conditioner; and metals to be returned to their respective industries.

Waste Haulers and Processors

The $25 billion waste management industry is dominated by two major publicly held companies: Waste Management, Inc. (WMI) and Browning-Ferris Industries (BFI). Not surprisingly, these companies are also involved in recycling in a big way. These two companies have increased their share of the industry even more so over the last several years by buying up many of the smaller companies in this branch of the industry.

The mega-companies in this industry tend to be involved in many aspects of waste management. In addition to hauling garbage, for example, they may own and operate sanitary landfills and incinerators, handle hazardous waste, and manage materials recovery facilities.

WASTE MANAGEMENT, INC.

Waste Management is the largest waste management company in this country. Its main business—hauling and disposing of garbage—serves nearly 8 million homes.

Waste Management's recycling subsidiary, established in 1986, is called Recycle America and is the nation's largest residential and commercial recycler, serving over 1 million homes with curbside collection. The company has established well over 200 recycling programs in the United States and Canada. In San Jose, California, for example, WMI collects approximately 2,000 tons of newsprint, aluminum, and ferrous metals monthly through its residential recycling program.

Among the materials collected by WMI through its various programs are glass, cans, newspapers, plastic containers, office paper, tires, corrugated paper, and yard wastes. In addition to its curbside collection, Waste Management is working with paper and plastic manufacturers to develop recycling of these materials. WMI also serves commercial customers with waste audits, waste reduction programs, and employee training.

WMI operates more than sixty processing plants (MRFs) throughout North America to handle the recyclables it collects through residential and commercial programs. These facilities process and package the collected materials and ship them to markets.

Recycle America also operates eleven tire shredding and recycling facilities nationwide. These facilities have shredded over 10 million tires since 1988. Processed tires are being used for road building materials and a variety of rubber products; whole tires are used as artificial reefs.

The company is active, as well, in other aspects of waste collection and treatment. WMI owns or operates over 125 sanitary landfills and is engaged in methane recovery programs. It also owns 55 percent of Wheelabrator Technologies Inc., through which it develops and operates waste-to-energy plants. The company's hazardous waste management subsidiary, Chemical Waste Management, is the nation's leading handler of toxic waste.

BROWNING-FERRIS INDUSTRIES

Browning-Ferris Industries is an international corporation with operations in North and South America, Europe, Australia, the United Kingdom, and the Middle East. In the United States, it is the second largest company in the waste processing industry. It collects garbage from over 5 million homes and owns and operates over 100 landfills.

BFI offers stiff competition to WMI in the field of recycling with its four RecycleNOW programs: residential curbside collection, recycling centers, commercial recycling, and landfills. The company has also developed an education program for elementary children to help teach them about recycling.

BFI has developed special programs for old corrugated cartons and high-grade office paper, because of the large volumes of these materials it collects. All other materials are collected through customer-designed programs that concentrate on the volume and markets for the customer's materials.

PROS AND CONS

These companies have not always received good press. The environmental community has often cited problems caused by the EPA's "revolving door policy" influencing these companies. Certainly there is a fair amount of movement by former EPA employees (including former administrators) into jobs in the industry they used to regulate (and vice-versa). William D. Ruckelshaus, for example, a former administrator of the EPA, is now BFI's chairman and CEO. Moreover, the companies or their subsidiaries are often in the news for illegal processing of their hazardous waste. According to Greenpeace, WMI was the leading recipient of EPA fines in the 1980s.

Although these companies are now well entrenched in the recycling business, they should not be given credit for the development of recycling across the nation. The big players in the waste industry only entered the picture after local groups and communities had struggled for years to develop successful recycling programs. These waste haulers, critics charge, have become involved only to keep control of what was becoming a larger—and potentially very profitable—sector of their overall industry. In many instances across the country they have managed to take over recycling projects that had been set up by local groups.

These companies owe a significant amount of their growth in recent years to an aggressive acquisitions policy. A *Business Week* article (12 September 1988, p. 112) noted that 250 small waste-hauling companies were bought the previous year. WMI and BFI reportedly did most of the buying.

That companies such as Waste Management, Inc. and Browning-Ferris Industries are regarded quite differently by different groups certainly helps to feed the controversy surrounding them. The EPA, for example, looks at these corporations as helping to solve our waste problems because they collect and dispose of waste. The environmental community, on the other hand, takes a rather different view: if these companies dispose of waste improperly or put corporate profits above the public's safety, they are actually making the problem worse. For better or worse, however, these companies currently dominate the waste processing industry and are responsible for a large portion of curbside and other recycling programs across the nation.

Consultants

Consultants to the recycling industry serve a very important purpose. As states and counties pass wide-ranging laws requiring local governments to implement stringent recycling policies, people who knew nothing about the subject are being required to develop and manage detailed recycling programs. Not surprisingly, they need help.

In many cases, these consulting firms had been involved in related industries and fields for many years. Thus the inclusion of recycling was a natural development. Engineers and companies associated with the solid waste disposal industry are common among consultants.

Services provided by consulting firms vary widely. From education and promotion, through feasibility analysis and planning, to program implementation and monitoring—all aspects of a recycling project are covered. Consulting firms can help a company or a county in market analysis, grant applications, systems design, and secondary materials marketing.

FRANKLIN ASSOCIATES

Franklin Associates, Ltd., one of the best-known consulting firms involved in the recycling industry, was founded in 1974. It is nationally known for its work in the various aspects of integrated solid waste management. Its studies are quoted widely throughout the recycling industry, by companies and government bodies alike.

Integrated solid waste planning, market analysis of recyclables, source reduction, and materials recovery for recycling and composting are among its areas of study. Franklin performs technical, environmental, and economic analysis for local governments to determine what management options are appropriate for that specific community.

In the area of source reduction, Franklin has done studies relating to both deposit laws and tax incentives. In developing materials recovery and recycling programs for clients, the firm helps quantify recyclables in the waste stream, analyzes markets for recovered materials, and provides technical evaluations of various collection and processing alternatives.

Franklin Associates' clients have included government agencies at the local, regional, state, and federal level, private firms, and trade associations. The company also prepares municipal solid waste characterization reports for the EPA.

GREEN CROSS

The Green Cross Certification Company is a not-for-profit advisory service that provides environmental consulting and independent certification services to the retail and manufacturing trade. Its purpose is to help companies in the formulation, implementation, and assessment of corporate environmental policies. It serves as a neutral third-party certifier of environmental product claims by independently investigating both product and industry environmental claims. Green Cross has no brokerage or ownership interest in the products it certifies and maintains complete financial independence from any special-interest organizations.

Green Cross certification means that specific environmental claims made about products have been thoroughly checked out and meet high standards of performance. Two levels of certification are awarded. Certification records must be updated on a quarterly basis in order for a company to maintain its product's certification status. Quarterly review enables Green Cross to ensure that the product is continuing to perform to the standards required under its certification requirements.

The first level of certification is awarded to a product that meets state-of-the-art performance standards in one or more categories. Claims such as "recycled content" (paper, glass, steel, plastic products), "biodegradable" (cleaning products), and "energy efficient" (light bulbs) are among those being evaluated. The Green Cross certification is accompanied by a statement of the specific achievement.

The second level of certification, the Environmental Seal of Achievement, is awarded to a product that undergoes a full "life-cycle" assessment and is shown to possess several significant environmental advantages over other products in its category. A "life-cycle" assessment involves an examination of the resources used, energy consumed, wastes produced, and emissions released as a result of the manufacture, distribution, use, and disposal of a product. To help consumers make the best informed decisions, documented advantages are always presented in detail along with each Seal of Achievement.

The Green Cross certification program is intended to support manufacturers in their efforts to achieve the highest standards of performance with respect to the environment. Additionally, it helps both retailers and consumers to distinguish between valid and invalid environmental claims.

INSTITUTE FOR LOCAL SELF-RELIANCE (ILSR)

The Institute for Local Self-Reliance is a nonprofit educational and research organization founded in 1974. The institute views recycling as merely one aspect of a policy regarding materials use. At the local or state level, the group works for the development of materials policies that strive for maximum efficiency in materials use (including energy efficiency) and that substitute direct solar energy or plant matter (stored solar energy) to produce fuels and industrial materials. ILSR regards materials policy development as well as recycling as strategies to achieve local self-reliance in urban areas.

The institute participates in a variety of activities to provide technical and decision-making information to city and state governments, environmental organizations, and industry. It publishes studies that furnish the information necessary for local governments or groups to develop alternatives for self-reliance and trains both community activists and government officials at regional and local workshops. It has also sponsored a national contest for communities across the nation who recycle high percentages of their waste stream.

ILSR's recycling projects include working in southern California with community organizations to halt plans for local waste incineration plants. Here the institute assisted local groups to form a coalition that successfully campaigned to have a series of mass-burn plants canceled in favor of recycling technologies.

GRASSROOTS GROUPS

In addition to these groups, a multitude of organizations are working at the community level throughout the nation to promote recycling and other activities beneficial to the local citizenry. Kentuckians for the Commonwealth and the Hoosier Environmental Council are examples of such groups.

Groups like these work at the grassroots level to protect their constituents from unsafe landfills or incinerators, to promote recycling, and to increase local activism. These groups represent an essential link in the chain of citizen, industry, and government participation in the development of recycling and similar programs.

Related Activities

Interest in recycling has spread far past the groups that focus solely on this one issue. From mail-order companies to the national press, this growing interest is causing a wide range of companies and organizations to take a serious look at recycling.

MAIL-ORDER COMPANIES

Across the nation retail stores have been very slow in providing a regular supply of recycled products—if any at all. Only recently has it become easier to find such recycled items as toilet paper, paper towels, tissues, or fluorescent light bulbs, and many communities still do not have access to these items in regular retail stores. As a result, many people have turned to mail-order companies for recycled and other "environmentally friendly" products.

In recent years both the number of mail-order supply companies and the variety of products they sell have increased dramatically. Mail-order companies range from those specializing in recycled products to those with a range of products that may be recycled, "cruelty-free," organic, or any combination of these.

Seventh Generation, started in 1988, is perhaps one of the best-known mail-order companies dealing in recycled products. Its product line includes everything from paper products, glass products, rechargeable batteries, and reusable shopping bags to undyed, unbleached cotton clothing. In addition to promoting recycled products, Seventh Generation has donated some $140,000 to groups working to better the planet. The company also has a board of advisors—including such well-known environmentalists as Peter Bahouth, executive director of Greenpeace, and Sandra Postel, vice-president of research at the Worldwatch Institute—who help Seventh Generation understand complex environmental issues.

Some mail-order companies sell cosmetics, personal products, and a variety of household products that are environmentally friendly and cruelty-free, such as Ecco Bella. Others specialize in a specific product range: Atlantic Paper Recycling Company specializes in stationery and paper products; Treekeepers, a southern California company, specializes in a range of reusable bags, from canvas and string shopping bags to canvas lunch bags and mesh produce bags.

SPREADING THE WORD

The growth of recycling has been greatly assisted in recent years by a gradual increase in the amount of information available about the issue. This is largely due to the establishment of conferences, such as that sponsored by the NRC, and because of the coverage recycling now gets in a variety of excellent journals. Such channels are vital for the spreading of information and development of new ideas.

Conferences allow delegates to learn from others in similar positions and from those with specific expertise. Not only on a national level, but at the state and local level, government employees, industry members, and concerned citizens meet on a regular basis. Delegates discuss strategies for developing recycling, new technologies, new legislation, and a host of other topics. Exhibitions running concurrently with these conferences allow visitors to see firsthand the technology and equipment they may need to purchase and give them a chance to speak with industry representatives.

Journals also play a vital role in the dissemination of recycling information today. They, too, are used as a forum for discussion and present an excellent medium through which to present the latest information in the recycling field. In addition to the journals listed in Appendix C, which focus specifically on recycling or environmental issues, articles on recycling appear in many publications. National periodicals such as *Time*, *The Smithsonian*, *Newsweek*, *National Geographic*, and *The Atlantic Monthly* are just a few that have covered our waste management problems and recycling. Likewise, national newspapers are increasing their coverage of the field.

WASTE-BASED MANUFACTURING

Waste-based manufacturing is an essential part of recycling. If recycling is not complete until a product or material goes full circle and becomes another product, then waste-based manufacturing is the final link in the recycling chain.

Its benefits to the community have been demonstrated clearly, particularly with respect to increased employment and revenues. A study from the Institute for Local Self-Reliance entitled "Getting the Most from Our Materials" cites some of the benefits New Jersey has gained from its waste-based manufacturing industry. This state's scrap-based manufacturers, together with other recycling and composting operations, employ over 11,000 people. The largest players in this industry alone bring in almost $1 billion in annual sales and employ close to 6,000 people.

Waste-based manufacturing can happen in two different ways. First, a product such as aluminum cans can be reformed into the same product continuously. Second, a product can be recycled into a completely different product. Glass being turned into glasphalt is such an example.

Although an essential step in the recycling process, waste-based manufacturing is not, however, going to happen overnight. Its successful development involves two separate aspects: changes in manufacturing habits and changes in consumer habits—both relating to reuse of materials and to collection of recyclable goods.

First, changes in manufacturing must happen. Traditionally, each manufacturing process or center in this country is dealt with, and treats itself, as a separate entity: it produces its own products and its own waste. This view must be transformed so that all manufacturing works together: one person's waste is another's raw materials. Only then can we be well on the way to severely curtailing the amount of waste we create. The whole industrial production process needs to be looked at not as a series of unrelated events but as a whole.

Examples of this system can already be found. The state of New Jersey, mentioned earlier, is developing a successful scrap-based manufacturing industry. Moreover, many individual companies are beginning to develop innovative solutions to their waste problems. But these solutions must be further developed and used across the board. Examples include Procter and Gamble, whose diaper scraps are used as stuffing in dolls; Anheuser-Busch, which uses some of its brewery sludge to make compost; and Dow Chemical, which turns some of its chemical by-products into dry-cleaning fluid. Likewise, in some instances wood scraps become chips for fragrance sachets; wastepaper becomes insulation; glass becomes asphalt, brick, and fiberglass. Experimental work is also being done on such products as the waste from sugarcane production, to turn it into methane, and apple waste, to make it into boiler fuel. Metals can also be recovered from power plant fly ash. The possibilities are almost endless.

To develop a successful, interdependent manufacturing system, more companies and individuals must start thinking like the inventive people who developed the preceding examples. Industry must begin to research new ways to reuse whatever waste cannot currently be used. Economic factors will certainly continue to spur them on.

Changes in consumer habits are equally important. As emphasized many times here, consumers must learn to reduce, reuse, recycle, and reject. We buy overpackaged, unnecessary, single-use items in quantities far too great to allow for our future standard of living to remain at its current level without drastically reducing the amount of materials we throw away.

The importance of purchasing recycled materials cannot be overstated. Apart from the simple fact that it's helping reuse otherwise wasted materials, it encourages manufacturers to used recycled materials. Often a manufacturer must make a major investment in new or adjusted machinery to use recycled materials in a product. Understandably, most manufacturers are reluctant to spend large sums of money if they can't be assured of a steady stream of reprocessed materials coming into their plant and a steady market for the new products once they are made. This is where the consumer comes in. The greater our effort to buy recycled whenever we possibly can, the stronger the case for manufacturers to produce such items.

Waste-based manufacturing can be developed in the traditional ways, such as steel and glass recycling, or it can be developed through any number of innovative approaches. We are seeing new developments constantly, such as new uses for tires, and can expect more to appear over the next few years.

Many innovative uses of waste have been in existence for years. Houses, for example, both experimental and practical, are made with quantities of used tires, glass bottles, aluminum and tin cans, used aluminum sheeting, discarded heavy cardboard cores from newsprint rolls, and any number of other materials. Although such projects are often looked at as solely experimental, many exist throughout the country and are fully functional.

The reasons to develop waste-based manufacturing are the same as those to develop the whole recycling chain. But perhaps there are even more specific reasons for industry, which is responsible for implementing this link in the chain. High costs of dumping waste are encouraging businesses large and small to minimize their waste or find alternative uses for it.

In recent years people have begun to discuss the concept of design for recyclability. This means that manufacturers design their products to be easily recycled when their useful life is over. The automobile industry, for example, both in the United States and Europe, is looking at designing cars with recycling in mind. High dumping costs and the potential for cheaper raw materials are making this industry reconsider how to use more recyclable materials in the first place. They are looking at substitutes for multiresin plastics, as in dashboards, which are difficult to recycle, and even at glass and plastic windshields to see how they could be made more practically recyclable.

The cost of dumping alone, however, won't change the habits of manufacturers who have done things the same way for decades. The development of products from recycled materials is going to depend largely on consumer demand: *your* demand. Buying recycled is the only sure way to get industry's attention and thereby to help develop waste-based manufacturing.

9 Recycling into the Future

There is no doubt that recycling will increase in significance as an integral part of our waste management processes in the future. We have seen ample evidence to sustain this belief: recycling offers a sound solution to many of the growing problems with our current system; the many benefits of recycling make it a logical option; and the continued creation of recycling legislation confirms its place as a solid waste disposal tool for generations to come.

We have seen recycling develop from a haphazard system of scavenging, through neighborhood recycling, to the current flourishing programs across the country with an attendant industry developing its own state-of-the-art technology. Over the past three decades our recycling rate has increased from less than 7 percent of our waste stream to today's 13 percent recycling rate.

The recycling rates for some of the major recycled products, like paper, glass, and aluminum, are gradually increasing, though plastics still lag behind. Even lesser-known recyclables, like tires, batteries, and various scrap metals, are getting more attention and hence more recycling. Legislation encouraging the development of markets for some of these less common recyclables is helping the situation.

Still, there's a great deal of room for growth. It has been demonstrated that individuals can make a difference—in home, school, and office recycling programs. Cities, counties, and states can run successful recycling programs also, whether they be mandatory or volunteer. Only a continued effort on the part of everyone concerned will ensure a satisfactory resolution to today's waste problems.

BARRIERS TO RECYCLING—
AND HOW TO OVERCOME THEM

For all the success stories about recycling, we still have many hurdles to overcome before it will develop to its full potential. Most of these obstacles have been noted throughout the previous chapters. Here we will look at some of the more common problems and discuss some possible solutions. With careful thought and organization, all of the obstacles are surmountable.

Financial Factors

If we hope to achieve a national recycling rate of 50 percent or higher, it will be necessary to make recycling economically viable. While we have certainly seen examples of recycling programs that are profitable, this is not always the case. In fact, there are many financial barriers that make recycling's financial viability extremely difficult.

THE PROBLEMS

One major hindrance to the development of markets for recycled products is the financial inequity that often exists between these recycled products and their virgin counterparts. Tax advantages for the manufacture and distribution of products made from virgin and nonrenewable resources in effect encourage the use—and depletion—of our limited natural resources.

Mining subsidies, for example, began much earlier this century. These depletion allowances have subsidized the cost of extracting minerals, oil, and gas from the earth. The U.S. timber industry is also highly subsidized. Subsidies were not initially established to discriminate deliberately against secondary industries but rather to guarantee the continued expansion of the extractive industries. Recently, however, they've had the unfortunate side-effect of severely restricting the development of recycling.

THE SOLUTIONS

There are a number of ways in which we can make the development of markets for recyclables more economically equitable in relation to that for virgin materials. Some of these have been mentioned throughout the book, particularly in the sections discussing legislation. Many more suggestions are being debated across the country as people look for ways to help the development of recycling.

Financial incentives for recycled products and businesses involved in recycling represent an important step in allowing these industries to develop and compete on an equal footing with those using raw materials or other nonrecycled products. While many believe that removing subsidies is not politically feasible, we must redress the balance by giving some advantages to recycled materials and products.

Many states have instituted certain tax credit or exemption schemes that represent a step in the right direction. In California, for example, tax credit for investment in recycling equipment is available for both individuals and corporations. Indiana allows certain tax exemptions. Maine, New Jersey, North Carolina, Oregon, Washington, and Wisconsin all offer some sort of financial incentives for recycling also.

The use of advance disposal fees on products that are nonrecyclable (or are not being recycled in large enough quantities) has increased in popularity in the last few years. States are using this cradle-to-grave fee system with tire recovery programs, for example, where the purchaser is charged a fee of anywhere from twenty-five cents to $2 per tire. The money typically goes into a fund to help manage the disposal of tires or to sponsor research on alternative uses for waste tires. Advance disposal fees represent a logical, environmentally responsible method of raising funds to deal with specific waste problems and can be used with any number of products.

Another suggestion is the creation of loans or bonds for recycling entrepreneurs, such as those developing new products or recycling processes. California, for example, offers development bonds for manufacturing products with recycled content.

Further suggestions to develop recycling through financial means include establishing a deposit charge for all kinds of containers, putting sales tax on disposable, one-time-only items, eliminating sales tax on goods with a set percentage of recycled content, and instituting full-cost accounting. In this last system, the original cost of an item would have to include its production and disposal in addition to compensation for the loss of any natural resources. Clearly, this approach would significantly increase the purchase price of goods with low recycled content and those that are hard to dispose of. Such a system would encourage the consumer to purchase more environmentally responsible products.

Markets

Recycling efforts cannot be successful until there are established markets for recycled materials. As we've noted many times, recycling does not just mean separating materials: the materials must be *reused*. So markets that take products made from recycled materials must be developed and they must be steady and assure reliable quantity and quality.

THE PROBLEMS

Current markets for recycled products are relatively unstable. The market for recycled-fiber newsprint, for example, fluctuates widely and has recently caused huge gluts of paper to be collected with nowhere to go. Highly publicized problems, particularly in the East, were caused by mandatory recycling orders that provided much more recycled paper than the market was ready to handle. The unwanted newsprint almost inevitably ends up in landfills or incinerators—all because the mandatory collection of newsprint was not balanced with equal requirements to use it.

Markets vary by region, also. On the West Coast, for example, paper is regularly shipped to the Far East in addition to being returned to local mills, both of which help to keep the market for used newsprint and cardboard steady. In the Midwest and the East, however, markets for used paper are not so easy to find. Plastic suffers from a similar problem: most of the few existing plastic recycling facilities are in the East, so other parts of the country have more difficulty recycling plastics.

Weak markets can affect all sorts of recycling efforts. Santa Monica, California, had to cancel the yard waste part of its recycling program not long after its inception—mainly because of the lack of markets. Even University City, Missouri, which considers its compost program a success, has to work hard to avoid a carryover of a small amount of compost from one year to the next.

THE SOLUTIONS

Buy recycled: this is ultimately the solution to underdeveloped markets. As individuals we can buy recycled products and we can encourage our businesses, schools, and governments to do the same. The problem with newspaper gluts, as mentioned above, is that there were requirements in force to collect the paper but no such requirements to use it. If all newspapers and the Government Printing Office (GPO) purchased recycled newsprint for use in their publications, for example, there'd be a steady market for the collected newsprint and much less chance for huge gluts.

But purchasing recycled materials is only part of the solution: collection and processing methods will have to expand also to handle the increased supplies of recyclables. This, too, will ensure manufacturers of a steady supply and they, in turn, will use the materials on a regular basis.

Setting recycling goals of 25 or 50 percent means nothing if equal or higher goals for *purchasing* recycled materials and products haven't been set. If governing bodies are going to set recycling goals, they must also set purchasing goals for recycled products. Mandatory government procurement could increase demand for recycled materials and products significantly.

Government procurement of products made from recycled materials is an essential element in the stabilization and development of these markets. Many state governments currently show some kind of preference for buying certain products made with recycled materials, but these procurement policies will need to be much more far-reaching to be effective. While many programs initially looked at paper, these preferential policies have expanded to include such materials as compost, tires, and oil products.

Texas and Louisiana provide good examples of useful preferential buying policies. In Texas, state agencies can pay up to 15 percent more for rubberized asphalt rather than conventional materials in road paving projects. In Louisiana, at least 5 percent of all purchases must be recycled products—and 25 percent of paper purchases must have recycled content by 1996.

Schools and universities must be encouraged to use recycled products whenever possible, as should all government offices. Their volume of stationery and computer paper could significantly affect the development of markets for recycled paper. The GPO alone, as the world's largest printer, could have a staggering impact if it purchased significant quantities of recycled products. Likewise, state highway maintenance agencies should purchase signs, cones, compost, and the like that is made of recycled materials in preference to those made of virgin materials.

These are examples of what can be done. Procurement programs must be more wide-ranging—demanding higher percentages of recycled content and larger numbers of purchases.

Technological Factors

Technological factors will play an important role in the future development of recycling. Investment in equipment and R & D is necessary, as are new design strategies. Both industry and government can contribute significantly to the advancement of recycling's technological infrastructure.

THE PROBLEMS

One of the main technological obstacles to the successful development of recycling is an inadequate capacity to process the *amount* of materials we will be recycling in the years to come. A lack of both recycling and processing facilities in large enough numbers across the country using state-of-the-art equipment will hamper the development of recycling as we begin to increase the demand for these materials.

Another important obstacle is that products are not manufactured with recycling in mind. Squeezable plastic bottles are nice, but their multiple layers make them practically impossible to recycle. Likewise, products made with multiple layers of different materials, like aseptic packaging, present equally difficult recycling problems.

Finally, there is no sophisticated research and development infrastructure for recycling in this country. This means that there is no automatic sharing of new information and no centralized system for organizing research into the problems that face the recycling industry.

THE SOLUTIONS

To meet the challenge of increasing the recycling capacity in this country, substantial investment in new recycling plants and equipment will be needed. As more recyclables are collected, the processing capacity will also need to increase to keep up with the demand from the developing markets.

The facilities needed include such things as new de-inking factories for newsprint and plants to recycle hazardous wastes like oil, lead-acid batteries, and tires. More widespread availability of new processing equipment for MRFs and composting plants will also be needed.

Obviously this kind of system enhancement involves significant cost, but the long-term benefits, financial and environmental, mean that it's worth the effort to overcome these obstacles. By insisting that government and businesses purchase recycled products, we can give the manufacturers the financial incentive necessary to invest in the equipment needed to further develop the markets.

Adjustments and advances can take many forms. Something as straightforward as encouraging manufacturers to produce things more uniformly, which would make recycling easier, can make a big difference without involving massive technological changes.

Design for recycling is another important factor in the future technological development of recycling. This strategy was mentioned in the last chapter in relation to the automobile industry. Design for recycling can be as simple as using glass milk bottles instead of wax-coated paper cartons or as complex as developing new methods of producing automobile parts.

In all industries, nonrecyclable components should be minimized.

Manufacturers should take responsibility for recycling everything possible and for the safe disposal, at the end of a product's life, of anything
that is not recyclable. This would certainly encourage design for recycling.

The federal government can play a key role in overcoming some of
the technical obstacles to recycling. Federal funding of research and
development and funding of information transfer for advances in recycling technology are possible projects for the government. Likewise,
the development of a national database to track available recyclables
and monitor national recycling rates would be extremely beneficial.

Public Habits and Attitudes

The attitude of the public toward recycling is another key factor, and
one that should not be underestimated. Although numerous recycling
efforts have been established with no profit motive and without legislative requirement, it must be accepted that this is not going to be the
case everywhere. Profit and legal pressure are often the two main motives to recycle.

THE PROBLEMS

Changing the public's habits can be one of the most difficult aspects of
developing a recycling program. Project ROSE, which recycles motor
oil in Alabama, cited changing the habits of do-it-yourselfers as one of
the toughest barriers to the success of its program. Likewise, Sauk
County, Wisconsin, noted one of its main obstacles as public apathy.

Many people have to be persuaded to recycle. It doesn't come natu-
rally because of the buy–use–dispose habits that are so well entrenched
in all of us. People also tend to get frustrated by misunderstandings and
misinformation about recycling, and so they may give up and stop
trying, either out of a sense of helplessness or even distrust. With the
type of information often available, this is not surprising.

Degradability and recyclability are two terms about which people
tend to be quite skeptical, and often rightly so. For example, there was
a period recently when "photodegradable" plastic bags were being ad-

vertised everywhere. When people realize, however, that plastic bags are not taken somewhere and laid out in the sun to degrade, but are usually taken to a landfill or incinerator just like the rest of your trash, they become skeptical. And packaging that is advertised as recyclable—but which can in fact only be recycled in a few very specific areas in the country—does not strengthen the public's faith in the information they receive.

Moreover, many people still believe that recycled products are of an inferior quality or may be dirty, or even dangerous. This is simply not true. Recycled products must pass the same quality tests as products from virgin materials.

THE SOLUTIONS

Education is the key to improving the public's recycling habits. People can be taught the benefits of recycling as part of the "reduce, reuse, recycle, reject" philosophy.

In school and at home, children can be taught not only how to recycle, but why it's important to recycle. Children have a great affection for nature that can be used to help them understand the benefits of recycling. If recycling is to become a normal part of our lives we must get children to participate in recycling today, for they are the recyclers of the future.

Of course, recycling, as a relatively new activity for most of us, is something adults need to learn about, too. It takes time for people to understand the reasons for recycling. It isn't obvious, for example, that by recycling bottles, cans, and newspapers we are saving energy, cutting down on pollution, and even providing new jobs as well as saving landfill space. As people become more aware of the wide-ranging benefits of recycling, however, we can be confident that participation will increase. Many recycling programs across the country that encountered public apathy or had trouble changing the public's recycling habits found that education helped tremendously.

Many things can be done to improve the public's faith in genuine recycling practices and in the quality of recycled products. A verifiable labeling system to tell consumers about the recycled content and recyclability of their purchases, such as that being developed by the Green Cross, will provide a reliable source of information about the quality and characteristics of recycled products.

Contamination

The contamination of recyclables has been a serious issue over the years. The amount of damage caused by contamination varies from material to material, but for many recyclables just a small amount of a noncompatible substance can ruin a whole batch.

THE PROBLEMS

Contamination can happen at various stages in the recycling chain. Materials may be contaminated by the households that put them out for curbside collection; they may get contaminated while being stored; or they may even become contaminated during the recycling process.

Any PVC plastic that gets into a batch of PET plastic, for example, can ruin it all because it fouls up the PET recycling process. Glass too must be treated carefully. Bits of ceramic, china, or metal that get into the furnace with recyclable cullet can ruin the quality of the final product. Newspapers must be kept separate from any glossy paper (as in magazines) or office and scrap paper. Unless specified that other paper is acceptable, a mixture will lower the quality of the final product. Likewise, mixing colored paper with high-grade office paper lowers the overall quality of the final product.

THE SOLUTIONS

Education and experience will play important roles in overcoming the obstacle of contamination. Most people, from participants in curbside programs to workers at MRFs, are still learning how to handle recyclables.

As manufacturers of recycled products must be able to rely on a certain quality level, contamination of the recycled materials must be kept to a minimum. This will be achieved on several levels. Shippers and handlers of recycled materials will learn methods to protect the integrity of the materials they deal with. Likewise, better storage facilities are now being built at MRFs that will reduce the likelihood of contamination at this stage of the chain.

Individual recyclers can make a big difference when we take our recyclables to a drop-off center or put them out on the curbside. It is simply a matter of taking care and keeping foreign objects separate from the recyclable goods. The cleanest materials always fetch the highest prices.

THE ROLE OF LEGISLATION

Although many people feel that legislation should be a last resort in our attempts to develop recycling, others say we are now at the point where it is indeed necessary. In many cases it looks as if nothing else will create a demand for recycled products or help find solutions to the reuse of items like tires and batteries. There are several initiatives pending that would attack some of the issues discussed in this book. Among these are several bills to develop recycling that have been proposed by Congressman Esteban E. Torres (D–CA).

The Newsprint Recycling Incentives Act (HR 873) is designed, as its name suggests, to increase the use of recycled newsprint. The bill would require newsprint manufacturers to produce a certain percentage of product with recycled-fiber content. The recycling requirement would be set at a rate only two percentage points higher than the current recycling rate and would increase by 2 percent a year for the next ten years. Manufacturers without the capacity to use recycled fibers (or to use enough to reach the quota) could purchase "recycling credits" from those manufacturers with excess capacity. The idea is to increase the demand for collected newsprint by stimulating the demand for paper with recycled content. The bill recognizes that current manufacturing plants are at or near capacity in using recycled fiber and thus provides an incentive to increase that capacity at a steady rate.

The Lead Battery Recycling Incentives Act (HR 870) is another example of pending legislation. Market forces currently dictate how much lead is recycled (more when virgin lead is expensive, less when it is cheaper), and the environment and our health lose out when lead is not recycled. This bill is designed to ensure lead recycling even when the price of virgin lead falls.

Working along the same lines as the newspaper recycling act, this measure would require battery manufacturers to produce batteries with a specified percentage of recycled lead. Again, the recycled percentage would begin at a rate two percentage points higher than the current rate of recycling and increase by 2 percent annually for ten years to a level of at least 95 percent.

This act as well would develop a system of credits. Any manufacturer producing in excess of the amount of reclaimed lead required could sell a "lead recycling credit" to those who produce batteries with less than the specified rate of reclaimed lead. The percentage of recycled lead content is set by law, but not the price of the credit. It is proposed to let the market establish the price. The recycling credit system intends to put more money in the hands of those producing batteries with the higher percentage of recycled lead. Then, if the price of virgin lead falls, this manufacturer is cushioned, by means of his credit income, from the relative high cost of recycled lead.

The recycling credit system was first introduced in Congress in 1989 as part of the Consumer Products Recovery Act (HR 2648/S 1181). It was later incorporated into other recycling incentive measures such as those mentioned here. This system, developed by Congressman Torres, Senator John Heinz (R–PA), and Senator Tim Wirth (D–CO), was based on work begun in Project 88, commissioned by Senators Heinz and Wirth.

Initiatives such as these may well pave the way for the development of equitable solutions to many of the barriers currently facing recycling in this country. While legislation may not be everyone's first choice as a method to encourage recycling, many current suggestions for legislative action do appear to offer realistic approaches to the problem. As in any new situation, a period of trial and error may be expected to smooth out unforeseen problems.

The ideas presented throughout this book will no doubt be tested, adjusted, and improved upon over the coming years. New and better ideas will come along to supersede or supplement these as participation in the debate becomes more widespread.

Because the environmental and social problems facing this country from our inadequate waste disposal system are very real and very urgent, discussion and education are essential. Only through hard decision making and creative solutions will we be able to clean up some of the mess we have created for ourselves and future generations.

Recycling is an environmentally sound and practical answer to a large part of our waste disposal problems. Its widespread application will depend on as many people as possible learning about its benefits and putting recycling to work. Only by understanding our problems and the options can we become part of the solution.

When you've read this book, please pass it on to a friend or colleague.

Appendix A:
Useful Addresses

General Resources

You can contact the organizations listed here for further information regarding recycling. (Many of these organizations do not focus solely on recycling issues.)

Aluminum Recycling Association
900 19th Street N. W., Suite 300
Washington, DC 20006
[202-862-5100]

American Iron & Steel Institute
1133 15th Street N. W., Suite 300
Washington, DC 20005
[202-452-7100]

American Paper Institute
260 Madison Avenue
New York, NY 10016
[212-340-0600]
[To order Paper Match: 800-878-8878]

Asphalt Recycling and Reclaiming Association
Three Church Circle, Suite 250
Annapolis, MD 21401
[301-267-0023]

Asphalt Rubber Producers Group
3336 North 32nd Street, Suite 106

Phoenix, AZ 85018
[602-955-1141]

Can Manufacturers Institute
1625 Massachusetts Avenue N. W.
Washington, DC 20036
[202-232-4677]

Citizens Clearinghouse for Hazardous Waste
P.O. Box 6806
Falls Church, VA 22040
[703-276-7070]

Concern, Inc.
1717 Massachusetts Avenue N. W., Suite 101
Washington, DC 20036
[202-265-1313]

Council for Solid Waste Solutions
1275 K Street N. W., Suite 400
Washington, DC 20005
[202-371-5319]

Direct Mail Marketing Association
11 West 42nd Street
New York, NY 10036
[212-768-7277]

Earthworm, Inc.
186 South Street

Boston, MA 02111
[617-426-7344]

Washington, DC 20009
[202-462-1177]

Environmental Action Foundation
1525 New Hampshire Avenue N. W.
Washington, DC 20036
[202-745-4870]

INFORM, Inc.
381 Park Avenue South
New York, NY 10016
[212-689-4040]

Environmental Defense Fund
257 Park Avenue South
New York, NY 10010
[212-505-2100]
[Recycling hotline: 800-CALL-EDF]

Institute for Local Self-Reliance
2425 18th Street N. W.
Washington, DC 20009
[202-232-4108]

Institute of Scrap Recycling

Franklin Associates, Ltd.
4121 West 83rd Street, Suite 108
Prairie Village, KS 66208
[913-649-2225]

Industries
1627 K Street N. W.
Washington, DC 20006-1704
[202-466-4050]

Friends of the Earth
218 D Street S. E.
Washington, DC 20003
[202-544-2600]

Keep America Beautiful
9 West Broad Street
Stamford, CT 06902
[203-323-8987]

Glass Packaging Institute
1801 K Street N. W., Suite 1105-L
Washington, DC 20006
[202-887-4850]

National Association of Solvent
Recyclers
1333 New Hampshire Avenue N. W.,
Suite 1100
Washington, DC 20036
[202-463-6956]

Global Tomorrow Coalition
1325 G Street N. W., Suite 915
Washington, DC 20005
[202-628-4016]

National Recycling Coalition
1101 30th Street N. W., Suite 305
Washington, DC 20007
[202-625-6406]

Green Cross Certification Company
1611 Telegraph Avenue, Suite 1111
Oakland, CA 94612
[415-832-1415]

National Soft Drink Association
1101 Sixteenth Street N. W.
Washington, DC 20036
[202-463-6732]

Greenpeace USA
1436 U Street N. W.

National Solid Wastes Management
Association
1730 Rhode Island Avenue N. W.
Washington, DC 20036
[202-861-0708]

Natural Resources Defense Council
40 West 20th Street
New York, NY 10011
[212-727-2700]

Plastics Recycling Foundation
P.O. Box 189
Kennett Square, PA 19348
[215-444-0659]

Sierra Club
730 Polk Street
San Francisco, CA 94109
[415-776-2211]

Solid Waste Alternatives Project
Environmental Action Foundation
1525 New Hampshire Avenue N. W.
Washington, DC 20036
[202-745-4870]

Steel Can Recycling Institute
Foster Plaza 10
680 Andersen Drive
Pittsburgh, PA 15220
[412-922-2772]

U.S. Environmental Protection
Agency
Office of Solid Waste Management
Programs
401 M Street S. W.
Washington, DC 20460
[Recycling hotline: 800-424-9346]

U.S. PIRG (Public Interest Research
Group)
215 Pennsylvania Avenue S. E.
Washington, DC 20003
[202-546-9707]

Worldwatch Institute
1776 Massachusetts Avenue N. W.
Washington, DC 20036
[202-452-1999]

State Recycling Offices

ALABAMA
Department of Environmental
Management
Solid Waste Division
1715 Congressman Wm. Dickinson
Drive
Montgomery, AL 36130
[205-271-7700]

ALASKA
Department of Environmental
Conservation
Solid Waste Program
P.O. Box O
Juneau, AK 99811-1800
[907-465-2671]

ARIZONA
Department of Environmental
Quality—OWP
Waste Planning Section, 4th Floor
Phoenix, AZ 85004
[602-257-2317]

ARKANSAS
Department of Pollution Control and
Ecology
Solid Waste Division

8001 National Drive
Little Rock, AR 72219
[501-562-7444]

CALIFORNIA
Recycling Division
Department of Conservation
819 19th Street
Sacramento, CA 95814
[916-323-3743]

COLORADO
Department of Health
4210 East 11th Avenue
Denver, CO 80220
[303-320-4830]

CONNECTICUT
Recycling Program
Department of Environmental
Protection
Hartford, CT 06106
[203-566-8722]

DELAWARE
Department of Natural Resources
and Environmental Control
89 Kings Highway
P.O. Box 1401
Dover, DE 19903
[302-736-4794]

DISTRICT OF COLUMBIA
Public Space and Maintenance
Administration
4701 Shepard Parkway S.W.
Washington, DC 20032
[202-767-8512]

FLORIDA
Department of Environmental
Regulation

2600 Blairstone Road
Tallahassee, FL 32201
[904-488-0300]

GEORGIA
Department of Community Affairs
40 Marietta Street N.W., 8th Floor
Atlanta, GA 30303
[404-656-3898]

HAWAII
Litter Control Office
Department of Health
205 Koula Street
Honolulu, HI 96813
[808-548-3400]

IDAHO
Department of Environmental
Quality
Hazardous Materials Bureau
450 West State Street
Boise, ID 83720
[208-334-5879]

ILLINOIS
Illinois EPA
Land Pollution Control Division
2200 Churchill Road
P.O. Box 19276
Springfield, IL 62706
[217-782-6761]

INDIANA
Office of Solid and Hazardous Waste
Management
Department of Environmental
Management
105 South Meridian Street
Indianapolis, IN 46225
[317-232-8883]

IOWA
Department of Natural Resources
Waste Management Division
Wallace State Office Building
Des Moines, IA 50319
[515-281-8176]

KANSAS
Bureau of Waste Management
Department of Health and
Environment
Topeka, KS 66620
[913-296-1594]

KENTUCKY
Resources Management Branch
Division of Waste Management
18 Reilly Road
Frankfort, KY 40601
[502-564-6716]

LOUISIANA
Department of Environmental
Quality
P.O. Box 44307
Baton Rouge, LA 70804
[504-765-0249]

MAINE
Office of Waste Reduction and
Recycling
Department of Economic and
Community Development
State House Station #130
Augusta, ME 04333
[207-289-5300]

MARYLAND
Department of Environment
Hazardous and Solid Waste
Administration
2500 Broening Highway, Bldg. 40

Baltimore, MD 21224
[301-631-3316]

MASSACHUSETTS
Division of Solid Waste Management
DEQE
1 Winter Street, 4th Floor
Boston, MA 02108
[617-292-5962]

MICHIGAN
Waste Management Division
Department of Natural Resources
P.O. Box 30028
Lansing, MI 48909
[517-335-1178]

MINNESOTA
Pollution Control Agency
520 Lafayette Road
St. Paul, MN 55155
[612-296-6300]

MISSISSIPPI
Non-Hazardous Waste Section
Bureau of Pollution Control
Department of Natural Resources
P.O. Box 10385
Jackson, MS 39209
[601-961-5047]

MISSOURI
Department of Natural Resources
P.O. Box 176
Jefferson City, MO 65102
[314-751-3176]

MONTANA
Solid Waste Program
Department of Health and
Environmental Science
Cogswell Building, Room B201

Helena, MT 59602
[406-444-2821]

NEBRASKA
Litter Reduction and Recycling
Programs
Department of Environmental
Control
P.O. Box 98922
Lincoln, NE 68509
[402-471-4210]

NEVADA
Energy Extension Service
Office of Community Service
1100 South Williams Street
Carson City, NV 89710
[702-885-4420]

NEW HAMPSHIRE
Waste Management Division
Department of Environmental
Services
6 Hazen Drive
Concord, NH 03301
[603-271-2900]

NEW JERSEY
Office of Recycling
Department of Environmental
Protection
CN 414
401 East State Street
Trenton, NJ 08625
[609-530-4001]

NEW MEXICO
Solid Waste Section
Environmental Improvement
Division
1190 St. Francis Drive

Santa Fe, NM 87503
[505-827-0197]

NEW YORK
Bureau of Waste Reduction and
Recycling
Department of Environmental
Conservation
50 Wolf Road, Room 208
Albany, NY 12233
[518-457-7337]

NORTH CAROLINA
Solid Waste Management Branch
Department of Human Resources
P.O. Box 2091
Raleigh, NC 27602
[919-571-4100]

NORTH DAKOTA
Division of Waste Management
Department of Health
1200 Missouri Avenue, Room 302
Box 5520
Bismark, ND 58502-5520
[701-224-2366]

OHIO
Division of Litter Prevention and
Recycling
Ohio EPA
Fountain Square Building, E-1
Columbus, OH 43224
[614-265-7061]

OKLAHOMA
Solid Waste Division
Department of Health
1000 N.E. 10th Street
Oklahoma City, OK 73152
[405-271-7159]

OREGON
Department of Environmental
Quality
811 S. W. Sixth
Portland, OR 97204
[503-229-5913]

PENNSYLVANIA
Waste Reduction and Recycling
Section
Division of Waste Minimization and
Planning
Department of Environmental
Resources
P.O. Box 2063
Harrisburg, PA 17120
[717-787-7382]

RHODE ISLAND
Office of Environmental
Coordination
Department of Environmental
Management
83 Park Street
Providence, RI 02903
[401-277-3434]

SOUTH CAROLINA
Department of Health and
Environmental Control
2600 Bull Street
Columbia, SC 29201
[803-734-5200]

SOUTH DAKOTA
Energy Office
217 1/2 West Missouri
Pierre, SD 57501
[605-773-3603]

TENNESSEE
Department of Public Health
Division of Solid Waste Management
Customs House, 4th Floor
701 Broadway
Nashville, TN 37219-5403
[615-741-3424]

TEXAS
Division of Solid Waste Management
Department of Health
1100 West 49th Street
Austin, TX 78756
[512-458-7271]

UTAH
Bureau of Solid and Hazardous
Waste
Department of Environmental
Health
P.O. Box 16690
Salt Lake City, UT 84116-0690
[801-538-6170]

VERMONT
Agency of National Resources
103 South Main Street, West
Building
Waterbury, VT 05676
[802-244-7831]

VIRGINIA
Department of Waste Management
Division of Litter Control and
Recycling
11th Floor, Monroe Building
101 North 14th Street
Richmond, VA 23219
[Inside VA: 800-KeepIt]
[804-367-1310]

WASHINGTON
Department of Ecology
Mail Stop PV-11
Olympia, WA 95804
[Inside WA: 800-Recycle]
[206-459-6000]

WEST VIRGINIA
Department of Natural Resources
Conservation, Education, and Litter
Control
1800 Washington Street East
Charleston, WV 25305
[304-348-3370]

WISCONSIN
Department of Natural Resources
P.O. Box 7921
Madison, WI 53707
[608-266-5741]

WYOMING
Solid Waste Management Program
Department of Environmental
Quality
Herschler Building
122 West 25th Street
Cheyenne, WY 82002
[307-777-7752]

Appendix B: Some Sources of Recycled Products

Acorn Designs
5066 Mott Evans Road
Trumansburg, NY 14886
[607-387-3424]
Printing and writing paper.

Atlantic Recycled Paper Co.
P.O. Box 39096
Baltimore, MD 21212
[301-323-2676]
Office paper and envelopes, computer paper, household paper goods (tissue paper, toilet paper, paper towels, napkins).

Central Paper Co.
1004 Whitehead Road Ext.
Trenton, NJ 08638
[609-883-7500]
Recycled paper products.

Conservatree Paper Co.
10 Lombard Street, Suite 250
San Francisco, CA 94111
[800-522-9200]
[415-433-1000]
Recycled office paper supplies.

Co-op America
2100 M Street N.W., Suite 403
Washington, DC 20063
[800-424-2667]
Catalog items include clothing, furniture made from scraps from the timber industry,

canvas grocery bags, recycled paper products, water conservation devices, household cleaners, and more.

Earth Care Paper, Inc.
P.O. Box 14140
Madison, WI 53714
[608-277-2900]
Catalog sales of recycled paper gift wrap, cards, calendars, stationery, posters, paper pads, printing paper, copy and computer paper, and more.

Ecco Bella
6 Provost Square, Suite 602
Caldwell, NJ 07006
[800-322-9366]
[201-226-5799]
A mail-order company that sells cruelty-free products, environmentally friendly products, and recycled products.

Ecological Fibers, Inc.
Pioneer Industrial Park
Lunenberg, MA 01462
[508-537-0003]
Recycled, acid-free paper.

Eco-Pack Industries, Inc.
7859 South 180th Street
Kent, WA 98032
[206-251-0918]
Alternative packing products.

Ecoprint
9335 Fraser Avenue
Silver Spring, MD 20910
[301-585-7077]
These printers specialize in printing on fine recycled papers and using environmentally friendly printing processes. They do not sell unprinted paper directly to the public.

Esselte Pendaflex Corporation
71 Clinton Road
Garden City, NY 11530
[516-741-3200]
A line of "Earthwise" recycled office products.

Lewmar Paper Co.
P.O. Box 490
Kenilworth, NJ 07033
[908-298-0800]
Recycled paper products.

Paper In Motion
P.O. Box 97
Newton Upper Falls, MA 02164
[617-964-2788]
Printing and writing paper.

Peacetree Recycled Paper
4134 N. Vancouver
Portland, OR 97214
[503-282-7266]
Printing and writing paper.

Pennsylvania Resources Council
P.O. Box 88
Media, PA 19063
[215-565-9131]
PRC has prepared a kit with a booklet entitled "Become an Environmental Shopper: Vote for the Environment" and a product list of 400 items in recyclable or recycled

packaging. The larger kit includes a poster. Kits are $3.50 and $5.00.

Quill Corporation
P.O. Box 50-050
Ontario, CA 91761-1050
[714-988-3200]
An office products mail-order company that sells some recycled products.

Recycled Paper Company
185 Corey Road
Boston, MA 02146
[617-277-9901]
Office paper supplies, including copy, computer, and fax paper, printed letterheads, and file folders.

Recycled Products Guide
P.O. Box 577
Ogdensburg, NY 13669
[800-267-0707]
Subscription service providing information on recycled products.

Seventh Generation
Colchester, VT 05446-1672
[800-441-2538]
A line of "Products for a Healthy Planet." Some of their products include large paper trash bags, recycled toilet paper, tissue paper, copy and computer paper, and composting equipment.

Treekeepers
249 South Hwy 101, Suite 518
Solana Beach, CA 92075
[619-481-6403]
Alternative shopping products — reusable canvas shopping bags and canvas lunch bags, for example.

Appendix C: Periodicals

American City and County
Communication Channels, Inc.
6255 Barfield Road
Atlanta, GA 30328
[404-256-9800]

American Metal Market
825 7th Avenue, 7th Floor
New York, NY 10019
[212-887-8580]

BioCycle
The JG Press
419 State Avenue
Emmaus, PA 18049
[215-967-4135]

Environmental Action
Environmental Action Foundation
1525 New Hampshire Avenue N. W.
Washington, DC 20036
[202-745-4870]

Environmental Decisions
National League of Cities
1301 Pennsylvania Avenue N. W.
Washington, DC 20004
[202-626-3000]

Everyone's Backyard
Citizen's Clearinghouse for Hazard-
ous Wastes
P.O. Box 6806
Falls Church, VA 22040
[703-276-7070]

*Garbage:The Practical Journal for the Envi-
ronment*
435 9th Street
Brooklyn, NY 11215
[718-788-1700]

Greenpeace Magazine
Greenpeace USA
1436 U Street N. W.
Washington, DC 20009
[202-462-1177]

NRDC Newsline
Natural Resources Defense Council
40 West 20th Street
New York, NY 10011
[212-727-2700]

Paper Match
American Paper Institute
Solid Waste Resource Center
260 Madison Avenue
New York, NY 10016
[800-878-8878]

Phoenix
Institute of Scrap Recycling Industries
1627 K Street N. W.
Washington, DC 20006-1704
[202-466-4050]

Recycling Times
National Solid Wastes Management
Association

1730 Rhode Island Avenue N. W.
Washington, DC 20036
[202-861-0708]

Recycling Today
GIE Publishing
4012 Bridge Avenue
Cleveland, OH 44113
[216-961-4130]

Resource Recycling
P.O. Box 10540
Portland, OR 97210
[503-227-1319]

Scrap Processing and Recycling
Institute of Scrap Recycling Industries

1627 K Street N. W.
Washington, DC 20006-1704
[202-466-4050]

Sierra
Sierra Club
730 Polk Street
San Francisco, CA 94109
[415-776-2211]

Waste Age
National Solid Wastes Management
Association
1730 Rhode Island Avenue N. W.
Washington, DC 20036
[202-861-0708]

Glossary

advance disposal fee: A per-container fee charged at the time of purchase. Proceeds typically go to support container recycling.

air classifier: A separating device that uses air to divide waste into lighter and heavier materials.

aseptic packaging: Used to make "drink boxes" (single-serving juice containers), these packages are made of aluminum foil, plastic, and paper. While convenient, they are extremely difficult to recycle because of their layers of different materials.

baghouse: A pollution control device in an incineration facility that collects airborne particles in large fabric filters.

baler: A machine that compacts waste materials to reduce volume.

bimetal container: A container made out of two metals. Typically, the body of the can is steel and the lid is aluminum.

biodegradable material: Waste material that is capable of being readily decomposed, especially by bacteria, into basic natural elements. Food wastes and paper are biodegradable.

bottle bill: Any mandatory beverage container deposit law or any law that encourages the use of recyclable glass containers rather than throwaway containers.

bottom ash: Small particles of ash and soot that fall to the bottom of an incinerator. Also called ground ash.

Btu: British thermal unit—the amount of energy generated by burning a given material. Literally, one Btu is the amount of heat required to raise the temperature of one pound of water by one degree Fahrenheit.

buy-back programs: Programs that purchase recyclable materials from the public.

closed-loop recycling: A system in which materials are continually recycled into the same product. Aluminum cans and glass bottles can be recycled in a closed-loop system.

combustibles: Materials from the waste stream that can be burned.

composting: A process that converts most organic materials, such as food and yard waste, to humus by microorganic activity.

crumb rubber: Rubber that has been cut up into small pieces.

cullet: Broken glass, typically in small pieces about the size of a pea, used in the manufacturing process. Glass is broken into cullet before being recycled.

curbside recycling: Any program that collects recyclable waste from residential curbsides.

degradable: Capable of being broken down into simpler compounds.

depletion allowance: A tax allowance for users of certain virgin materials in compensation for the depletion of these materials.

digester: A large drumlike vessel used to compost organic solid waste. As the waste is continuously mixed and aerated, composting is more rapid than other methods such as windrows.

electrostatic precipitator: A pollution control device in an incineration facility that collects airborne particles by using an electrical charge.

EPA: The U.S. Environmental Protection Agency.

ferrous metals: Metals that contain iron. Most common ferrous metals are magnetic.

flint glass: Clear glass.

fly ash: Small particles of ash and soot that are caught in the pollution control equipment of an incinerator.

ground ash: Another term for bottom ash.

HDPE: High-density polyethylene. This plastic is best known as the material from which milk and water jugs and soft drink bottle bases are made.

IPC: Intermediate processing center. Another term for a MRF.

IPF: Intermediate processing facility. Another term for a MRF.

Leachate: Liquid that has filtered down through the waste in a landfill and become contaminated.

Magnetic separator: A device that uses magnets to separate metals from waste.

Mass burn: Incineration of solid waste with no preprocessing to remove recyclables.

Methane: A gas produced by the decomposition of waste in a landfill. It is odorless, colorless, and extremely flammable.

MRF: Materials recovery facility (pronounced "murf"). An intermediate processing center that cleans and separates mixed recyclable materials and otherwise prepares them for final markets. (See also IPC and IPF.)

MSW: Municipal solid waste. All waste generated in a given municipality from residential, industrial, or commercial sources.

Nonferrous metals: Metals that contain no iron, such as aluminum, copper, brass, and bronze.

PET: Polyethylene terephthalate. This is the type of plastic used in the two-liter soda bottle. Qualities include resistance to moisture and good insulation.

photodegradation: Deterioration from the ultraviolet radiation in sunlight.

Post-consumer waste: Waste generated from residential or commercial sources that has completed its intended use.

Pre-consumer waste: Waste from any manufacturing process, such as glass broken in the factory or paper offcuts from a paper mill. It specifically refers to waste materials that never reach the consumer.

Precycling: Another term for waste reduction or source reduction.

Price preferential: A policy that allows an entity to pay a specified amount more for a product with recycled content than it would pay for the equivalent product from virgin materials.

PVC: Polyvinyl chloride. A type of plastic used in flooring, records, vinyl siding, shower curtains, and garden hoses.

Pyrolysis: The process of decomposing waste by heat action in an oxygen-deficient atmosphere.

Raw materials: Materials that are still in their natural, preprocessed state.

RDF: Refuse-derived fuel—that is, fuel derived from the incineration of municipal solid waste. It is usually burned to create electricity.

recycling: Any process by which materials otherwise destined for disposal are collected, separated or processed, remanufactured, and reused.

recycling credit: A proposed method of encouraging manufacturers to recycle certain materials. Those using more than a required amount of recycled materials in their products could sell credits to manufacturers not meeting the minimum standards, therefore earning money from their recycling efforts.

resource recovery: A term that used to mean the extraction of reusable materials from the waste stream but now often refers to the incineration of mixed waste to create energy.

scrubbers: Pollution control devices in incineration facilities that neutralize acid gases by mixing them with a lime solution.

source reduction: Another term for waste reduction.

Superfund site: Superfund is the common name for the Comprehensive Environmental Response Compensation and Liability Act (CERCLA), an act passed in 1980 by Congress that allocated funds to the EPA to begin cleaning up the nation's worst toxic dumps. A Superfund site is any location that has been allocated cleanup funds through this program.

TPD: Tons per day. Used as a measurement of solid waste capacity at a MRF or an incineration facility, for example.

virgin materials: Another term for raw materials.

waste reduction: A policy of creating less waste in the first place—by using fewer disposable products or products with less packaging, for example. Also called source reduction or precycling.

waste stream: The waste output of any area, facility, or other entity.

waste-to-energy incineration: The process of burning municipal solid waste to produce energy.

windrow composting: Composting in long piles that are turned regularly to speed decomposition.

Bibliography

In addition to the publications cited here, the state recycling offices of the following states were all contacted to verify recycling legislation and statistics: California, Connecticut, Florida, Illinois, Indiana, Iowa, Louisiana, Maine, Maryland, Michigan, Minnesota, Missouri, New Jersey, New Mexico, New York, North Carolina, Ohio, Oklahoma, Pennsylvania, Rhode Island, Tennessee, Texas, Vermont, West Virginia, Washington, Wisconsin, and the District of Columbia.

Acott, Mike. "Hot Mix Asphalt Changes Are on the Horizon." *American City & County*, January 1990, pp. 42–44.

Aguilar, Marlene. "Trash Recycling Daily Routine for People of Wellesley, Mass." *Waterbury Sunday Republican*, 20 August 1989, p. A-10.

Alcoa. "Aluminum Cans Make Sense!" Pittsburgh: Alcoa, 1989.

"A Look at Plastic Wastes." *Reusable News* (EPA), Spring 1990, p. 3.

Aluminum Association. "Aluminum Recycling: America's Environmental Success Story." Washington, DC: Aluminum Association, 1990.

———. "U. S. Aluminum Can Recycling—72–88." Washington, DC: Aluminum Association, 1990.

American Newspaper Publishers Association. "Read. Then Recycle." Washington, DC: American Newspaper Publishers Association, 1990.

American Recovery Corporation. "Sorain Cecchini Technology." Washington, DC: American Recovery Corporation, 1990.

Anderson, Carol. "Governing Guide: Recycling." *Governing*, August 1990, pp. 5A–28A.

Apotheker, Steve. "Animal Bedding—a Capital Idea." *Resource Recycling*, July 1990, p. 42.

———. "Fine Printing and Writing Paper—It's Recycled, Too." *Resource Recycling*, May 1990, pp. 30–33.

———. "Market Quality Issues Loom for MRFs." *Resource Recycling*, May 1990, pp. 28–29.

Arnold, Dana, et al. "EPA Guidelines Emphasize Recycling." *American City & County*, May 1989, p. 64.

"Aseptic Packaging Recycled into Plastic Lumber." *Recycling Times*, 14 August 1990, p. 15.

Asphalt Recycling and Reclaiming Association. "Guideline Specifications for

Cold Planing." Annapolis, MD: Asphalt Recycling and Reclaiming Association, 1986.

———. "Guideline Specifications for Hot In-Place Recycling." Annapolis, MD: Asphalt Recycling and Reclaiming Association, 1988.

———. "Guidelines for Cold In-Place Recycling." Annapolis, MD: Asphalt Recycling and Reclaiming Association, 1986.

———. "Proven Guidelines for Hot-Mix Recycling." Annapolis, MD: Asphalt Recycling and Reclaiming Association, 1986.

Asphalt Rubber Producers Group. "Texas Asphalt-Rubber Survey." Phoenix: Asphalt Rubber Producers Group, 1990.

———. "Uses of Asphalt Rubber." Phoenix: Asphalt Rubber Producers Group, 1989.

Beck, Melinda, et al. "Buried Alive." *Newsweek*, 27 November 1989, pp. 66–76.

Bennack, Frank A., Jr. "A Look at Newsprint Recycling: Today & Tomorrow." Speech at the Rochester Institute of Technology, Rochester, NY, 11 April 1990.

Breen, Bill. "Landfills Are #1." *Garbage*, September/October 1990, pp. 42–47.

Bremmer, Brian. "Recycling: The Newest Wrinkle in Waste Management's Bag." *Business Week*, 5 March 1990, pp. 48–49.

Cadwallader, Mark. "Landfill Liner Systems Keep Waste from Water." *American City & County*, May 1988, p. 46.

Caplan, Ruth, et al. *Our Earth, Ourselves*. New York: Bantam Books, 1990.

Casey, Nancy. "Garbage Prevention and Recycling: An Analysis of State Legislation." A Greenpeace Action Report. Washington, DC: Greenpeace Action, 1990.

Center for Plastics Recycling Research. "Market Research on Plastics Recycling." Technical Report 31. Washington, DC: Plastics Recycling Foundation; Pascataway, NJ: Center for Plastics Recycling Research, 1989.

Citizen's Clearinghouse for Hazardous Wastes. *Recycling . . . the Answer to Our Garbage Problem*. Arlington, VA: Citizen's Clearinghouse for Hazardous Wastes, 1987.

Coakley, Michael. "In Wellesley, People Wouldn't Dream of Trashing the Dump." *Chicago Tribune*, 24 June 1986.

Concern, Inc. *Household Waste: Issues and Opportunities*. Washington, DC: Concern, Inc., 1989.

Cooper, Gary (AARP). Telephone conversation with author, June 1991.

Council for Solid Waste Solutions. "How Modern Waste-to-Energy Plants Work." Washington, DC: Council for Solid Waste Solutions, 1989.

Crampton, Norm. *Complete Trash*. New York: M. Evans and Company, 1989.

"Curbside Recycling Programs Take Off But We Need More Ways to Re-use Our Refuse." *Audubon Activist*, May/June 1989, p. 11.

Dadd, Debra Lynn, and Andre Carothers. "A Bill of Goods? Green Consuming in Perspective." *Greenpeace*, May/June 1990, pp. 8–12.

"The Degradable Plastics Debate." *Reusable News* (EPA), Spring 1990, p. 3.

"The Dow–Huntsman–National Park Service Recycling Program: A Report on the Program's First Summer Season." Report presented for the director, National Park Service, December 1990.

EarthWorks Group. *50 Simple Things You Can Do to Save the Earth*. Berkeley: EarthWorks Press, 1989.

———. *The Recycler's Handbook*. Berkeley: EarthWorks Press, 1990.

Federal Register. Vol. 53, no. 120, 22 June 1988, Environmental Protection Agency, 40 CFR Part 250, 23555–23556.

———. Vol. 54, no. 32, 17 February 1989, Environmental Protection Agency, 40 CFR Part 248, 7345.

Fins, Antonio, and George Coats. "Meet the Kings of the Garbage Heap." *Business Week*, 12 September 1988, pp. 112–116.

Foote, Jeffrey R. (National Soft Drink Association). Letter to author, 7 May 1990.

Forsell Stauffer, Roberta. "Energy Savings from Recycling." *Resource Recycling*, January/February 1989, pp. 24–25.

———. "Recycle While You Play." *Resource Recycling*, May 1990, pp. 46–50.

Franklin Associates. "Integrated Solid Waste Management." McLean, VA: Franklin Associates, 1991.

"From Shower to Scour: Waste Stopper: Pumice on Copper." *Ideas: A Compendium of 3P Success Stories*. Saint Paul: 3M, 1990.

"From Trash to Cash." *Business Week*, 18 June 1990, p. 30.

Frosch, Robert A., and Nicholas E. Gallopoulos. "Strategies for Manufacturing." *Scientific American*, September 1989, pp. 144–152.

Gallagher, Mark (Curry Company, Yosemite). Telephone conversation with author, 5 June 1991.

Gibboney, Douglas L. "Closing the Loop with Glass Recycling." *BioCycle*, April 1990, pp. 90–92.

Gibson, Susan. "National Park Service Pilots Plastic Recycling." *Recycling Today*, August 1990, pp. 62–63.

———. "Recyclers Find Alternate Methods for Curbside Success." *Recycling Today*, July 1990, pp. 54–56.

Glass Packaging Institute. "How to Curb the Solid Waste Crisis." Washington, DC: Glass Packaging Institute, 1988.

Glenn, Jim. "Curbside Recycling Reaches 40 Million." *BioCycle*, July 1990, pp. 30–37.

———. Telephone conversation with author, June 1991.

Glenn, Jim, and David Riggle. "Where Does the Waste Go?" *BioCycle*, April 1989, pp. 34–39.

Goldstein, Nora. "Solid Waste Composting in the U.S." *BioCycle,* November 1989, pp. 32–37.

Goldstein, Nora, and Bob Spencer. "Solid Waste Composting Facilities." *Bio-Cycle,* January 1990, pp. 36–39.

Gorino, Bob (ISRI). Telephone conversation with author, June 1991.

Green, Mark. "Recyclable . . . or Just Fraudulent?" *New York Times,* 21 April 1991, p. 11.

Green Cross Certification Company. "The Green Cross Certification Company: Setting a New Standard for Environmental Excellence." Oakland, CA: Green Cross, 1991.

————. "Green Cross Recycled Content Certification Standards." Oakland, CA: Green Cross, 1991.

Greenpeace Action. "Greenpeace Action Community Recycling Start-Up Kit." Washington, DC: Greenpeace Action, 1989.

————. "Municipal Solid Waste Incinerators." Washington, DC: Greenpeace Action, 1989.

————. "Toward a Chlorine-free Pulp and Paper Industry." Washington, DC: Greenpeace Action, 1990.

————. "Waste Reduction and Recycling." Washington, DC: Greenpeace Action, 1990.

Grogan, Peter. "Nine Legislatures Choose Weapons." *Waste Age,* February 1990, pp. 52–58.

Haylen, Peter (Encore!). Telephone conversation with author, June 1991.

Hecht, Shaun (Environmental Action Coalition of New York). Telephone conversation with author, June 1991.

Institute for Local Self-Reliance. *Beyond 40 Percent: Record-Setting Recycling and Composting Programs.* Washington, DC: Island Press, 1991.

————. "Institute for Local Self-Reliance, Environmentally Sound Economic Development." Washington, DC: Institute for Local Self-Reliance.

Institute of Scrap Recycling Industries. "Recycling Nonferrous Scrap Metals." Washington, DC: Institute of Scrap Recycling Industries, 1990.

————. "Recycling Paper." Washington, DC: Institute of Scrap Recycling Industries, 1990.

————. "Recycling Scrap Iron and Steel." Washington, DC: Institute of Scrap Recycling Industries, 1990.

————. "Recycling Scrap Materials Contributes to a Better Environment." Washington, DC: Institute of Scrap Recycling Industries, 1991.

Kermode, George E. (Bumper Recycling Association of North America). Letter to author, 2 April 1990.

Kimball, Bob (XTree Company). Telephone conversation with author, June 1991.

Kraten, Steven. "Market Failure and the Economics of Recycling." *Environmental Decisions*, April 1990, pp. 20–25.

Kroesa, Renate. *The Greenpeace Guide to Paper.* Vancouver, BC: Greenpeace, 1990.

Kurtz, Connie (National Park Service). Telephone conversation with author, 3 June 1991.

Logsdon, Gene. "Agony and Ecstasy of Tire Recycling." *BioCycle*, July 1990, pp. 44–45.

Luoma, Jon R. "Trash Can Realities." *Audubon*, March 1990, pp. 86–97.

MacEachern, Diane. *Save Our Planet: 750 Everyday Ways You Can Help Clean Up the Earth.* New York: Dell Publishing, 1990.

MacLean, Alair. "Clouds and Silver Linings: Paper Recycling and Pollution." Paper presented at the National Recycling Congress, San Diego, 22 August 1990.

Marinelli, Janet. "Composting: From Backyards to Big-Time." *Garbage*, July/August 1990, pp. 44–51.

McClanahan, Michael F., and Kathleen E. Kelly. "The Largest Public MRF in Florida." *BioCycle*, July 1990, p. 79.

Miller, Krystal. "On the Road Again and Again and Again: Auto Makers Try to Build Recyclable Car." *Wall Street Journal*, 30 April 1991, p. B-1.

Mitchell, Adam. *Once Is Not Enough: A Citizen's Recycling Manual.* Boston: National Toxics Campaign (for Northeast People Organized to Win Environmental Rights), 1989.

Morris, David, et al. *Getting the Most from Our Materials: Making New Jersey the State of the Art.* Washington, DC: Institute for Local Self-Reliance, 1991.

National Association for Plastic Container Recovery. "Recycling PET: A Guidebook for Community Programs." Charlotte, NC: National Association for Plastic Container Recovery, 1989.

National Oceanic and Atmospheric Administration, Marine Debris Information Office. "Our Water Planet Is Becoming Polluted with Plastic Debris . . ." San Francisco: NOAA Marine Debris Information Office, 1990.

National Recycling Coalition. "Membership." Washington, DC: National Recycling Coalition, 1990.

———. "The National Policy on Recycling." Washington, DC: National Recycling Coalition, 1989.

National Soft Drink Association. "Cans." Washington, DC: National Soft Drink Association, 1988.

———. "Glass." Washington, DC: National Soft Drink Association, 1988.

National Solid Wastes Management Association. "At a Glance: Recycling Solid Waste." Washington, DC: National Solid Wastes Management Association, 1989.

———. "At a Glance: Recycling Solid Waste." Washington, DC: National Solid Wastes Management Association, 1990.

————. "At a Glance: Solid Waste Disposal Overview." Washington, DC: National Solid Wastes Management Association, 1991.

————. "Garbage Then and Now." Washington, DC: National Solid Wastes Management Association, 1990.

————. "Special Report: The Future of Newspaper Recycling." Washington, DC: National Solid Wastes Management Association, 1990.

————. "Special Report: Landfill Capacity in the Year 2000." Washington, DC: National Solid Wastes Management Association, 1989.

————. "Special Report: Recycling in the States, Update 1989." Washington, DC: National Solid Wastes Management Association, 1989.

National Wildlife Federation. *Your Choices Count.* Vienna, VA: National Wildlife Federation, 1990.

"125-Plus Recycling Laws Enacted." *Waste Age,* January 1990, p. 8.

Oregon Department of Environmental Quality. "Oregon's Recycling Program(s)." Portland: DEQ, 1990.

————. "Update: Oregon's New Recycling Act." Portland: DEQ, 1989.

Paper Stock Institute. "Recycling Paper." Washington, DC: Institute of Scrap Recycling Industries, 1990.

Pierson, Robert W., Jr. "Eight Steps to Block Corner Success." *Waste Age,* November 1988, pp. 147–158.

————. "Low-Cost Recycling: Block Corner Pickup." *Waste Age,* October 1988, pp. 126–128.

"Plastic Bans Proliferate, Prodding Industry onto Recycling Bandwagon." *Audubon Activist,* May/June 1989, p. 10.

Pollock, Cynthia. *Mining Urban Wastes: The Potential for Recycling.* Washington, DC: Worldwatch Institute, 1987.

Powell, Jerry. "All Plastics Are Not Created Equal." *Resource Recycling,* May 1990, pp. 38–41.

"Putting Our Agenda into Action: Source Reduction and Recycling." *Reusable News* (EPA), Spring 1990, p. 7.

Rathje, William L. "The History of Garbage." *Garbage,* September/October 1990, pp. 32–39.

————. "Rubbish!" *Atlantic Monthly,* December 1989, pp. 99–109.

"Recycling Offers Benefits, Opportunities . . . and Challenges." *Waste Age,* January 1988, pp. 54–60.

"Recycling Plastics: A Forum." *Environmental Action,* July/August 1988, pp. 21–26.

"Recycling Program of Yosemite Park and Curry Co." Yosemite, CA: Curry Company, 1991.

Root, Jon (Santa Monica Recycling Office). Telephone conversation with author, June 1991.

Rosenberg, Arnie. "Glass Makers Are Perfectly Clear on Cullet's Rise to Prominence." *Recycling Today!*, December 1989, pp. 93–95.

Royster, Patty (BFI, Santa Clara County). Telephone conversation with author, 4 June 1991.

Rubber Manufacturers Association. "Scrap Tires Fact Sheet 1988." Washington, DC: Rubber Manufacturers Association, 1988.

Sanjour, William. "Why EPA Is Like It Is." Paper presented to the meeting of the Coalition for Health Concern at Kenlake, KY, 17 November 1990.

Schwartz, Anne. "Drowning in Trash, We Begin to Discard Our Wasteful Ways." *Audubon Activist*, May/June 1989, p. 1.

Schwartz, John, et al. "Turning Trash into Hard Cash." *Newsweek*, 14 March 1988, pp. 36–37.

"Scrap: America's Ready Resource." *Phoenix Quarterly* (special issue), April 1989.

Seldman, Neil. "Community Recycling: Its Past, Present and Future." *Building Economic Alternatives*, Winter 1989, p. 7.

———. Telephone conversation with author, 28 October 1991.

Serumgard, John R. "Special Waste: Scrap Tires." Speech presented at the Recycling Business and Technology Conference, Washington, DC, 22 February 1990.

Sibbison, Jim. "Revolving Door at the EPA" *The Nation*, 6 November 1989, pp. 524–528.

Simon, Ruth. "Alchemy, 1990s Style." *Forbes*, 24 July 1989, pp. 92–96.

Slipek, Stephen (National Park Service). Telephone conversation with author, 3 June 1991.

"Solvent Saver: Film Unit Develops Pollution Solution." *Ideas: A Compendium of 3P Success Stories*. Saint Paul: 3M, 1990.

Spano, Nicholas A. "Wheels of Fortune." Report. Albany: New York State Legislature, January 1990.

Stark, Fred (Rubber Research Elastomerics, Inc.). Telephone conversation with author, June 1991.

"State Initiatives: The Driving Force in U.S. Recycling Policy." *Environment Week*, 30 November 1989, p. 10.

"The Steel Can: An American Classic." *Food & Beverage Marketing*, November 1989, pp. 23–42.

Steel Can Recycling Institute. "Steel: Building on a History of Recycling Leadership." Pittsburgh: Steel Can Recycling Institute, 1989.

———. "Steel: It's a Natural Friend of the Environment." Pittsburgh: Steel Can Recycling Institute, 1989.

Stoga, Susan (Hyatt Hotels). Telephone conversation with author, June 1991.

Tharp, Joan (Hewlett-Packard). Telephone conversation with author, June 1991.

Torres, Esteban E. "Lead Battery Recycling Incentives Act, (proposed), H.R. 870." U.S. Congress. Photocopy.

———. "Newsprint Recycling Incentives Act, (proposed), H.R. 873." U.S. Congress. Photocopy.

Treadaway, Dan. "Is Recycling the Answer?" *American City & County*, May 1989, pp. 40–54.

U.S. Department of Energy. "Recycling Waste to Save Energy." FS 227. Washington, DC: DOE, 1989.

U.S. Environmental Protection Agency, Office of Solid Waste. *Decision-Makers' Guide to Solid Waste Management.* EPA/530-SW-89-072. Washington, DC: EPA, 1989.

———. *How to Set Up a Local Program to Recycle Used Oil.* EPA/530-SW-89-039A. Washington, DC: EPA, 1989.

———. *Recycling Works! State and Local Solutions to Solid Waste Management Problems.* EPA/530-SW-89-014. Washington, DC: EPA, 1989.

———. (Solid Waste Information Clearinghouse). Telephone conversation with author, May 1990.

Walton, Jim. "Asphalt Recycling: An Alternative." *American City & County*, August 1988, p. 80.

Waste Management, Inc. "An Introduction to Waste Management, Inc." Oak Brook, IL: Waste Management, Inc., 1991.

Watson, Tom. "Mixed Rigid Plastic Containers: Making the Grade." *Resource Recycling*, May 1990, pp. 22–25.

Wellesley, Massachusetts. Department of Public Works. "Wellesley's Recycling Program." 19 December 1989.

XTree Company. "The XTree Green Pages." San Luis Obispo, CA: XTree Company, 1991.

———. "XTree's Greenprint." San Luis Obispo, CA: XTree Company, 1991.

Yaskin, Judith A. "Recycling Update: Recycling in Review—Year III." *New Jersey Municipalities*, January 1991, pp. 12–13.

Index

About the Author

Jennifer Carless has written previously on international political and defense issues. She holds a bachelor's degree in French and Spanish and a master's degree in international policy studies.

She has lived in London, Paris, Madrid, and Geneva, and currently resides in northern California. She is a member of the Author's Guild and an avid traveler and music lover. Her next book, evaluating renewable energy sources, is due to be published in late 1992.

Also Available from Island Press

Balancing on the Brink of Extinction: The Endangered Species Act and Lessons for the Future
Edited by Kathryn A. Kohm

Better Trout Habitat: A Guide to Stream Restoration and Management
By Christopher J. Hunter

Beyond 40 Percent: Record-Setting Recycling and Composting Programs
The Institute for Local Self-Reliance

Coastal Alert: Ecosystems, Energy, and Offshore Oil Drilling
By Dwight Holing

The Complete Guide to Environmental Careers
The CEIP Fund

Death in the Marsh
By Tom Harris

Farming in Nature's Image
By Judith Soule and Jon Piper

The Global Citizen
By Donella Meadows

Healthy Homes, Healthy Kids
By Joyce Schoemaker and Charity Vitale

Holistic Resource Management
By Allan Savory

Inside the Environmental Movement: Meeting the Ledership Challenge
By Donald Snow

Learning to Listen to the Land
Edited by Bill Willers

The Living Ocean: Understanding and Protecting Marine Biodiversity
By Boyce Thorne-Miller and John G. Catena

Making Things Happen
By Joan Wolfe

Media and the Environment
Edited by Craig LaMay and Everette E. Dennis

Nature Tourism: Managing for the Environment
Edited by Tensie Whelan

The New York Environment Book
By Eric A. Goldstein and Mark A. Izeman